LIBERATION THEOLOGY AT THE CROSSROADS

LIBERATION THEOLOGY AT THE CROSSROADS

Democracy or Revolution?

Paul E. Sigmund

New York   Oxford
OXFORD UNIVERSITY PRESS
1990

Oxford University Press

Oxford   New York   Toronto
Delhi   Bombay   Calcutta   Madras   Karachi
Petaling Jaya   Singapore   Hong Kong   Tokyo
Nairobi   Dar es Salaam   Cape Town
Melbourne   Auckland

and associated companies in
Berlin   Ibadan

Published by Oxford University Press, Inc.,
200 Madison Avenue, New York, NY 10016

Oxford is a registered trademark of Oxford University Press

Library of Congress Cataloging-in-Publication Data
Sigmund, Paul E.
Liberation theology at the crossroads : democracy or revolution? /
Paul E. Sigmund.
p.   cm.
ISBN 0-19-506064-4
1. Liberation theology.   2. Democracy—Religious aspects—
Christianity.   3. Revolutions—Religious aspects—Christianity.
4. Catholic Church—Doctrines.   I. Title.
BT83.57.S58   1990
230'.2—dc20   89-36761   CIP

9 8 7 6 5 4 3 2 1

Printed in the United States of America
on acid-free paper

To Ignacio Ellacuria S.J.,
rector of the Central American University of El Salvador
and liberation theologian,
who was killed because he believed that
Christians have a special duty to the poor and the oppressed

Contents

LIBERATION
THEOLOGY
AT THE
CROSSROADS

Introduction

DURING THE Extraordinary Synod of Bishops in Rome in November–December 1985 there was an unusual public display of disagreement among the Latin American bishops. It focused on attitudes toward liberation theology, the new theological current that had originated in Latin America at the end of the 1960s. On Saturday, November 30, Bishop Dario Castrillon Hoyos, the secretary of the Latin American Bishops Conference (CELAM), denounced the liberation theologians, saying, "When I see a church with a machine gun, I cannot see the crucified Christ in that church. . . . Some lines of liberation theology . . . are based on the use of instruments that are not specific to the Gospel. We can never use hate as a system of change. The core of being a church is love" (*New York Times,* December 1, 1985). Two days later, in a formal statement presented to the synod, the president of the Brazilian Bishops Conference, Bishop José Ivo Lorscheiter, replied, "Liberation theology is not a theology of violence. . . . It is not a theology that assumes or justifies Marxist ideology. [It] presupposes a new consciousness of the context of oppression . . . a conversion toward the poor and a commitment to their liberation. Liberation theology is indispensable to the church's activity and to the social commitment of Christians" (*New York Times,* December 4, 1985).

The Lorscheiter statement was not only a response to Bishop Castrillon, but more fundamentally it was an attempt to answer the criticisms of liberation theology contained in *The Instruction on Certain*

3

Aspects of the "Theology of Liberation," issued in September 1984 by the Vatican Congregation for the Doctrine of the Faith over the signature of its prefect, Cardinal Joseph Ratzinger. That document had accused the liberation theologians of using "concepts uncritically borrowed from Marxist ideology and . . . theses of a biblical hermeneutic marked by rationalism," resulting in a "new interpretation which is corrupting whatever is authentic in the generous initial commitment on behalf of the poor."

It was not only the church hierarchy that felt compelled to choose up sides on the controversy. In the United States the *National Catholic Reporter* took a strongly favorable position to liberation theology.[1] The *National Catholic Register* attacked it, quoting the statement by the Catholic novelist Walker Percy that the liberation theologians "are saying that the only way to correct an evil . . . is by violence, violent revolution. And toward that end they justify not only killing, but also joining Marxist-Leninist revolutions. Liberation theology is a perversion of Christianity" (*National Catholic Register,* January 6, 1986). Internationally, a book-length interview by an Italian journalist with Cardinal Ratzinger was published in many languages (U.S. title, *The Ratzinger Report,* San Francisco: Ignatius Press, 1985), which included a private memorandum critical of liberation theology written by Ratzinger in early 1984 that had been published by an Italian magazine. The *Instruction* and the Ratzinger book in turn produced responses by Latin American liberation theologians, including a book by the Uruguayan Jesuit Juan Luis Segundo S.J., which accused the Vatican of making "constant allusions to Marxism [as] a mere publicity gimmick to diminish liberation theology in the eyes of those who are not sufficiently sensitive to the profound and subtle methods of theology."[2] More conservative Latin American bishops began to meet and promote a "theology of reconciliation" as an answer to the liberationists. In July 1985, they issued a *Declaration of Los Andes* in Chile calling for reconciliation rather than liberation, and in January 1986 they met again in Lima. In the wake of the Vatican statement, a network of Latin American and European bishops and theologians developed who were opposed to liberation theology and committed to countering its influence. They held meetings and published articles and books, many of them in Bogota, under the auspices of the Center for the Study of Latin American Development and Integration (CEDIAL).

Responding to popular interest in the subject, the prolific American sociologist, priest, and novelist Andrew Greeley published a best-selling paperback novel in 1985, *Virgin and Martyr,* the story of a nun who becomes involved in revolution in Latin America as a result of exposure to the teachings of the liberation theologians. One of the book's main characters describes the liberation theologians:

> They are characterized by the following: A fierce hatred of the United States. An innocence of the complexities of international economics. A bland assumption that Marxism has been validated as a solution to social problems. A poverty of serious theological reflection. And the pretense that no Marxist society exists anywhere in the world by which Marxist "praxis" (their word—if you say "practice," you are horribly out of fashion) could be evaluated. [pp. 383–84]

The controversy over liberation theology is not new. Indeed, the publication in 1973 of the English translation of *A Theology of Liberation,* the book by a Peruvian priest, Gustavo Gutierrez, that gave the movement its name, immediately produced strong adverse reactions. Thomas Sanders, a Latin Americanist with theological training, published an attack on liberation theology in the liberal Protestant magazine *Christianity and Crisis,* in which he accused the liberation writers of "utopian moralism" that ignores the reality of sin and moral ambiguity in all human structures, and contradicts the central affirmations of the Pauline-Augustinian tradition developed in the Christian realism of Sanders's mentor Reinhold Niebuhr. In turn, Sanders's article was denounced by the Brazilian Protestant theologian Rubem Alves for its "ideological bias and unambiguous relationships with colonialism, racism, and economic exploitation. We believe that your theology to a great degree is part of cultural imperialism" (*Christianity and Crisis,* September 17, 1973). Similar attacks and defenses have been published in Europe, Latin America, and the United States for many years, with some theologians describing liberation theology as the "cutting edge" of theological thinking and others viewing it as a dangerous "politicization" or "horizontalism" in theology.

What accounts for the intensity of the feeling for and against liberation theology? Who gives a more accurate description of its content and implications? To answer these questions it is necessary to examine the origins, content, and development of a movement that is now two decades old. During the last twenty years, it has emerged as an identifiable school, with a method of doing theology and a set of assumptions and doctrines that have become both influential and controversial. An examination of its history, method, and doctrines may help us to make a balanced judgment on the validity of the conflicting claims.

As a preliminary answer to the question of why so much attention has been given to what are, after all, the writings of fairly minor Latin American clergymen, one may say that we now realize—as we did not, say, twenty years ago—that religion in the Third World, and in the United States as well, has tremendous political potential. That potential can be activated, however, in different directions. It can give support to the status quo, it can call for reform and social change, or it can fuel a revolution. Catholicism in Latin America has played the first role, the justification of the status quo, throughout most of its history. In the last thirty or forty years, however, it has also promoted reform, especially in the areas of human rights, labor organization, and support for democracy. It is only in the last twenty years, however, that some Latin American theologians have moved one step further and begun to call for radical solutions to Latin American social problems. That opening to the left by the Latin American church has as its theoretical underpinning liberation theology. It represents a type of Catholic radicalism that was almost unknown in Latin America prior to the middle and late 1960s. Its emergence was possible only because of the changes that took place in the Catholic church worldwide during and after the Second Vatican Council (1962–1965), and because of the heightened sense of the political and economic crisis in Latin America produced by the challenge of the Cuban Revolution and the American-sponsored reforms of the Alliance for Progress. That it was a radicalism linked to the oldest and strongest continent-wide institutional structure in Latin America—the Catholic church, for so long a bulwark of the status quo—made it all the more challenging—and to some, threatening. Later, when it seemed to have played a part in supporting and promoting two revolutionary movements in Latin America, the attempt at a transition to socialism in Allende's Chile (1970–1973), and the revolutionary turmoil in Central America involving the overthrow of Somoza by the Sandinistas and the emergence of guerrilla movements in El Salvador and Guatemala, it became the subject of positive and negative discussions, not only in religiously related media, but also in the world press and secular organs of opinion.

Liberation theology in Latin America is radical both in its method and its content. A radical is one who goes to the root (*radix*) of a problem. Those roots are identified in the writings of the liberation theologians in several different ways.

1. First, it is argued that it is necessary to make a radical break with earlier ways of doing theology. Rather than developing a series of abstract and deductive propositions about the relation (*religio*) of man to God, theologians engage in their profession as a "second act," following after the experience of involvement with the poor at a given moment in history. Theology grows out of the combination of theory and practice that the liberation theologians call *praxis* rather than through some formal, systematic, organized study.

2. The locus for doing this theology is the poor, and theologians must both be committed to the poor and work with them if they are to do theology. God has a particular love for the poor, and those who wish to follow him must exercise what the church has called "the preferential option for the poor."

3. This theology must be related directly to the Word of the Bible. That is the primary source of religious knowledge, although always in relation to the experience of the poor. In fact, the very title of the liberation theology movement is derived from the Bible. The text on which it is based is the scene in the fourth chapter of the Gospel of St. Luke in which Christ announces his mission in the synagogue in Nazareth by reading from the Old Testament prophet Isaiah, chapter 61: "The Spirit of the Lord is upon me because he has anointed me to preach the Gospel to the poor . . . to bid prisoners to go free . . . to liberate those who are oppressed, to preach the acceptable year of the Lord, a day of retribution." According to Luke, after Jesus finished reading those words he closed the book and stated, "This day the scripture is fulfilled in your ears" (Luke 4:18–21). Other biblical texts that are frequently cited include Matthew 11:5, in which Jesus tells the disciples of John the Baptist to report as evidence that he is the Messiah the fact that "the poor have the Gospel preached to them"; Mary's statement in the Magnificat, "He has put down the mighty from their thrones and raised up the humble; he has filled the hungry with good things, the rich he has sent away empty-handed" (Luke 1:52–53); Christ's account of the Last Judgment, in which eternal life is the reward of those who feed the hungry, clothe the naked, and care for the sick and imprisoned (Matthew 25:31ff.); and the liberation of the Jews from Egyptian bondage in the Book of Exodus.

4. What the poor experience in Latin America is oppression. Theologians therefore are to concern themselves with liberation, in the sense of the removal of the causes of oppression. One can thus sum up the first four elements in the words that appear near the end of the first chapter of Gustavo Gutierrez's book that launched the movement. Liberation theology is "critical reflection on Christian praxis in the light of the Word" (*A Theology of Liberation*, Maryknoll, NY: Orbis Books, 1973, p. 13).

5. If liberation theology were nothing more than a call for involvement with the poor as one's Christian duty, and relating the biblical message to their experience, it would not have produced the storm of controversy that surrounds it. However, besides the grass-roots radicalism in method, there are significant substantive elements that are radical in content. The liberation theologians argue that theology should make use of "the social sciences" in their attempt to analyze the obstacles to oppression. When they say "the social sciences," however, the liberation theologians usually mean Marxist methods of analysis. At least at the outset, therefore, there was a close association between liberation theology and Marxism—in the form of the claim that the root cause of the oppression of the poor in Latin America is "dependent capitalism"—and that the way to remove that oppression and to achieve the liberation of the poor is through socialism. Liberation theologians drew on the theory of *dependencia* that had recently been developed in Latin America, and linked it to Marxist theories of the class struggle and exploitation to argue that the church should concern itself with the poor in a specific way—by commitment to the (self-) liberation of the poor from dependent capitalism.

6. If this seemed to be a reductionist and simplistic approach to a complicated problem, it was. Over time and in dialogue with like-minded Christians, the liberation theologians later became aware that capitalism was not the only obstacle to liberation. By the mid-1970s they were reminded often that in a continent in which Indians, mestizos, and women had been exploited for centuries, the problem of liberation involved psychological, ethnic, racial, and gender factors as well as economic structures. As in mainstream Marxism, it was possible to relate those oppressions to economic causes—but since the commitment was to Marxism as a tool of analysis rather than a metaphysics, or philosophy, there began to be a willingness to consider other types of oppression as independent variables.

7. Early in the development of the liberation theology movement, it became clear that the emergence of Christian Base Communities in a number of countries in Latin America offered an instrument for the liberation of the poor that was in keeping with the fundamental principles of liberation writings, and they became incorporated into its message. Linked to the *anticapitalist* quasi-revolutionary *structuralism* of liberation theology was a *grass-roots populism* that had begun separately, and was theoretically distinct—but soon became closely associated with it. In such countries as Brazil, Chile, Nicaragua, and El Salvador, the Ecclesial Base Communities (CEBs) became an important force to press for social change and to develop among the poor an awareness (*conscientização*) of their spiritual and material problems, and of the possibilities of taking collective action to remedy them.

The experience of popular participation within the Roman Catholic church challenged older hierarchical models of church authority, but the reforms associated with the Vatican Council and the acute shortage of priests gave them a kind of legitimacy. Protestant observers such as Richard Shaull might call the liberation theologians *The Heralds of a New Reformation* (Maryknoll, NY: Orbis Books, 1984) but in such countries as Brazil the growth of the Base Communities was seen as a positive application of the church's continuing concern with the evangelization of the poor within, rather than against the institutional church. Brazilian theologian Leonardo Boff put forward a more uncompromisingly democratic model of the church in *Church, Charism, and Power* (English translation, New York: Crossroad, 1985), making use of quasi-Marxist terminology to do so (the hierarchy was accused of "the gradual expropriation of the spiritual means of production from the Christian people"—p. 112), and brought down upon him the wrath of the Vatican. Yet Boff continued to insist that the papacy has a special position in the church constitution in maintaining doctrinal unity on the basis of the emerging consensus of the community. Along with other liberation theologians, he also reaffirmed (and reinterpreted) such traditional doctrines as the Trinity, the special position of Mary, and the central importance of the Eucharist. If it was a new reformation, it was very different from the one that occurred in the sixteenth century.

There was no question, however, that it was radical. Besides the radical character of its approach to theology, its structural anticapitalism and its grass-roots populism related it to two long-standing traditions of Western radical thought—Marxist socialism and Rousseauian populist democracy—but in both cases those traditions were refocused upon the poor. The socialist revolution was to be carried out by the poor (not the proletariat) and the local community was to be made up of the poor and marginalized.

The combination of two different radical strains—anticapitalism, and the promotion of popular participation in church and state—helps to explain the ambivalent reaction that liberation theology has produced. Supporters of liberation theology point to its concern for the liberation of the poor, and view opposition to its teachings as inspired by a desire to defend positions of wealth and power in church and state. Opponents, on the other hand, highlight its Marxist terminology and class analyses and its readiness to blame capitalism for all of Latin America's problems and to endorse an undefined socialism as the cure-all for the evils of exploitation and oppression. In fact, the writings of the liberation theologians combine both types of radicalism, although they do so in different ways and the relation of the two elements has changed in the last twenty years.

The tensions between the two types of radicalism were not evident, however, as long as most of Latin America was governed by authoritarian military dictatorships. Things changed, however, in the 1980s. By the end of that decade only Chile and Paraguay remained as rightist dictatorships and they were both beginning democratic transitions. On the left Cuba and, in the view of some, Nicaragua used a combination of Marxism and nationalism to keep the ruling *caudillo* or *comandantes* in power.

How are religiously motivated radicals who are concerned with the liberation of the poor in Latin America to respond to this situation? Will they continue to argue for "revolutionary" structural changes leading to the overthrow of the capitalist system, or will they make use of the Base Communities and the institutions of "bourgeois" democracy to promote the welfare of the people? How helpful to the poor is revolutionary rhetoric and action when the lessons of the 1970s in Chile, Uruguay, and Argentina seem to have been that such rhetoric and action lead only to counterrevolution by the armed forces? This is the choice that the liberation theologians face today. Will they make use of the structural and ideological resources of the Christian tradition to bring about a genuine participation by the poor and oppressed in bettering their condition, or will they retreat into a sterile revolutionism that may be emotionally satisfying but does not help the poor?

The choice was posed all the more dramatically with the publication of the "Instruction on Christian Freedom and Liberation" on April 6, 1986, by the Vatican Congregation for the Doctrine of the Faith. The Instruction abandoned the negative tone of its 1984 predecessor and asserted that the "quest for freedom and the aspiration to liberation which are among the principal signs of the times in the modern world, have their source in the Christian heritage" (*New York Times,* April 6, 1986). While rejecting "the systematic recourse to violence as the necessary path to liberation" (although in extreme cases "recourse to armed struggle" may be permissible "to put an end to an obvious and prolonged tyranny") the Instruction argued that "it is perfectly legitimate that those who suffer oppression on the part of the wealthy and the political powerful should take action through morally licit means, in order to secure structures and institutions in which their rights will be truly respected." The Instruction endorsed "a preferential love for the poor on the part of the church" and a "Christian practice of liberation" that recognized the natural rights and duties of the individual but linked them to the principle of social solidarity and the common good, while opposing all forms of collectivism.

Shortly after the Instruction was published, a letter from the pope to the Brazilian bishops made the church's commitment to liberation all the more clear. The pope endorsed the Brazilian bishops' efforts to find responses to the problems of poverty and oppression that are "consistent with the teachings of the Gospel, of the living tradition and of the ongoing *magisterium* [teaching] of the Church. As long as this is observed, we are convinced, we and you, that the theology of liberation is not only timely but useful and necessary." Both documents clearly identified the central teaching of the church with the "special option for the poor," while at the same time they rejected class struggle and violence.

The challenge was thus posed as to the future development of liberation theology. Gustavo Gutierrez, the founder of the movement, recognized this when he welcomed the Vatican documents and described them as "ending a chapter" in the history of liberation theology. The Brazilian bishops were also enthusiastic about the apparent resolution of the conflict that had divided the Latin American and

Brazilian church. Others, however, were less willing to abandon earlier Marxist-influenced rhetoric, and raised questions as to whether the earlier radicalism of the liberationists was being coopted by the church establishment.

The conflict seemed to parallel the earlier problems of the socialist movement in Western Europe. The Social Democratic parties were for a long time ambivalent about the parliamentary system and reluctant to abandon the revolutionary tradition of Karl Marx. It is true that Marx had made some grudging concessions to the possibility that the workers might take power peacefully (Speech to the Second International, The Hague, 1882) but the basic thrust of his analysis seems to have been that in normal circumstances only a revolutionary upheaval can resolve the inherent contradictions of capitalism.

For Marx that transformation was to be carried out by the overwhelming majority of the population, but in the hands of Lenin, Marx was used to justify the imposition of the rule of a revolutionary vanguard party bent on eliminating the traces of "false consciousness" among the masses that had led them to support reformist trade unionism and bourgeois democracy. In Western Europe, however, socialists such as Jean Jaurès in France and Eduard Bernstein in Germany argued that parliamentary democracy was an important component of the Marxist tradition.

Which way will the liberation theologians go? Will they abandon or fundamentally alter the utopian revolutionism that they adopted in the late 1960s and early 1970s? Will they listen to the "praxis" of the poor and respond to their expressed needs and specific problems, or will they continue to believe in the necessity of "conscientization" by means of a naive and reductionist anticapitalism? If liberation theology is committed to "using the tools of social analysis" and "learning from the social sciences," *which* tools and *which* social science will they utilize?

It will be the argument of this book that it is time for liberation theologians to distinguish between the *method* and the *content* of the theology that they have developed. It is entirely in keeping with their own emphasis on "praxis" that the liberation theologians should continue to utilize the methods and promote the goals that they developed nearly two decades ago, but be willing to alter the content of their socioeconomic analysis, on the basis of experience, to recognize that there may be other sources of oppression (racial, sexual, and cultural) besides economics, and to reassess the liberal democratic and constitutionalist tradition that the liberation theologians rejected in the late 1960s. This is especially important at a time when democracy and human rights need "all the help they can get" in Latin America—and the possibilities for the development of genuinely participatory policies and institutions are greater in Latin America than ever before. At the outset, liberation theology was both a demand for true democracy and a protest against the exploitation and external domination associated with dependent capitalism. In its more extravagant rhetoric, its original formulations seemed to emphasize the need for an anticapitalist and antiimperialist revolution more than the need for empowerment and participation of the poor. Today there is less emphasis on structuralist criticisms and more on participatory involvement. (For examples, compare Gutierrez's first book, *A Theology of Liberation,* published in Spanish in 1971, with his recent books, for example, *We Drink from Our Own Wells,* the Spanish edition of which was published in 1983—or contrast the arguments of the 1970 and 1984 articles by the same author, published as appendices to this book.) The question for the future is whether this commitment to involvement of, and with, the poor can take place without the heavy overlay of pseudo-Marxism that produced such a strong reaction against the movement in the 1970s. At a time when the American Catholic bishops are actively engaged in criticism of the shortcomings of the American system because of a concern for social justice that is based on both the Christian and liberal traditions, it is time for a new North-South dialogue on the part of Christians, concerning both the accomplishments and the shortcomings of liberal democracy and the mixed economy as it has developed in the Americas. It is in the hope of contributing to this dialogue that this book has been written.

1

The Catholic Church and Politics: Historical and Institutional Background

THE MESSAGE of the Bible is not an overtly political one; it is about the relation of God to the Chosen People, and the redemption of mankind by Jesus Christ. Christ did not endorse any particular political system, and the political implications that have been drawn from his message are diverse and even contradictory. Part of the message of the liberation theologians is an argument for a new relationship between Christianity and politics that is more faithful to the Bible than earlier theory and practice. To understand in what respects this relationship is new, and why it emerged at the time it did, it is necessary to begin with an historical overview of the way in which Christianity—especially Roman Catholicism—has been related in the past to political, economic, and ecclesiastical structures in Europe and Latin America. In an organization with an institutional memory spanning nearly 2000 years, this is not easy to do. Yet for the bishops and theologians of Latin America in 1968, the year of the birth of liberation theology as a distinct current of Catholic thought, that memory is important as a source of both legitimation and differentiation.

At the time of Christ, Palestine was under Roman rule, but the Jews continued to be restive, and a nationalist revolutionary movement called the Zealots called for liberation from Roman rule. It is believed that one or more of Jesus' followers was or had been a member of the Zealot movement, and Barabbas, who was set free by Pilate in response to popular demand, is usually considered to have been condemned for participating in a Zealot uprising or political assassination. Yet when Christ was asked whether a Jew should pay taxes to the Romans he replied, "Render to Caesar the things that are Caesar's and to God the things that are God's" (Matthew 22:21), an answer that has been variously interpreted as calling for separation of the spiritual and the temporal, submission to existing rulers, or complete disinterest in politics.[1]

In response to what appear to have been anarchic tendencies in the early church, Paul wrote in his Epistle to the Romans (ch. 13), "Be subject to the powers that be. The powers that be are ordained of God. He that resists the power, resists God." Yet from the outset there were clear limits on the Christian's political obligation. St. Peter refused an order from the Sanhedrin to stop preaching because "we must obey God rather than man" (Acts 5:29), and the early Christians repeatedly defied Roman orders to give divine honors to images of the emperor. Faced with Roman persecution, the Christians organized their own underground religious communities, and as early as the writings of St. Paul it is evident that there were problems of organization and authority within these communities. There is debate about the emergence of the distinction between bishops (*episcopoi,* "overseers") and priests (*presbyteroi,* "elders"), the relation of their authority to that of the apostles (the "apostolic succession"), and the respective powers of the successors of the other apostles and those of the successor of Peter ("Thou art Peter, and upon this rock I will build my church," Matthew 16:18), but there is evidence for monarchical, aristocratic, and democratic elements in the early church constitution, with the Bishop of Rome, the patriarchs and bishops, and the local Christian communities representing each of the three classic forms of government.

As a persecuted sect, the early church developed independently of the political structure, but it could not fail to be affected both by Jewish and Roman legal theories (transmission of authority by the laying on of hands, the theory of ordination) and by the philosophical currents of the contemporary world. The church fathers wrote in an intellectual context that was deeply affected by two major philosophical schools, Stoicism and Platonism. After the legalization of Christianity by Constantine in 313 AD and its subsequent adoption as the official religion of the empire, the Christian fathers, notably St. Augustine (354–430), drew upon Stoicism and Platonism to forge a world view that emphasized the hierarchical and ordered nature of God's creation ("the Great Chain of Being") and the immanence of God's moral purposes in the structure of the world that he created ("the natural law"). While it is true that as a consequence of the Fall the world had been corrupted by sin and one could hope for happiness not in the "earthly city" but only in the "City of God" to come, it was the duty of Christians in positions of authority, such as rulers or judges, to impose a minimal order on a sinful world (*The City of God,* bk. XIX, chs. 6–13), just as it was the duty of the subjects of those in authority to obey them. Augustine's views provided the basis for an essentially conservative Christian world view that emphasized order, obedience, hierarchy, authority, and the divine origin of spiritual and temporal rule.[2]

These were the underlying assumptions of the traditional, legalistic, and feudal society of the Middle Ages. The translation of the works of Aristotle into Latin in the thirteenth century threatened the stability of this order, but Thomas Aquinas (1225–1274), in his great synthesis the *Summa Theologiae,* endeavored to prove that the claims of reason as represented by "the Philosopher" (Aristotle) could be harmonized with Christian revelation. The political implications of the Thomistic synthesis were not threatening to the medieval order since monarchy in church and state was endorsed as reflecting the divinely intended order in the universe, although typically a place was also given to the participation of the nobles and the people as well and to the restraints of basic law upon the ruler.[3]

In the late Middle Ages the development of representative institutions out of earlier feudal consultative bodies did not challenge the principle of monarchy, since parliaments were perceived as primarily consultative bodies with a *duty* to "advise and consent" to taxes and legislation. It is true that in the fourteenth and fifteenth centuries a constitutional crisis in the church produced the conciliar movement that argued for a structure of representative bodies in the church, deriving their legitimacy both from the succession of the bishops to the apostles, and from a belief in the council as the corporate representative of the whole body of believers (*congregatio fidelium*). Once the crisis was past, however, the course of papal centralization continued—and it was intensified by the challenge of the Protestant Reformation. Monarchy and hierarchy were the prevailing models of Catholic Christendom, and the earlier competing aristocratic and democratic principles formed the basis of the rival episcopalist and congregationalist theories in Protestantism. Concordats—diplomatic agreements between the Vatican and the monarchs of Catholic Europe—regulated the respective rights of pope and king, and part of the legitimacy of the Catholic ruler was derived from his or her religious duty to spread the faith (for example, *Isabela la Catolica* of Spain).

This was the religio-political outlook that was brought to Spanish and Portuguese America by the era of colonial conquest. The spread of the faith by missionaries and soldiers ("the cross and the sword") was but a further extension of the crusading spirit that had only recently (1492) liberated southern Spain from Moslem rule. While there were a few courageous churchmen who criticized the quasi-genocide of the native Indian populations, the exercise of the *patronato,* or nominating power, by the Spanish monarch guaranteed that Catholic bishops would be faithful servants of the Spanish throne. When the Spanish colonies revolted in the early nineteenth century, the papacy denounced the uprisings and called upon the Latin Americans to return to obedience to the Bourbon monarchs. While the lower clergy in Latin America (for example, Fathers Morelos and Hidalgo in Mexico) often supported independence, the church hierarchy was sympathetic to the continuation of Spanish rule. After independence the principal political division between conservatives and liberals often focused on the status of the church in the areas of education, marriage, and landholding.

In Latin Europe, the anticlericalism of the liberal movement in revolutionary France and the desires of liberal nationalists in Italy to annex the papal states (they formed a band across central Italy from south of Venice to north of Naples, blocking Italian unification) led the papacy to issue repeated condemnations of liberalism and democracy in the nineteenth century. Initially the papacy under Pope Pius IX (1846–1878) had responded to the challenge of modern liberal democracy with condemnations (see, for example, Proposition 69 of the Syllabus of Errors [1864]—"It is an error to believe that the Roman pontiff can or should reconcile himself to, and agree with progress, liberalism, and modern civilization"), but under Pope Leo XIII (1878–1903) it began to develop a Catholic alternative to the main politico-economic movements of the nineteenth century, liberalism and socialism. Drawing on the thinking of St. Thomas Aquinas, the teaching of which he had made the basis of theological instruction in Catholic seminaries, Leo XIII published his famous labor encyclical, *Rerum Novarum,* in 1891, supporting the workers' right to earn a living wage and to form trade unions, and condemning both "the misery and wretchedness" of the workers under economic liberalism, and the collectivist materialism of an undifferentiated—but presumably, from the description, Marxist—socialism. The pope's criticism of socialism emphasized the "natural right" of man to the fruits of his labor and in effect adopted the argument of John Locke that when a man mixes his labor with the fruits of the earth he is entitled to their ownership. Leo also stressed, however, the social obligations that accompany private ownership and the limits that the community could place upon it. Rejecting the class struggle, Leo called on labor and employers to cooperate since "it is ordained by nature that these two classes should exist in harmony and agreement, . . . so as to maintain the equilibrium of the body politic" (par. 15).

The social Catholicism that was propounded by the papacy still was not combined with an endorsement of political democracy, despite the fact that Christian Democratic and Catholic parties were being formed in many European countries. Pius XI's labor encyclical, *Quadragesimo Anno* (1931), seemed to propose a decentralized form of corporatism, based on intermediate and professional associations ("subsidiarity"). It was not until the end of World War II that the papacy formally supported democracy as morally and religiously justified (Pius XII, Christmas Message, 1944). Official papal endorsement of democracy as the form of government most in keeping with the "dignity of the human person" took place only during the pontificate of John XXIII, with the publication of *Pacem in Terris* (1963) and in the declaration on *The Church in the Modern World* of the Second Vatican Council (*Gaudium et Spes*) adopted in 1965.[4]

Pope John's encyclical *Pacem in Terris* was addressed to "all men of good will." And the Vatican Council's declaration, *Gaudium et Spes* [The Church in the Modern World], stated that it was aimed at "the whole of humanity," expressing an attitude toward the modern world very different from that of the nineteenth-century popes. In *Gaudium et Spes,* Vatican II called for a continuing dialogue between the church and the world, denounced economic inequality and disparities between rich and poor nations, and based human freedom and interdependence on the dignity of man and his creation by God. This freedom can be attained, said the council, only in solidarity with others since by divine intention all human beings constitute one family and are endowed with a social nature, and "since all men possess a rational soul and are created in God's likeness, . . . the basic equality of all must receive increasingly greater recognition" (par. 29). Thus, after more than a century of resistance to democracy, liberty, and equality, the Roman Catholic church formally endorsed all three as religiously and biblically based.

The council alluded to atheistic doctrines that anticipate "the liberation of man through his economic and social liberation," warning that "when the proponents of this doctrine gain governmental power they vigorously fight against religion" (par. 21). While "rejecting atheism, root and branch," the council declared that "all men, believers and unbelievers alike, ought to work for the rightful betterment of this world in which all alike live. Such an ideal cannot be realized, however, apart from sincere and prudent dialogue" (par. 21). The passage recalled the famous statement of Pope John XXIII in *Pacem in Terris* (par. 158–59), "One must never confuse error and the person who errs, not even when there is a question of error in the moral or religious field. . . . Neither can false philosophical teachings regarding the nature, origin, and destiny of the universe and of man be identified with historical movements that have economic, social, cultural and political ends, not even when those movements have originated from those teachings." The council's call for dialogue and Pope John's distinction between philosophy and historical movements were later to be cited by those who favored collaboration with the Marxist left in Europe and Latin America.

The Second Vatican Council thus moved international Catholicism from a generally conservative and even authoritarian position to one that supported democracy, human rights, and social justice. It also endorsed dialogue with the Marxist left, but the only reference to "liberation" was made in the context of a discussion of the Marxist critique of religion. Marxist-Christian dialogues had been taking place in Europe for more than ten years before the council's statement, but the most serious efforts along these lines never arrived at anything approaching a synthesis, and except in Yugoslavia such discussions ended with the Soviet invasion of Czechoslovakia in 1968. In France there had also been sporadic efforts to link Catholics of the left with the Communists but their principal result had been the expulsion of the most prominent Marxist participant involved in that effort, Roger Garaudy, from the French Communist party.[5]

The council also encouraged the reading of the Bible by the laity, and it promoted ecumenism—that is, cooperation with adherents of other faiths, whether Orthodox, Protestant, Moslem, or Jew. It modified the highly centralized church structure that had been adopted at the time of the Council of Trent and Counter-Reformation in the sixteenth century and reinforced by the decrees of the First Vatican Council (1870–1871). *Lumen Gentium* [The Dogmatic Constitution of the Church] defined the church as "the people of God" and stated that "the order of bishops is the successor to the college of the apostles in teaching authority. . . . Together with its head, the Roman Pontiff,—and never without this head—the episcopal order is the subject of supreme and full power over the universal church" (ch. III). The following chapter also discussed the role of the laity, concluding that "the laity are gathered together in the People of God and make up the Body of Christ under one Head" (ch. IV). While these decrees did not transform the church into a democracy, they promoted a significant decentralization of authority and legitimacy. Papal monarchy was no longer the model, but a mixed constitution that involved the bishops, clergy, and laity in the decision-making of the church, without rejecting papal primacy in the areas of the definition of dogma and the administration of the church. Thus in addition to a political opening to democracy and human rights and a philosophical opening to dialogue with other points of view, there was a religious and ecclesiological opening to models of church government other than the centralized authoritarianism that had prevailed for a century or more.[6]

The Vatican Council and the pontificate of John XXIII marked a significant movement of the international Catholic church towards political pluralism. The hierarchical integralism and the fortress mentality of the nineteenth-century papacy was replaced by a new openness to dialogue, not only with other religions but also with atheists, including Marxists. While the movement had been basically from conservative authoritarianism toward a more favorable attitude to democracy and human rights, the very fact that such a shift had taken place indicated a new openness that allowed themes and attitudes to be discussed in Catholic circles that had not been permitted earlier. One of those themes was the relation of Christianity and Marxism, and more specifically the parallelism between the Marxist criticisms of capitalism and some of the anticapitalist elements in the Vatican social encyclicals. It was suddenly possible for devout Catholics, both clerical and lay, to study and discuss Marxism more sympathetically, in the interests of dialogue. Among those who did so were a number of Latin American seminarians pursuing advanced study in Europe before and during Vatican II.

In the earlier part of the twentieth century the Latin American church had begun to move away from its alliance with conservative elements and to develop a reformist response to modern democracy. These included the beginnings of a Catholic trade union movement, the foundation of a number of Catholic universities (except for Javeriana University in Bogota [1939] and the Catholic University of Chile [1888], all were founded after World War II), and the organization of Catholic youth, student, and peasant organizations modeled on European Catholic Action.[7] Christian Democratic parties were formed that looked to the European parties and to European Catholic writers such as Jacques Maritain for their inspiration. Eduardo Frei, later president of Chile (1964–1970), heard Maritain lecture in Spain on his way to a Catholic student meeting in Rome, and in 1938 Maritain himself went to Latin America to lecture in Brazil and Argentina. One of his lectures, *A Letter on Independence,* which argued for a "third position" between right and left, was reprinted in Chile at the time and formed part of the continuing argument between the Conservative party leaders and a party youth group, the Falange, that left the Conservatives and later formed the core of the Chilean Christian Democratic party. In Venezuela a student group with a progressive Catholic orientation formed a Committee for Independent Elections (COPEI) that became the present Venezuelan Social Christian party. Parties were also founded in the post–World War II period in many other countries and they have had significant electoral success in El Salvador (Salvador's former president, José Napoleón Duarte, was repeatedly elected mayor of San Salvador long before he was elected president in 1984) and Guatemala (where the first civilian presidential elections in nearly twenty years led to the election of a Christian Democrat, Vinicio Cerezo, in December 1985, with 68 percent of the vote).

The emergence of Christian Democratic parties and auxiliary organizations influenced by the social teaching of the church signified a movement away from the old integralist hierarchical model that anticipated and reinforced the changes in worldwide Catholicism associated with the Vatican Council. With strong support from Catholic student groups and trade unions, the Christian Democrats provided a mass base for social reform and democracy in a number of Latin

American countries, as well as a democratic alternative to the challenge of the Cuban Revolution after 1959. When the dictatorship of Marco Perez Jiménez was overthrown in Venezuela in 1958 the COPEI Social Christian Party agreed to enter the government of the social democratic *Acción Democratica* president Romulo Betancourt. In 1958 as well, Eduardo Frei ran on the Christian Democratic ticket for president of Chile and although he did not win, his party began a meteoric rise that culminated six years later in his election to the presidency by an absolute majority, a very rare occurrence in Chile's multiparty system. Also in 1958, Pope John XXIII was elected pope and the Cuban Revolution entered its final year, ending with the triumphal entry of Fidel Castro into Havana on New Year's Day of 1959. When the Cuban Revolution veered sharply to the left over the next two years, the newly elected American president, John Kennedy, announced the initiation of a ten-year program of assistance to Latin America, the Alliance for Progress, which was intended to demonstrate that reform and development could best be carried out under democratic auspices. The natural candidates to carry out this program were the Social Democratic and Christian Democratic parties of the center-left in Latin America.

The Catholic church also viewed the Cuban Revolution as a challenge that required a response, especially after its relatively weak presence in Cuba was almost totally eliminated with the shutdown by Castro of the entire system of private education and the combined expulsion and withdrawal of the foreign clergy that accounted for the bulk of the priests and nuns in Cuba. Elsewhere in Latin America, the church established a number of socially oriented research institutes, the best known of which was the Centro Belarmino in Chile. A spin-off from the Centro Belarmino, DESAL, was organized by the Belgian Jesuit Roger Vekemans, who had been specially sent to Chile for this purpose. It became the major "think tank" to develop the program of Eduardo Frei's "Revolution in Liberty" for the 1964 presidential election.

In the United States as well, a major effort was made to recruit missionaries to go to Latin America, as the pope asked the American and Canadian churches to send 10 percent of their new clergy to Latin America. The Maryknoll order, in particular, which had originally been concerned mainly with missionary activity in China, now reoriented its activities principally toward Latin America. There were critics of these programs (see, for example, Ivan Illich, "The Seamy

Side of Charity," *America,* January 21, 1967) but large numbers of young committed missionaries from the United States and Europe began to work among the rural and urban poor of Latin America; the church hierarchy in Chile, Brazil, and Venezuela began to take a greater interest in social and agrarian reform; and the church turned its attention to what were now beginning to be described as the "marginalized" sectors of society—the peasantry, the inhabitants of the shantytowns in and around the major cities made up of immigrants from the countryside, and in general, the poor and downtrodden.

The most important single influence to modernize and galvanize the Latin American church was the Second Vatican Council. The Latin American bishops had already established a continent-wide organization, the Latin American Bishops Conference (CELAM), in 1955, but its members had not held a general conference since then, although a small bureaucracy had been established and smaller assemblies were held annually. However, from October 1962 until December 1965, almost the entire Latin American hierarchy—600 in all—met in the last three months of each year in Rome as participants in the Council's sessions. They held their own annual CELAM assemblies there, and were advised by several hundred Latin American *periti* (experts) and younger clergy, many of them students or recent graduates of the theological faculties of Europe. The updating and opening that were taking place at the council had a particularly strong effect on the Latin American bishops. They discussed with each other their common problems, thought about the application to Latin America of the Council's teachings, and returned resolved to apply these teachings in their own national conferences, which had become much more significant bodies now that expanded air travel possibilities made it easier for the bishops of a given country to meet. The most important decision that they made was to hold a Second General Conference of Latin American Bishops at Medellín, Columbia in 1968.

The period between the beginning of the Second Vatican Council in 1962 and the CELAM meeting in Medellín in 1968 was one of turmoil in the Latin American church. One can perceive in these years the beginnings of the radicalization that ultimately produced the liberation theology movement. Brazil was the country that seemed to be moving leftward most radically, particularly in the church. When President Janio Quadros resigned in 1960 and his leftist vice-president, João Goulart, succeeded him—although only after he had been denied many of the normal constitutional powers of the presidency—Brazil began a process of polarization that finally culminated in the military coup of April 1, 1964. Among Catholic groups an identifiable Catholic left emerged with roots in the student and trade union movements, that was willing to work with the (outlawed) Communist party in pursuit of social change. The hierarchy also promoted the organization of Catholic peasant unions (the *sindicais rurais*) to compete with the Communist-dominated peasant leagues (*ligas componesas*) in the depressed Northeast. The church also supported a peasant literacy campaign through the Basic Education Movement (MEB), which had begun in the late 1950s and utilized the new educational methods of the Brazilian educator Paulo Freire, who devised a system of *conscientização* ("consciousness raising") to encourage the peasantry to relate their literacy education to their current problems in a systematic way. The MEB became more controversial in the 1960s as its work began to acquire a distinctly anticapitalist flavor, at the same time that *Acão Popular,* an offshoot of the University Catholic Action Organization, moved rapidly leftward.

The church hierarchy in Brazil moved to respond to the situation by becoming more involved in social action, and publicly supporting agrarian reform, rural unions, and Catholic Action by laymen. It issued statements calling for social change, and warning against the possibility of violence and civil war. The bishops pursued a middle course between the radical students and peasant leaders, and the more conservative middle and upper classes in the cities. Right-wing Catholic groups such as the "Society for Tradition, Family, and Property" emerged, and one of the precipitants of the 1964 military coup was a mass march for "God, Country, and the Family" in São Paulo, which was interpreted by the military as an invitation to carry out a coup. After the coup, student and peasant leaders were arrested, the military took over the universities and dissolved many leftist organizations and publications, and a new era of takeovers by the military as an institution, rather than by individual *caudillos,* began in Latin America.[8] At this time, one can perceive the beginnings of the organization of Ecclesial Base Communities (CEBs), small groups of 20 to 30 lay people who met on a regular basis to discuss scriptural passages and to apply them to daily experience. The CEBs were first established in Brazil and Panama in the early 1960s with the support of the hierarchy. In Brazil the movement grew to the point that estimates of their number today range up to 100,000 CEBs involving 4 million participants. While decentralized, the CEBs are part of the structure of the Catholic church in the sense of acknowledging, and being approved and supported by, the clergy and hierarchy. They are a response to the problem of the shortage of priests in Latin America, the need for a closer relationship between the Christian message and the lived experience of the lower classes, and the new openness of the church to the world. They form part of the experiential background to the emergence of liberation theology in Latin America in the late 1960s and have been incorporated into the thinking that we will examine in later chapters.

Colombia was also becoming radicalized in the mid-1960s, but with very different results. In 1962 Father Camilo Torres returned from theology studies in Louvain (where he had been a fellow student of the priest who was later to found liberation theology, Gustavo Gutierrez) to become chaplain to the students at the National University. Colombia had returned to democracy in 1957 after a period of dictatorial rule, but it was operating under the so-called National Front system, whereby power was shared by the traditional Conservative and Liberal parties. Torres, who came from a well-known oligarchical family, denounced the arrangement and attempted to organize a national movement to carry out major social reforms. When that movement did not succeed, he joined a Marxist guerrilla movement. Three months later, in early 1966, he was killed in a skirmish with the armed forces. Along with Che Guevara, who was murdered after his capture in Bolivia in 1967, Torres became a kind of patron saint of the newly emerging Catholic left, as well as a symbol of the dangers of such leftism to Catholic conservatives. The Colombian church was divided in its reaction to Torres, and the statements quoted in the Introduction by a Colombian bishop concerning the inappropriateness of Christ carrying a machine gun clearly referred to Camilo Torres's death.[9]

Between the ending of the Second Vatican Council in 1965 and the Medellín CELAM General Conference of 1968, Pope John XXIII's successor, Paul VI, published the encyclical *Populorum Progressio* [On the Development of Peoples] in March 1967. While expressing great hope for the improvement of the human condition through development, the encyclical also attacked the abuses of the international economic system in language stronger than that of earlier papal statements and differing from them also in failing to balance papal criticism of capitalism with attacks on Communism. The pope described capitalism as a system "which considers profit as the key motive for economic progress, competition as the supreme law of economics, and private ownership of the means of production as an absolute right that has no limits and carries no corresponding social obligation." In Paul's view this "unchecked liberalism" leads to dictatorship rightly denounced by Pius XI (in *Quadragesimo Arno,* 1931) as producing the international imperialism of money (par. 26). The pope decried "situations whose injustice cries to heaven where whole populations destitute of necessities live in a state of dependence [in which] recourse to violence as a means to right these wrongs to human dignity is a grave temptation" (par. 30). He followed this with a cryptic paragraph, often quoted in later years, that seemed at once to endorse and condemn revolution:

> We know, however, that a revolutionary uprising—save where there is manifest long-standing tyranny which would do great damage to fundamental personal rights and dangerous harm to the common good of the country—produces new injustices, and brings on new disasters. A real evil should not be fought against at the cost of greater misery. [par. 31][10]

Yet after his negative comments (for example, "The world is sick," par. 66) the pope concluded, "Development is another name for peace."

By the time of the 1968 Medellín meeting, therefore, the issue of the moral validity of the present economic and political system in Latin America was squarely before the church. Marxist criticisms of capitalism and the "dependence" of which the pope spoke were being analyzed by social scientists in Latin America. Latin Americans were growing impatient with the meager results of the "development" that had been promised as a solution to Latin America's problems by the Alliance for Progress. Besides the 1964 coup in Brazil, civilian governments had been overthrown in Honduras, Argentina, Bolivia, and Ecuador, and another would be overthrown in October 1968 in Peru, while the armed forces or personalist dictators governed most of Central America. The question of the legitimacy of revolutionary violence, the abuses of capitalism, and the appropriate response to poverty and oppression had to be faced by the bishops at the Medellín meeting. To assist them in doing so a series of working papers had been prepared, and preliminary meetings held. One of those who helped to prepare those papers was a priest from the Lima archdiocese who had been educated at the Catholic universities of Louvain (Belgium) and Lyons (France) and had returned, like Camilo Torres, to work with university students in Lima. His name was Gustavo Gutierrez.

2

The Birth of Liberation Theology: Medellín and Beyond

MANY WRITERS have seen anticipations of the characteristic elements of liberation theology in writings by Latin American theologians in the early and middle 1960s. Such elements can be found, for example, in the earlier writings of Juan Luis Segundo S.J., an Uruguayan Jesuit. In 1962, Segundo published an essay in Spanish, "The Function of the Church in the River Plate," which developed a dialectical vision of the church as a small community in tension with the mass society of modernity but continually engaged with it in a common struggle of transformation. Others have pointed to the World Council of Churches' Conference on Church and Society, "The Christian in the Technical and Social Revolutions of Our Time," held in Geneva in June 1966—in particular, to the call by Richard Shaull, then a professor at the Princeton Theological Seminary, for a theology of revolution that could be applied to the urgent needs of Latin America (in particular to Brazil, where he had taught for a number of years). However, the clearest beginning of the new line of theological speculation is in the writings of Gustavo Gutierrez in the period leading up to and following the 1968 Medellín meeting of the Latin American bishops. What the meeting did was to legitimate a new kind of Catholic radicalism in Latin America that could now cite the official statements of the bishops in support of their arguments.

Even before the end of the Second Vatican Council there had been meetings of theologians who were concerned to develop a theologically grounded response to the problems of Latin America. In 1964 at a meeting in Petropolis, Brazil (which was also attended by Segundo), Gutierrez first presented his conception of theology as scripturally based critical reflection on experience (*praxis*), and he outlined similar ideas to a group of Catholic student leaders in 1967. A more developed version, "Towards a Theology of Liberation," was presented at a meeting in Chimbote, Peru, in July 1968 shortly before Medellín, but it was only after Medellín that his ideas began to receive wide attention. He was himself in attendance at the Medellín meeting and he influenced some of the texts that were finally adopted. Thus there was something of a circular process at work in which the ideas associated with liberation theology were developed before the Medellín meeting, the bishops at Medellín adopted certain key elements and phrases, and then the bishops in turn were cited to give additional legitimacy to the new theological currents.

What is most striking in the conclusions of the Medellín meeting are the frequent references to two concepts that had not appeared in earlier church documents of the Latin American church—"dependence" and "liberation"—and its discussion of the problem of violence in Latin America. In the section entitled *Justice,* the bishops speak of the need for "profound conversion" in order to achieve "authentic liberation" (par. 3). While they endorse the need for "new and reformed structures," the bishops assert that "there will be no new continent without new men who know how to be truly free and responsible according to the light of the Gospel." The transformation of man in the light of the Gospel is described as "an action of integral human development and liberation" (par. 4), thus linking the developmental theme of the 1967 papal encyclical, *Populorum Progressio,* to a new emphasis on liberation. When they discuss the economy the bishops employ the "third position" tactic so common in Catholic social thought to criticize "liberal capitalism" and the "temptation of the Marxist system," both of which are described as "against the dignity of the human person," with Latin America "caught between these two options" and "dependent on one or the other centers of power" (par. 10). The bishops call for a social and economic change "to liberate the authentic process of Latin American development and integration" (par. 11). In the section entitled *Poverty in the Church,* the bishops speak of a "deafening cry . . . from the throats of millions asking their pastors for a liberation that reaches them from nowhere else" (par. 2), and in a phrase that in slightly altered form was to become central (and controversial) in later discussions, the bishops declare that the church must act in a way "that effectively gives preference to the poorest and most needy sectors" (par. 9).[1]

The work of the Ecclesial Base Communities was specifically endorsed by the conference. It referred to *concientización* in favorable terms and called upon the church to promote the establishment of small basic communities "in order to establish a balance with minority groups in power" and to support "the downtrodden of every social class so that they might come to know their rights and how to make use of them" (*Justice*, par. 20).

In these sections, it seemed that a political reading of the conclusions of the conference would have the church deeply involved in organizing the poor and restructuring the economy in a humanist fashion. But suppose, as was the case in many countries at the time, this is not possible because of the nature of the groups in power—in particular, military or authoritarian governments in league with foreign interests? The most famous Medellín document, *Peace*, criticizes "realities that constitute a sinful situation" in Latin America (par. 1) and the Latin American countries' "dependence on a center of economic power around which they gravitate . . . so that our nations frequently do not own their goods or have a say in economic decisions affecting them" and it asserts that "the principal guilt for the economic dependence of our countries rests with powers inspired by uncontrolled desire for gain" (par. 8).

In the same document the bishops deal with the most controversial issue to be discussed at the conference—violence. While claiming that "violence is neither Christian nor evangelical," the bishops proceeded to make the most famous (or infamous) assertion of the meeting:

> In many instances, Latin America finds itself faced with a situation of injustice that can be called institutionalized violence, when because of a structural deficiency of industry and agriculture, of national and international economy, of cultural and political life, whole towns lack necessities and live in such dependence as hinders all initiative and responsibility as well as every possibility for cultural promotion and participation in social and political life, thus violating fundamental rights. This situation demands all-embracing, courageous, urgent, and profoundly renovating transformations. We should not be surprised therefore that the temptation to violence is surfacing in Latin America. [par. 16]

The bishops then quote Paul VI's ambiguous statements on revolution although they reverse the order of his discussion, thus giving more emphasis to the case for revolution, before concluding that violence is usually less effective and more danger-prone than "the dynamism of the awakened and organized community at the service of justice and peace" (par. 19).

Gustavo Gutierrez was an expert advisor (*peritus*) to the committee that drafted the document, *Peace*. One writer asserts that he was its principal author.[2] A revised version of Gutierrez's Chimbote paper was published in Montevideo in 1969 and presented at a conference in Switzerland. The English translation of that paper appeared in the Jesuit journal *Theological Studies* in June 1970, as "Notes for a Theology of Liberation." This seminal article, a slightly condensed version of which appears as Appendix I in this book, led to the writing of the most important and influential work on liberation theology, *A Theology of Liberation,* published in Spanish in 1971 as *Teologia de la Liberación* (Lima: Perspectivas, CEP) and translated into English in 1973 (Maryknoll, NY: Orbis Books).

Who is Gustavo Gutierrez and why did his article and book have such an impact? Gutierrez is a Peruvian who was born in Lima in 1928. After a period as a medical student at San Marcos University he entered the priesthood and was sent to Europe to study philosophy and theology at Louvain, Belgium, and Lyons, France, in the mid-1950s. Although this was before the calling of the Second Vatican Council, new currents were stirring within the European church that would have an effect on the council. Father Emile Houtart at Louvain was developing the study of religious sociology as an important instrument for the use of the church. Biblical studies were being carried out by Catholics on a more ecumenical basis. At Lyons, Henri de Lubac S.J. was interested in the relationship between Christianity and Marxism. A more historical approach was being taken to philosophy than the deductive abstract Thomism that had dominated Catholic theology since the nineteenth—and some would argue the sixteenth—century. The most interesting new figures in theology were two Germans—a Lutheran, Juergen Moltmann, and a Roman Catholic, Johann Baptist Metz, both of whom had developed theological theories intended to relate theology more directly and critically to the problems of the modern secular world ("the theology of hope" and "political theology"). Gutierrez was also influenced by the attempts of the Austrian Jesuit Karl Rahner to recast Thomistic philosophy in existentialist terms that would take account of modern criticisms of the "essentialism" of scholasticism. However, as Gutierrez describes it, until he returned to Peru he was not moved to question the traditional theological education he had received, however updated. In Peru he was ordained in 1959 and took up a position in the Theology Department of the Pontifical University, although he lived (and lives) in Rimac, a slum area of Lima. His confrontation with the poverty of the area led him to three discoveries: "That poverty was a destructive thing, something to be fought against and destroyed . . . that poverty was not accidental . . . but the result of a structure . . . [and] that poor people were a social class. It became crystal clear that in order to serve the poor, one had to move into political action."[3] These discoveries took place at a time of increasing radicalization of Latin American intellectuals and students, and of disillusion with the models of development that had been proposed by the architects of the Alliance for Progress. An important element in their thinking was the theory of *dependencia,* then being developed by Brazilian and Chilean social scientists, which argued that the reason for Latin America's continuing underdevelopment was its dependence on the metropolitan powers—first Spain, then Great Britain, and now the United States. A related (although conceptually distinct) approach that was shared by most Latin American social scientists was a Marxist-influenced class analysis explaining the problems of Latin America in terms of the dominance of bourgeois capitalism and international imperialism. And linking all of these was an international communications network among socially committed Latin American theologians who exchanged information on their insights and experience. The result was the beginning of a new approach to Latin American theology that was based on Latin American experience, and marked a rejection of European and American models, whether in theory (the neo-Thomism of the French Catholic philosopher Jacques Maritain, as well as the developmentalism of the Alliance for Progress) or in practice (the church-influenced Christian Democratic parties, trade unions, and youth and student organizations of the Catholic Action variety).

"Notes for a Theology of Liberation," Gutierrez's 1970 article in the Jesuit journal *Theological Studies,* struck many of these themes, and summarized what were to be the recurring elements in later debates. It began by asserting that theology should be regarded only as "secondary"—as reflection upon the experience of commitment to service in the life of the church. Then it contrasted development, which it equated with economic growth, with liberation, which Gutierrez described as "a dynamic and historical concept of man as looking towards his future, doing things today to shape his tomorrow" (p. 247). Unlike development, liberation implies a need to attack the causes of Latin America's social problems, which can be summed up as "oppression" and "domination."

> Among the central ones is the economic, social, political, and cultural dependence of some peoples on others. That domination involves the complicity of national oligarchies with foreign centers of power which leads to the creation of greater wealth for the few and of greater poverty for the many. To emerge from this situation Latin America needs a social revolution that will radically change the conditions it lives in at present. Today a more or less Marxist inspiration prevails among those groups and individuals who are raising the banner of the continent's revolution. And for many in our continent this liberation will have to pass, sooner or later, through paths of violence. [p. 250]

Where does the church fit into this picture? Generalizing from the students and intellectuals with whom he has been in contact, Gutierrez observes that Catholic youth movements no longer support Christian Democratic parties or else become part of their radical wing. (He is probably thinking of the "rebelde" wing of the Chilean Christian Democratic party that left the party in 1969 to form the Movement for United Popular Action—MAPU—and joined the Allende Popular Unity leftist coalition when it was created in early 1970.) The choice for the church in Latin America is reform or revolution, and it must "break its ties with the present order" and commit itself to the poor, because the Gospel message is "radically incompatible with an alienated society" (p. 254). The church's mission is not only to exercise a social critique but to "stimulate and radicalize the dedication of Christians to history about them" (p. 259). There is a danger in this that theology will become a new ideology, but it is impossible to work out in advance the exact guidelines for the conduct of the church because "there are certain chapters of theology that can only be written afterwards" (p. 258).

Significantly absent until the end of the article are references to the Bible. The first part of the article footnotes Marx, Hegel, W. W. Rostow, and the dependency theorists, and when it turns to more specifically theological themes, the references are to the Medellín document on peace and to the new European theologians, especially Moltmann and Metz. The article concludes with a biblical reference to the coming of the kingdom of peace and justice, and a call for "a new man" (p. 257) involving "a total break with the unjust order to which it is bound in a thousand conscious and unconscious ways," "making oneself one with the poor" by being "dedicated to the revolutionary cause" (pp. 260–61).

This is heady stuff—and it is radical in its formulation, if somewhat vague about details of its execution. It poses the problem—revolution or reform—without answering it directly but with a clear tilt in the direction of the revolutionary alternative. The problem of the use of violence is alluded to, although without the nuances of Paul VI or Medellín. Marxist methodology is accepted as the common instrument of social analysis of Latin America, although more emphasis seems to be placed on dependence as the cause of underdevelopment rather than, as in classical Marxism, exploitation. While the word *praxis* is not used, the concept of theology as reflection that *follows after* rather than *guides* experience seems to be related to the Hegelian-Marxist notion of praxis. Yet implicit in Gutierrez's discussion is a question that would continue to haunt the liberationists: What are the means to achieve the ending of domination or oppression? Have alternative institutions of social change, including democratic participation, pressure group politics, and party competition, proven to be as bankrupt as the radicals of the late 1960s believed? Is the only alternative a violent revolution against capitalism and dependency? And what does theology have to contribute to answering that question?

What had been only outlined in a preliminary paper was amplified and given definitive form in the single most important statement on the subject, which gave the whole movement its name—the book *A Theology of Liberation.* In its very opening chapter, Gutierrez acknowledges two principal influences on his attempt to reformulate the task of theology—the Second Vatican Council and Marxism. The council's call (*Gaudium et Spes,* no. 44) for the church to take account of "signs of the times" is seen as implying an effort to reflect on the actual life of the church rather than in abstract theological categories, and to consider historical experience in the interpretation of the Christian message. In the case of Marxism, Gutierrez speaks of theology's "direct and fruitful confrontation with Marxism . . . in reflecting on the meaning of the transformation of this world and the action of man in history" (p. 9). Gutierrez refers specifically to the Marxian notion of *praxis,* which is based on the *Eleventh Thesis on Feuerbach* ("Philosophers have only interpreted the world; the point is, to change it.") and concludes that "theology fulfills a prophetic function in so far as it interprets historical events with the intention of revealing and proclaiming their profound meaning" (p. 13). He then concludes that theology for him is "critical reflection on Christian praxis in the light of the Word."

How is this to be achieved? In his next chapter Gutierrez suggests that theology should make use of "advances in technological and scientific knowledge," and analyzes the development of ideas of human liberation in Hegel, Marx, and Freud, concluding that their ideas have received specific embodiment in the contemporary "aspiration to liberation" in places as diverse as Vietnam, Brazil, New York, and Prague—the last a reference to the Prague spring of 1968, which experimented with a "socialism with a human face," only to be crushed by direct Soviet intervention in August of that year. These philosophical and historical references are then linked to the two encyclicals of Pope John, *Mater et Magistra* (1961) and *Pacem in Terris* (1963), and Paul VI's *Populorum Progressio* (1967), which for the first time gave a theological interpretation to the concept of development. For Gutierrez's purposes in legitimating his theological project, however, the Second Vatican Council's 1965 decree, *Gaudium et Spes* [The Church in the Modern World] is more important. He finds two key words in the document that are relevant to his argument—dependence and liberation. In paragraphs 9 and 85 he finds references to the continuing dependence of the poor nations on the rich, while he also notes that the word *liberation* is used in paragraphs 10 and 20 (although he does not observe that they are used in discussions of false views of naturalistic humanism and of atheism).[4] After citing one of the very few biblical references in the first half of the book (Galatians 5:1, "For freedom, Christ has set us free"), Gutierrez concludes that liberation is to be understood on three levels, "the aspirations of oppressed peoples and classes, the understanding of history, and as Christ's action in liberating man from sin, the ultimate root of all injustice and oppression" (p. 37).

The next step in Gutierrez's argument is to contrast the "radical change in perspective," which he is proposing, with earlier Catholic social thought, especially that represented by the neo-Thomism of Jacques Maritain and the conception of Christian social and political involvement contained in European and Latin American Catholic Action movements and Christian Democratic parties. Gutierrez criticizes these movements for their "naive reformism," and their attempt to confine the message of the church to preaching the Gospel and providing a source of inspiration for laymen who are to apply its insights to politics. This "distinction of planes," he argues, ignores the fact that "everything has a political color" (p. 47), and that in the Third World the conflict between oppression and liberation makes the conciliatory approach of the Christian Democrats "only a justifying ideology for a profound disorder, a device for the few to keep living off the poverty of the many" (p. 48). Politics is necessarily conflictual, and it is necessary to attack economistic and humanistic visions of reality. An emphasis on the conciliatory aspects of the Gospel overlooking its political and conflictual dimensions interferes with "a scientific and structural knowledge of socio-economic mechanisms and historical dynamics" (p. 49).

How is one to achieve that knowledge? In a later chapter we learn that, in the case of Latin America at least, the key to liberation is provided by a recognition that the cause of the region's underdevelopment is its dependence on the developed world and "the domination exercised by the great capitalist countries, and especially by the most powerful, the United States of America" (p. 89). And that dependence is explicable only in terms of "the worldwide class struggle between oppressed countries and dominant peoples" (p. 87). Latin America because of its experience in the 1960s has entered into a "full-blown process of revolutionary ferment" with guerrilla efforts, the stimulation provided by the example of the Cuban Revolution, the failure of developmentalism and populism to provide effective solutions, and a search for new solutions "most frequently of socialist inspiration" that "represents the most fruitful and far-reaching approach" (p. 90). This socialism will take a variety of different approaches, involving a "broad rich, and intense revolutionary praxis" that seeks "a qualitatively different society" and "the building of a new man" (pp. 90–91).

Among those approaches Gutierrez briefly mentions one that would later become central to the thrust of liberation theology—the work of the Brazilian educator Paulo Freire in developing *A Pedagogy of the Oppressed* (English translation, New York and London: Herder and Herder, 1970). In the process of using Freire's methods of literacy training, the oppressed person becomes aware of his or her situation and is able to find a language with which to become "less dependent and more free, as he commits himself to the transformation and building up of society" (p. 91).

How does the church relate to the revolutionary process that has just been described? In the next chapter Gutierrez calls on the laity, priests, and bishops to become involved in politics. In Latin America "the oppressed and those who seek to identify with them face ever more resolutely a common adversary [capitalism? the United States?], therefore the relationship between Marxists and Christians takes on characteristics different from those in other areas" (p. 104). Some priests have organized to express their own commitment to liberation, and some (Gutierrez is presumably thinking of Camilo Torres) have joined revolutionary groups. On the episcopal level, the main action has been through statements of national bishops conferences and the Latin American Bishops Conference (CELAM) as a whole. At this point, Gutierrez refers once more to the Medellín Conference of Bishops. Ignoring the qualifications contained in the original statement by the bishops, he quotes them as describing the situation in Latin America as one of "institutionalized violence"—and cites the bishops' discussion of dependence as demonstrating that the Latin American church has moved from discussing development to the new theme of liberation. He also cites more radical Latin American priests and bishops to support the moral superiority of socialism over capitalism, and "the abolition of the private ownership of capital which leads to the dichotomy of capital and labor, and the exploitation of man by man" (p. 112). Both earlier (p. 26) and later (p. 274) Gutierrez identifies himself with the need to establish a socialist society in Latin America that is "more just, more free, and more human" (p. 274), and to abolish the private ownership of capital because it is based on "the exploitation of man by man" (p. 111), replacing it with "the social ownership of the means of production" (p. 112).

The reason that such action is necessary is given in the most controversial section of *A Theology of Liberation*, entitled "Christian Brotherhood and the Class Struggle" (pp. 272–79). Insisting that "the class struggle is a fact and neutrality in this question is not possible," Gutierrez demands that the church express its love for the rich by "liberating them from their condition as oppressors, by liberating them from themselves."

> To love one's enemies presupposes recognizing and accepting that one has class enemies and that it is necessary to combat them. . . . To participate in the class struggle . . . leads to a classless society without owners or dispossessed, without oppressor and oppressed. . . . There are growing numbers of Christians who challenge the mythical notion

of the Christian community . . . and who believe that the authentic
unity of the church necessarily implies the option for the oppressed and
exploited of this world.

What has been outlined so far is an insistence that true Christianity involves the overthrow of capitalism and its replacement by a
socialism that will overcome the class struggle—the opposition of
capital and labor inherent in the private ownership of the means of
production. This may appear to be a call for a socialist revolution in
Latin America—through the act of baptizing the revolution. Yet
Gutierrez insists that this is not his intention. He maintains that proponents of the theology of the revolution, such as Richard Shaull,
have not engaged in the level of political analysis that is necessary to
determine whether a revolution is either necessary or desirable. He
also insists throughout the book that the poor and oppressed rather
than a revolutionary elite are to be the agents of their liberation,
and quotes Medellín on the need for more grass-roots organizations
(*organizaciones de base*) to promote the rights of the poor and secure
social justice (pp. 113–14).

So far we have summarized the argument of the first half of the
book as well as a controversial section near its close. Once again one
is struck by the lack of scriptural discussion and the saliency of
Marxist argumentation, although this is not unmixed with a populist
appeal to the need for the organization and participation of the poor.
In the last half of the book Gutierrez discusses more specifically
biblical and spiritual themes, including the significance of the story
of the Exodus in the Old Testament, Christ's role as liberator, and
the ways in which God manifests himself in history.

Particularly striking is the discussion of "a spirituality of liberation" (pp. 203–8), which Gutierrez was to develop in the 1980s.
Here the deeply religious basis of his commitment to the poor shines
through as he argues that "conversion to God implies conversion to
neighbor, in an act of gratuitousness which allows one to encounter
others fully, the universal encounter which is the foundation of communion of men among themselves, and of men with God" producing
a joy and celebration that is "a feast of the Christian community"
(p. 207). Those who view liberation theology as nothing more than
a Christianized Marxism should read these passages of the book, and
the rest of the second half of the work.

A Theology of Liberation set forth most of the major themes of later writings by liberation theologians—the emphasis on praxis as the close interrelation between theory and experience, the role of history, the ideological critique of religion, the importance of the participation of the poor especially through Christian base communities, the use of "social science" (that is, dependence theory and Marxism) to explain Latin American underdevelopment, and the need to work toward overcoming the class struggle and exploitation through the establishment of socialism. Gutierrez's writings contain both of the elements that we singled out at the beginning of this work: a radical critique of domestic and international capitalism, and a call for more active participation of the poor and the oppressed in the work of their liberation. In *A Theology of Liberation,* however, the emphasis is much more upon the former than the latter in the sense that the structuralist anticapitalism is discussed at much greater length than the participatory populism. This emphasis is an understandable product of the time at which the work was written—the late 1960s and the early 1970s. As the book was being completed Chile elected a Marxist president, Salvador Allende, with the support of a coalition that also included Christians and parties of a more secular orientation. Allende's Popular Unity seemed to embody the commitment to the poor and oppressed—and to socialism—that liberation theology argued was the logical conclusion to be drawn from the message of the Scriptures.

3

Revolution and Counterrevolution in Chile

WHAT MADE the Chilean example all the more attractive was that it did not seem to involve a choice between political democracy and a socialist revolution carried out and dominated by a minority. While Allende had received only 36 percent of the votes in the September 1970 popular election, he gained a majority in the congressional runoff (after agreeing with the Christian Democrats to the adoption of a constitutional amendment containing a statute of democratic guarantees) and very close to a majority in the municipal elections of April 1971. In Argentina the military regime was tottering, and it appeared that the country would be required to hold elections that the Peronists, long excluded from the vote, would win; in Peru the military coup of 1968 was now becoming more radicalized, nationalizing many foreign firms and attempting to establish a system of popular participation called SINAMOS ("Without Masters") to channel popular participation; while in Bolivia a left-wing military ruler, Juan José Torres, was being swept along in a wave of popular euphoria that created a popular assembly to replace traditional representative institutions. It was easy to think, at this point, that socialism was the wave of the future in Latin America, and that the newly radicalized church should be in the vanguard of that movement.

This was clearly what the Group of Eighty Priests (at a meeting in which Gutierrez participated) had in mind in Chile when they issued a statement in April 1971 in support of the "accession of the People's Government to power" and declared themselves in favor of "socialism," describing it as involving "the social appropriation of the means of production . . . which overcomes the division of society into antagonistic classes" and generates "new values which will pave the way for a society which evinces more fellowship and brotherhood." The priests called for a "more active participation of Christians in the implementation of socialism."

Six weeks later the bishops of Chile issued an important "Working Paper" entitled "The Gospel, Politics, and Socialisms," which seemed to be intended as a reply to the Eighty. In that document the bishops used a phrase that was to become central to the future debates—the "option for the poor." While rejecting the use of the phrase to mean an "exclusive" choice of the poor over other sectors of society, the bishops described the church's policy as involving "a very special preference for the poor," but said that the choice of economic system that would express that option—that is, between socialism and capitalism—was to be left to the individual Christian, since while the church encouraged Christians to participate in politics and represented basic social and moral values, its role did not include choosing among the many different types of capitalisms and socialisms. However, after saying that a Christian might legitimately opt for socialism as the best system to help the poor, the bishops warned that in Chile the "real agents" of socialism were the Marxist parties, and that this raised special problems. Marxism was not only a method but an all-embracing philosophy, an atheistic world view, and, in practice, an ideological "monolithism" that led to the imposition of totalitarianism and the single party. Both Marxist socialism and capitalism, said the bishops, are materialist in orientation and manipulate the many for the benefit of the few. As for those who see Marxism as a "scientific" approach to history, sociology, and economics, the bishops recalled that

history has demonstrated as false many of the laws that Marx held to be scientific, necessary, and inevitable. The Marxist approach, with its economic determinism and exclusivity, cannot be reconciled with Christianity although a sincere Christian can collaborate with the present government if he: 1) believes that it offers the best possibilities for opening the history of Chile to the liberating power of Christ's resurrection, 2) maintains a critical attitude towards his decision and recognizes that he should avoid making his commitment into an absolute value, and 3) is aware of the risks involved in his choice.[1]

Besides their general statement on the issue of the participation of Christians in the Allende government, the bishops also issued a specific reply to the Eighty discussing a question that was to become increasingly important in Latin America in later years—the role of the priest in politics. While defending the right of the clergy to make political choices, the bishops warned that to give this choice the "moral backing that stems from his character as a priest" may "threaten to disrupt the unity of the Christian people with their pastors" and if his choice is "presented as a logical and inescapable consequence of this Christian faith, as in this case, then it implicitly condemns every other option and thus it is an attack on the liberty of other Christians."

In the same month that the bishops published their declaration on socialism, Pope Paul VI issued an encyclical, *Octagesima Adveniens,* to celebrate the eightieth anniversary of Leo XIII's labor encyclical, *Rerum Novarum.* After discussing the church's support for the rights of the human person and its "preferential respect for the poor" (par. 3), the encyclical devoted considerable attention to contemporary ideologies. Taking the customary "third-position" stance of the Vatican, it argued that

> the Christian cannot without contradicting himself adhere to ideological systems which radically go against his faith and his concept of man. He cannot adhere to Marxist ideology, to its atheistic materialism, to its dialectic of violence and to the way it absorbs individual freedom in the collectivity, at the same time denying all transcendence to man and his personal and collective history; nor can he adhere to the liberal ideology which believes it exalts individual freedom by withdrawing it from every limitation, stimulating exclusive seeking of interest and power, and by considering social solidarity as more or less automatic consequences of individual initiatives. [par. 25]

While recognizing that Marxism and liberalism have adopted different forms, the Pope warns that "careful judgment is called for. Too often Christians attracted by socialism tend to idealize it in terms which apart from anything else, are very general: a will for justice, solidarity, and equality. They refuse to recognize the limitations of the historical socialist movements which remain conditioned by the ideologies from which they originated" (par. 25). There is a danger "of accepting the elements of Marxist analysis without recognizing their relationships with ideology and of entering into the practice of class struggle and its Marxist interpretations while failing to note the kind of totalitarian and violent society to which this process leads" (par. 34).

In the case of liberalism, while there has been a "renewal of liberal ideology in the name of economic efficiency and of the defense of the individual," it too calls for "discernment" because "at the very root of philosophical liberalism is an effective affirmation of the autonomy of the individual, his activity, his motivation and the exercise of his liberty" (par. 35).[2]

If both Marxism and liberalism are seriously flawed, what is the Christian to do? The encyclical noted at the outset (par. 4) that

> in the face of such widely varying situations it is difficult for us to utter a unified message and to put forward a solution which has universal validity. Such is not our ambition, or is it our mission. It is up to the Christian communities to analyze with objectivity the situation which is proper to their own country, to shed on it the light of the Gospel's unalterable words and to draw principles of reflection, norms of judgment, and directions for action from the social teaching of the Church.

The pope then reviewed the changes that have taken place since the encyclicals of his predecessors in 1891 and 1931, asserting that

> today men yearn to free themselves from need and dependence. But this liberation starts with the interior freedom that men must find again with regard to their goods and their powers. They will never reach it except through a transcendent love for man, and in consequence through a genuine readiness to serve. Otherwise as one can see only too clearly, the most revolutionary ideologies lead only to a change of masters. [par. 54]

The encyclical concludes that "in concrete situations and taking account of solidarity in each person's life, one must recognize a legitimate variety of possible options. The same Christian faith can lead to different commitments" (par. 50).

The encyclical thus appears to be making the same argument as the Chilean bishops, although its warnings against the dangers on the left seem stronger, socialism appears to be more quickly and directly identified with Marxism than in the Chilean document, and the overall tone seems more admonitory than that of the Chileans.

Six months after the publication of the encyclical the Second General Synod of Bishops was held in Rome with "Justice" as its theme.

In preparation for the meeting, national bishops' conferences prepared presentations on the synodal theme that reflected the general radicalization of social criticism by the Latin American church. In the case of the Peruvian bishops, their statement—in the preparation of which Gustavo Gutierrez had a major role—no longer left it up to the individual or local community to decide on the capitalism-socialism question. Beginning from a "personal and communal commitment" "to opt for the poor and marginalized," the Peruvians state in straightforward fashion, "The humanist understanding of work and the experience of our people leads to the rejection of capitalism both in its economic form and its ideological basis which favors individualism, profit, and the exploitation of man by man." Following the usual balancing act of Catholic social thought, the bishops also denounced "certain bureaucratic, totalitarian, and atheistic socialisms," but the influence of Gutierrez became much clearer when they argued for "a real democracy with effective political participation and social ownership of the means of production." The military government of Peru had already instituted a method for giving workers a share in profits and ownership through the so-called Industrial Community, which was ultimately aimed at a fifty-fifty sharing between workers and investors, and it was also planning to establish some experimental worker-owned firms. (Both programs were substantially modified after an internal military coup in 1975.) However the bishops went much further when they announced as their goal the establishment of "a socialist society with a humanist and Christian content" (p. 245).[3]

The second General Synod of Bishops did not make as clear a statement as the Peruvians but it clearly was influenced by the liberation themes that had been stated by the Latin American bishops. "Scrutinizing 'the signs of the times,' " the final document, "Justice in the World," echoes at the outset the structuralist critique of Medellín when it speaks of "the cry of those who suffer violence and are oppressed by the unjust systems and structures" and even quotes without attribution chapter 4 of St. Luke's Gospel, the biblical proof text of the liberationists, when it speaks of "the Church's vocation to be present in the heart of the world by proclaiming the Good News to the poor, freedom to the oppressed, and joy to the afflicted" (par. 5). The bishops repeatedly warn of the disastrous consequences "if the developing nations and regions do not attain liberation through development" (par. 16), God is described as "the liberator and defender of the poor" (par. 30), and the bishops conclude that "the mission of preaching the Gospel dictates at the present times that we should dedicate ourselves to the liberation of man even in this present existence in the world" (par. 35).[4]

When it comes to specific recommendations the bishops speak mainly of the need to support the United Nations and promote human rights. Their only controversial recommendation is a paragraph that supports giving less developed nations "full and equal participation in organizations concerned with development," criticizing the developed nations' "almost total domination of economics, research, investment, freight charges, sea transport, and insurance"—an anticipation of later proposals at the U.N. that were to be described by their proponents as the New Economic Order. The new vocabulary of liberation did not therefore translate itself into a radical demand for revolution on the part of the bishops, nor did it, as in the case of the liberation theologians, mean that the earlier interest in development had been abandoned. It did, however, mark a stronger interest in the problems of poverty, violence, and oppression, at a time when all three were increasingly visible in areas such as Latin America, and its concluding paragraph continued the Medellín program by expressing special concern for "the poor, oppressed, and afflicted" (par. 77).

At the end of 1971 Fidel Castro made a lengthy visit to Chile during which he met priests who were sympathetic to the Cuban Revolution. In his speech to the students at the University of Concepción he discussed the relation between the revolution and the church, arguing that religion was not at the root of the church-state conflicts in Cuba but that the problem was the utilization by the bourgeoisie of religion as a political instrument. He claimed that the Cuban Revolution had never been antireligious, and that within the church there were now revolutionary and progressive currents favoring liberation, which made it possible for there to be a "strategic alliance" between Marxists and Christians. In his farewell speech in the Chilean National Stadium, Castro specifically referred to his discussion with the Group of Eighty Priests on the necessity of uniting Marxist revolutionaries and Christian revolutionaries in an alliance based on the "enormous points of coincidence between the most pure precepts of Christianity and objectives of Marxism."[5] There was no mention of the fact that Christians in Cuba are excluded from many professions and from party membership, or of the closure of the Catholic schools and the expulsion of foreign priests in the early years of the revolution. Castro's discussion was important because it opened up a topic that was to be much discussed in later years—in particular after the Nicaraguan Revolution in which "revolutionary Christians" took an active part, and following which several priests participated in a Marxist-led government.

At the time of Castro's visit, the Eighty Priests decided to form a permanent organization, and called a meeting of the Christians for Socialism to be held at the same time as the worldwide UNESCO Conference scheduled for April 1972 in Santiago. The draft agenda for the meeting was clear in its political commitment: "We must make explicit our revolutionary option in favor of the implementing socialism through the rise of the proletariat to power." Santiago's Cardinal Raúl Silva Henriquez declined an invitation to participate, charging the meeting's organizers with reducing Christianity to the revolutionary class struggle and to a "single dimension: socioeconomic transformation." The preparatory report to the conference presented by the Chilean delegation was a lengthy document that traced the history of Christian participation in politics from Christian conservatism through Christian reformism or Social Christianity (the Christian Democratic Party), to a dialectical "revolutionary Christianity." On the subject of violence it asserted that "the preference of the Christian is for peace, but the battle often does not conform to his preference. The dosage of violence is determined by those who resist being deprived of their privileges."

The conference was attended by 400 delegates from all over Latin America. When questions were raised about its financing, it was said that much of it had come from a "Foreign Missions Board of a major Protestant church," but opposition Chileans assumed that there had been financial assistance from the Allende government. The Final Document of the conference adopted a distinctly Marxist line and did not contain a single reference to the Bible or to the social teaching of the Church—not even to the Medellín conference. It endorsed Castro's proposal of a strategic alliance between Marxists and revolutionary Christians "within the liberation process on this continent," and stated that there were only two possible alternatives, dependent capitalism or socialism.

> Socialism presents itself as the only acceptable option for getting beyond a class-based society [since] social classes are a reflection of the economic base which in a capitalistic society sets up an antagonistic division between the possessors of capital and those who are paid for their labor. To attain socialism we need . . . a revolutionary praxis

of the proletariat. . . . Operating through the takeover of power by the exploited masses, this praxis leads to social appropriation of the means of production and financing and to comprehensive rational economic planning.

The document concluded by quoting Che Guevara's statement, "When Christians dare to give full-fledged revolutionary witness, then the Latin American revolution will be invincible." Just at the time that the Final Document was being written, the Allende government's "comprehensive rational planning" was beginning to produce the economic breakdown and political polarization that ultimately produced the September 1973 coup. By June 1972 the inflation rate in Chile was over 100 percent; by the next July it was 323 percent. Massive government deficits and the collapse of industry and agriculture, as well as social tension heightened by increasing violence on both sides and an attempt by the Allende government to impose a prescribed curriculum on the private schools ("the Unified National School") finally led the armed forces to overthrow the Allende government on September 11, 1973.[6]

In a period of increasing social conflict, in April 1973 the bishops met to consider what attitude they should take toward the Christians for Socialism. They drafted a document that was formally approved only two days after the September 1973 coup. Entitled "Christian Faith and Political Activity," it harshly criticized the Christains for Socialism on the grounds that although the movement used the name of Christians and was organized and directed by priests, it took "positions so clearly and decidedly political that it is indistinguishable from political parties of similar currents of opinion." The organization does not distinguish between the role of the laity and the clergy, and it makes judgments that are based on "the Marxist-Leninist method of interpreting history in economic terms [which] reduces the religious life of humanity to an ideology reflecting the economic infrastructure and the class struggle. . . . Where religion claims to be above and beyond conflicting dialectics in the social struggle . . . this method sees alienation and complicity with the dominant social groups." Although the church is not neutral in the struggle for justice, it does not offer any political model per se as its own and does not exercise political power, "while the Christians for Socialism identify the people of God with a proletarian class that is conscious of its situation." The lengthy document concludes, "we prohibit priests and religious from belonging to that organization; and also from carrying out the kinds of activity that we have denounced in this document." When the document was finally adopted in September, the prohibition was no longer necessary since all organizations of its type had been outlawed and its principal leaders had been driven into exile.

There had been earlier exiles. Shortly after Allende came to power, the Belgian Jesuit Roger Vekemans S.J., who had been an advisor to the Christian Democratic president Eduardo Frei before his election in 1964, and the director of an influential "think-tank" in Santiago, left the country. He first went to Caracas, but finding it inhospitable set up a similar research group in Bogota, the Center for the Study of Development and Integration in Latin America (CEDIAL), which was largely staffed with Chileans and principally dedicated to fighting liberation theology. A short book by Vekemans that was written at the start of the Allende period, *God and Caesar, The Priesthood in Politics,* has been published in English (Maryknoll, NY: Orbis Books, 1972). It is an attempt to draw a middle line between an otherworldly "verticalism" and a politicized "horizontalism" in deciding what is the proper role for the priest in politics, and it devotes particular attention to the problem of ideology and its relation to the social teachings of the church. In Bogota Vekemans began organizing seminars and a monthly publication (*Tierra Nueva*), and wrote books and articles to combat the new theological trends in Latin America. His extraordinarily well-documented *Teología de la Liberación y Cristianos por el Socialismo* (Bogota: CEDIAL, 1976) argued, as the title implies, that the revolutionary lyricism of the Christians for Socialism was linked theoretically to the heavily Marxist content of the theology by which it was inspired. To demonstrate the links between liberation theology and the Christians for Socialism, Vekemans cited Gutierrez's role as "godfather" (*padrino*) to the original Declaration of the Eighty and his lecture on "Marxism and Christianity" at the ceremony establishing the secretariat of the organization. Vekemans also observed that the research organization of another liberation theologian, Hugo Assmann (discussed below) served as secretariat and publicity center for the Chilean group, and that Assmann himself was the author of its initial document.[7]

Vekemans has been portrayed as a sinister *bête noir* by the liberation theologians, but they feel even more threatened by Alfonso Lopez Trujillo, then auxiliary bishop (now cardinal) of Medellín, Colombia. In November 1972, at the Fourteenth Ordinary Assembly of CELAM,

Lopez Trujillo was elected Secretary General of the organization and thereafter a number of personnel changes were made to put more moderate bishops in charge of key departments. For the supporters of liberation theology this amounted to a counterrevolution in which, in the words of a letter of a number of German theologians "the driving force behind this campaign is Roger Vekemans . . . supported especially by the Colombian auxiliary bishops, Alfonso Lopez Trujillo and D. Castrillon."[8]

Yet Lopez Trujillo did not take the rabidly antiliberation stance of Vekemans (who in his book described the writings of the liberation theologians as "promiscuities" and "feverish ravings"). In 1973 he sponsored a meeting of a theological reflection team that involved a dialogue between Gutierrez and other liberationists, and their major Latin American critics. Because the meeting distinguished among the liberationist writers on issues such as acceptance of Marxist theories of the class struggle and support for revolution, it has been interpreted by one writer as an attempt to deradicalize liberation theology by promoting divisions among them, but an examination of the publication that resulted from the meeting reveals a sincere attempt to distinguish the elements of liberation theology that are or are not compatible with Catholic social thought.[9]

In a later book published after he had become Archbishop of Medellín and President of CELAM, Lopez Trujillo engages in a more detailed and nuanced analysis of liberation theology.[10] There he attacks the notion that liberation theology is a logical consequence of the statements of the Medellín conference—either in its basic theses, its conduct, or its Marxist content (p. 99). However, he notes that unlike earlier European efforts at a theology of revolution, the theology of liberation recognizes the necessity of establishing a certain autonomy for theology and does not simply place itself at the service of any and all revolutionary movements. He distinguishes between the notions of liberation put forward at Medellín, emphasizing sin and conversion, and those put forward by the liberationists, emphasizing politics and conflict. Even among the latter group he finds that Gutierrez's writings are primarily pastoral in intention while those of Hugo Assmann, for example, are "fiery and bellicose" (p. 236). Lopez notes that after the 1972 meeting of the Christians for Socialism in Santiago, another meeting held in El Escorial in Spain seemed to indicate that at least some of the liberation wirters were moving away from the heavily politicized writing that concentrated on the class struggle to more directly theological themes. This was particularly true, in his view, of Gutierrez, whose presentation seemed to indicate "a desire to save theology from the temptation of ideologization" (p. 248). Lopez Trujillo's "hidden agenda" was thus not really hidden. He was attempting to reclaim the notion of liberation from the heavily Marxist interpretation that had been given it by the theologians of the new school.

This was necessary because the term *liberation* was becoming more and more widely used both in Latin America and in papal documents. An example of its new prominence that demonstrates the difference between the rhetoric of the 1960s and that of the 1970s appears in two successive editions of a book by the French theologian René Laurentin. When it was published in French in 1969 it was entitled *Developpement et Salut,* but the English translations (Orbis Books, 1972) was called, *Liberation, Development, and Salvation,* with an introduction that explained the reason for the change. While the final declaration of the Second General Assembly of the Synod of Bishops in November 1971 had attempted to link the two notions when it spoke of "liberation through development" ("Justice in the World," par. 16), at the next meeting of the Synod's General Assembly in 1976, the word *liberation* was sprinkled throughout the discussions. In their 1976 final declaration the bishops spoke of "the social consequences of sin which are translated into unjust social and political structures," but noted that "the Church does not remain within merely social and political limits (elements which she must take into account) but leads towards freedom under all its forms—liberation from sin, from collective or individual selfishness."[11] By 1976, when Pope Paul VI published *Evangelii Nuntiandi* [On Preaching the Gospel], liberation had become an important concept in Catholic theology but by then it was linked directly to the Gospels and purged of its Marxist and revolutionary connotations. Thus Paul states that the Gospel proclaims "liberation from everything that oppresses people particularly liberation from sin." This liberation is neither exclusively spiritual nor exclusively political since "it cannot be limited to any restricted sphere whether it be economic, political, social, or cultural. It must rather take account of the totality of the human person" (par. 33). Also, it is not limited to this world or the next, because the hereafter is "both in continuity and in discontinuity with the present situation" (par. 27).[12]

Liberation had thus become theologically respectable, but its content had been broadened and an attempt was being made to break its association with Marxist analysis and solutions. Henceforth the argument would be over the theological content of the term rather than its relevance to contemporary theology.

In his book Lopez Trujillo also alluded to another problem that was to become much more significant in later writings of the liberation theologians. This was the opposition he noted in some documents of the Christians for Socialism between the institutional church—that is, the hierarchy—and the "popular" church—that is, the people, who in turn were identified with the poor, who then became the proletariat (p. 101).[13] He linked this to the spread of the Ecclesial Base Communities, which he observed should be seen as instruments of evangelization and not of politicization or opposition to ecclesiastical communion. Again, an attempt was being made to distinguish between the positive and negative aspects of the new movements and to de-radicalize them both in terms of their ideology—Marxist elements—and their conduct—the danger of organizational opposition to the hierarchy.

4

The Development of Liberation Theology:
The Marxist Phase

THE EFFORT to counteract, moderate, or co-opt liberation theology took place at a time of increasing polarization in Latin America. Not only had the Allende government in Chile been overthrown in September 1973, but in late 1971 the radical Torres government in Bolivia had been replaced by a right-wing government under General Hugo Banzer, the long-standing democracy of Uruguay ("The Switzerland of Latin America") had been undermined and then abolished by the military in 1973, the progressive military government of General Juan Velasco in Peru had been replaced by a more conservative regime under General Francisco Morales Bermudez in 1975, the military government of Ecuador had moved to the right in 1976, and in the same year in Argentina the government of Isabel Perón was overthrown by a particularly repressive military junta under General Rafael Videla. In fact, if one looked at a map of Latin America in the mid-1970s only Venezuela, Costa Rica, Colombia, and Mexico had relatively free governments. The church took varying positions toward the new military regimes, but in most countries it was active in the protection of human rights, providing shelter and help to the victims of military repression. This was particularly true in Brazil, Chile, and El Salvador, where the church vigorously opposed the violation of human rights, both in its statements and actions. The liberation theologians became more radicalized as they viewed the terrible plight of Latin America, and the Latin American left began to argue that the ideological source of the military intervention was the doctrine of the National Security State, an American-imposed ideology that justified any action, however monstrous, if it was done in the name of the defense of "the free world" against the Communist threat.

José Miguez Bonino

An example of the continuing radical character of liberation theology in the period following the Chilean coup and the most influential Protestant work on the subject is the book by José Miguez Bonino, *Doing Theology in a Revolutionary Situation* (Philadelphia: Fortress Press, 1975). In the introduction to his book Miguez Bonino refers to the Christians for Socialism meeting in Santiago (in which he participated) and acknowledges his use of "sociological science indebted to Marxist analysis." What follows is much Marxist sociology and almost no theology. Rejecting the populism of the 1960s, which emphasized the "people" rather than a class analysis, Miguez argues that while Marxist dogmatism is to be avoided, theologians of liberation will employ "a strict scientific-ideological analysis, avowedly Marxist" to aid them in reflecting on "historical praxis," unmasking "enslaving political options" such as theologies of development and "third positions," and forcing them to deal with problems of conflict and violence, while also including specifically theological elements such as "death, fellowship, and sacrifice" that the Marxists ignore (p. 73). The use of Marxism therefore does not involve abstract or eternal theory or dogmatic formulae but "scientific analysis and a number of verifiable hypotheses. . . . [I]t seems to many of us that it has proved and still proves to be the best instrument available for an effective and rational realization of human possibilities in historical life" (pp. 85–97).

Miguez Bonino also devotes considerable attention to hermeneutics—that is, the theory of interpretation (from Hermes, the messenger of the gods), originally developed in connection with nineteenth-century interpretation of the Bible, but now given more general application. For the liberation theologians hermeneutics means "an identification of the ideological frameworks of interpretation implicit in a given religious praxis" (p. 94). He argues that one must be self-conscious about the way in which one's commitment affects one's reading of the Bible, since "all we have today in Latin America are reactionary, reformist, or revolutionary readings of what we have called the germinal events of the Christian faith." It is clear which reading he favors, but the book devotes little or no attention to developing such an interpretation. Indeed, as he admits (p. 61), the first half of the book is simply a rehash of the familiar arguments of the secular left concerning the failures of developmentalism, "the hoax of democracy" (p. 15), and the continuing exploitation of Latin America by multinational corporations.

> The capitalist form of production as it functions in today's world in the dependent countries (perhaps not only in them) creates a form of human existence characterized by artificiality, selfishness, the inhuman and dehumanizing pursuit of success measured in terms of prestige and money, and the resignation of responsibility for the world and for one's neighbor. [p. 31]

The solution is to recognize that "the class struggle is a fact" and abandon "the ideology of conciliation at any price" so that

> we love the oppressed, defending and liberating him; the oppressor by accusing and combating him. Love compels us to fight for the liberation of those who live under a condition of objective sin . . . in this way, paradoxically, class struggle does not only not contradict the universality of love, but becomes demanded by it. [pp. 119–22]

Only in the last two chapters of the book does Miguez Bonino touch specifically theological themes (without citing a single biblical reference until the last sentence), when he analyzes the writings of the German theologian Juergen Moltmann. He is aware that Moltmann has been critical of liberation theology as "seminary Marxism" and he returns the compliment by accusing Moltmann of failing to give a "coherent socioanalytical account of oppression" while insisting at the same time that the Christian must identify with the poor, the oppressed, and the humiliated: "But the poor, the oppressed, the humiliated are a class and live in countries. . . . [I]s it possible to claim a solidarity with the poor and to hover above right and left as if that choice did not have anything to do with the matter?" (pp. 147–48). Having then identified Christian solidarity toward the poor with a leftist quasi-Marxist commitment, Miguez Bonino concludes—almost as an afterthought—with a discussion of the importance of Christian base communities, although even here he feels it necessary to warn that they run the danger of moving into the subjectivity of bourgeois religiosity rather than involving themselves politically and relating "their communal Christian experience to a concrete political and ideological praxis" (p. 172).[1]

Hugo Assmann

Hugo Assmann's *Theology for a Nomad Church* (Maryknoll, NY: Orbis Books, 1976) was a product of the same period, having first been published in Spain in 1973 as *Teología desde la praxis de la Liberación* (only the first half of the Spanish edition was translated) and written during Assmann's days in Allende's Chile. Like Miguez Bonino, Assmann attacks the reformists: "The concept of 'development' has been shown up for the lie that it is" (p. 49). Also like Miguez Bonino, he criticizes the European theologians for not being specific enough, not daring to use the word *imperialism* and failing to "rise to the challenge of openly naming the components of the infra- and super-structures of power, and the implications of strategic and tactical attacks on them" (p. 34). "In view of the appalling political naivete of much theology it can at least be suggested that using secular science as a basis for theological reflection may be the only realistic way of dragging theology out of its ghetto" (p. 64). That reflection must be related directly to the goal of liberation, since—and here Assmann quotes one of the sillier statements made by an earlier liberation theologian, the Brazilian Protestant Rubem Alves—"Truth is the name given by the historical community to those actions which were, are, and will be effective for the liberation of man" (p. 76).

Citing the Medellín references to sinful social situations and appealing to the example of the Exodus of the Jews from slavery in Egypt, Assmann argues that in a world in which two-thirds of the population lives in a situation of oppression, theologians must become politically involved. While he denies that this requires them to develop a full-blown theory of revolution, he believes that this calls for "theoretical reflection on the demands of the historical movement and the implications of the fact of revolution in practice for liberating Christian faith" (which seems to be the same thing) so as to maintain "a critical consciousness at the heart of the revolutionary process" (pp. 90–91).

To do so one must "look at the given situation as our primary and basic reference point. . . . The Bible, tradition, the *magisterium* or teaching authority of the Church, history of dogma and so on, even though they need to be worked out in contemporary practice, do not institute a primary source of 'truth in itself' unconnected with the historical now of 'truth in action'" (p. 104).

This sounds like a quasi-fascist antiintellectualism, rather than the application of social science to theology. Yet in the next chapter Assmann begins to develop more specific categories that are drawn from dependence theory and Marxism. There he argues that liberation is the "political correlative" of dependence and "for most of those who use this language, this implies the use of a sociological analysis derived from Marxism, and a strategy that will lead to a form of socialist society" (p. 116). This will require a "total break with the ways sought through development in its various guises, including those masquerading as: 'Third World roads' (state capitalism, revolutionary nationalism and so on)" (p. 131). It is not clear what the strategy and tactics of that break are to be, for example, whether they will involve the electoral road to power as in Allende's Chile, or what a given set of circumstances require. One is obliged to commit oneself on such tactical questions as what one means by "party," "proletariat," "vanguard," "methods of action," but the basic minimum for liberation is "the anti-development option" (p. 131).

If the Bible and church teaching are not a source of truth, and a total break is to be carried out under the guidance of Marxist sociological analysis, what is the specifically Christian role? Christians committed to revolution realize that

> the traditional contributions of Christian social teaching . . . are wholly inadequate for action on the more radical implications of faith as the practice of liberation . . . [and that] their commitment to liberation means introducing the class struggle into the Church itself. They know that they are not *with* other Christians but *in open conflict* with the majority of them. [p. 138]

While committed Christians will use Marxist sociological categories, they recognize that "orthodox Marxism often seems incapable of appreciating the features peculiar to the Latin American situation," which include both petit-bourgeois values and a passivity that is based on "pseudo-Christian" traditions and values. The revolutionary Christian recognizes that there is a special place for faith in this process—for a revolutionary ethic that "was Che Guevara's constant dream . . . that makes use of most specific channels for the efficacy of love" (p. 141). Assmann concludes by calling for Christians to develop "plans for the objectives of liberation in the form of a historical project" and recognizes that Christians of middle-class extraction can be "a humanizing influence on the revolutionary process" although the oppressed and the exploited are the ones who must become the revolutionary vanguard. While

> neither the structures of the Church nor the theology in vogue offer resources for a specifically Christian contribution for liberation . . . A truly historical reading of the Bible, particularly of the message of Christ, leads to a whole series of radical questions to which Marxism has not paid sufficient attention, of which perhaps the most significant is the Christian affirmation of victory over death, that final alienation to which Marxism can find no satisfactory answer. [pp. 143–44]

As in the case of Miguez Bonino's book, *Theology for a Nomad Church* is significantly lacking in biblical analysis (there is only one biblical citation), and its theology is really methodology—a discussion of how to do theology rather than an effort to do it. It oscillates between an action-oriented antiintellectual pragmatism, and a derivative Marxism, with occasional references to dependence theory thrown in. It is easy to see why Assmann is often regarded as one of the most radical of the liberation theologians.[2] His position did not make his life easy for him. Born in Brazil of German extraction, he was subsequently expelled from that country, Bolivia, and Chile, and spent years of exile in Costa Rica. He is now teaching at a small Methodist-sponsored university near São Paulo, Brazil, and in 1988 was the object of an assassination attempt that left four bullets in his body.

José Porfirio Miranda

While the liberation theologians of this period all acknowledge their debt to Marxist analysis—in particular, to the class struggle, the role of conflicting economic interests, the importance of history and of actual experience (praxis) in evaluating one's theoretical position, as well as a certain progressivist interpretation of stages of consciousness in history—few of them actually confront Marx's writings directly. The exception would be José Porfirio Miranda, a Mexican ex-Jesuit, who has written a number of books on the relation of the New Testament to Marx's writings, especially in his early "humanist" phase. His best-known work, *Marx and the Bible* (Maryknoll, NY: Orbis Books, 1974), was originally published in Spain in 1971. It attempts to show that the Bible shares Marx's opposition to private property, his dialectical method, and his historical vision. Most significant for the development of liberation theology is its analysis of the similarities between St. Paul's concept of the "new man" who is transformed by conversion to the Christian faith and "the Marxist hope that the world will be transformed when the relationships among men become true bonds of love and justice" (p. 277). He recognizes that Marx was an atheist and therefore both avoided the problem of death and "did not even glimpse the possibility of resurrection" (p. 278), but then quotes the German Marxist philosopher Ernst Bloch to the effect that the logical next step in the dialectic would be a transcendence (*Aufhebung*) of the order of nature not unlike the Christian belief in the resurrection. In a later book, *Marx Against the Marxists* (Maryknoll, NY: Orbis Books, 1980), he repeats a claim that had been made often by European participants in the Christian-Marxist dialogue— that Marx's opposition was not to religion as such, but to the specifically bourgeois version of Christianity of nineteenth-century Europe that used the Christian message as an ideological justification for capitalism. Marx, he notes, described religion not only as "the opiate of the people" but also as "the sigh of the oppressed creature" and "the heart of the heartless world." This argument was to become more important at the end of the 1970s in Central America when Marxists and Christians began active collaboration in revolutionary activity. Miranda's direct influence on the other liberation theologians was very limited, however. He did not participate in their meetings, and eventually he abandoned both his Jesuit vocation and his Catholic faith. Moreover, his interpretations of both the Bible and Marx are unconvincing. Marx's atheism was genuine and did not spring only from opposition to bourgeois religion. As a young man he wrote of his sympathy for Prometheus in rejecting submission to the gods, and argued that "the criticism of religion ends with the doctrine that for man the supreme being is man." As the English Catholic theologian Nicholas Lash concludes, Miranda's "reading of the Bible in *Marx and the Bible* seems as tendentious as his reading of Marx in *Marx Against the Marxists*" (*A Matter of Hope: A Theologian's Reflections on the Thought of Karl Marx*, Notre Dame, IN: University of Notre Dame Press, 1981, p. 4).

Juan Luis Segundo

A much more influential writer on liberation theology is Juan Luis Segundo S.J., a Uruguayan Jesuit who, as noted earlier, has been writing on related themes since the early 1960s. He is the only liberation theologian on whom two doctoral theses and books have been published. (Alfred T. Hennelly, *Theologies in Conflict: The Challenge of Juan Luis Segundo,* Maryknoll, NY: Orbis Books, 1979, and Anthony J. Tambasco, *The Bible for Ethics: Juan Luis Segundo and First World Ethics,* Lanham, MD: University Press of America, 1981.) He is the most prolific of the liberation theologians, although the quality of his writing does not always match its quantity.

Two of his writings, however, are widely acknowledged to be important contributions: *The Liberation of Theology* (Maryknoll, NY: Orbis Books, 1976), a revised version of lectures given at Harvard Divinity School in early 1971, and "Capitalism and Socialism: A Theological Crux," an article originally published in *Concilium,* vol. 6, no. 10: Claude Geffré and Gustavo Gutierrez, eds., *The Mystical and Political Dimensions of the Christian Faith* (New York: Herder and Herder, 1974), pp. 78–91. The article, which has been reprinted in many studies and collections on liberation theology, is considered important because it articulates most clearly what the liberation theologians mean by *socialism* and why they choose it over capitalism:

> By socialism we do not mean a long-term social project endowed with a particular ideology or philosophy. We give the name of socialism to a political regime in which the ownership of the means of production is removed from individuals and handed over to higher institutions whose concern is the common good. By capitalism we understand the political regime in which the ownership of the goods of production is open to economic competition. . . . Today the only thing we can do is decide whether we are going to leave to individuals or private groups, or to take away from them, the right to possess the means of production which exist in their countries. That is what we call the option for capitalism or socialism. [p. 115]

To the criticism that the details of such a transformation should be described, Segundo unconvincingly replies that to demand that "Latin Americans put forward a project for socialist society which will guarantee in advance that the evident defects of known socialist societies will be avoided" is like asking Christ before he cures the sick man to guarantee that "the cure will not be followed by even graver illnesses" (p. 121). Segundo concludes,

> The sensibility of the left is an intrinsic feature of an authentic theology. . . . In the face of the options between racial separation and full community of rights, free international demand and supply and a balanced market (with an eye to the underprivileged countries), or capitalism and socialism, what is at stake . . . is the eschatalogical Kingdom itself, whose realization and revelation are awaited with anguish by the whole universe. [p. 123]

The Liberation of Theology is a more sophisticated statement of Segundo's views. It opens with a chapter on hermeneutics that develops Segundo's theory of "the hermeneutic circle," the continuing change in our interpretation of the Bible that is "dictated by the changes in our present-day reality, both individual and social" (p. 8). He follows this with an application of his method to the writings of Harvey Cox, Karl Marx, Max Weber, and the black theologian James Cone. Particularly interesting is his analysis (pp. 13–19) of the Marxian critique of religion, in which he criticizes Marx for not continuing to develop the thinking that inspired the less well-known lines that followed his famous claim that religion is "the opiate of the masses"—"Religious suffering is at the same time an expression of real suffering and a protest against real suffering" (*Contribution to a Critique of Hegel's Philosophy of Right*). Segundo believes that if Marx had pursued that strain he would have realized that ideology had warped the thinking of contemporary Christians in nineteenth-century Europe so that "they ended up unwittingly interpreting it in a sense that served the interests of the ruling class," and perhaps he would have been able to ask whether "a new interpretation favoring the class struggle of the proletariat might be possible or even necessary" (p. 17). Today, Segundo says, "Marx's work is such a stimulus for theology that new methods and profound questions in present-day theology are an inheritance from him, even though Marx rejected theology" (p. 18). Segundo's own method, the "hermeneutics of suspicion" of the ideological content of religious and philosophical theories is, of course, a good example of Marxist influences on theological interpretation.

Another example would be his analysis of the ideological elements in the original Christian message about the necessity of turning the

other cheek, which he interprets as an attempt to deradicalize the political implications of Christianity. While Segundo agrees that Jesus
was not a political revolutionary as were his contemporaries the Zealots, he believes that Jesus' death was caused by Jewish fears concerning the implication of his message for their relationship with the
Roman occupiers (pp. 110ff.). Even the command to love one's
neighbor and the prohibition against killing are reinterpreted by Segundo in a complex and unpersuasive fashion to mean that Jesus is
"urging us to use the least amount of violence compatible with effective love" (p. 166). The Ten Commandments are described "not as
the intrinsic exigencies of a moral code but rather as a complex of
behavior patterns required to maintain and preserve a particular group
of people in a particular historical setting" (p. 165). Christianity becomes a process of "learning to learn" or "deutero-learning" (Bate-
son) rather than a set of dogmas.

What does this mean in terms of concrete political action? Segundo
quotes Moltmann that it requires "a dialectical process of opting for
the oppressed." This in turn leads to the question of means. Violence,
he says, is not the main problem; it is rather "whether or not we must
manipulate human masses and turn them into tools before we can
raise their consciousness" (p. 88). Having said this Segundo then
moves off in another direction to criticize those who feel that they
can derive from Christianity an absolute standard for judging political systems. He then proceeds to develop such a standard implicitly
himself in saying that when Marxist regimes are criticized by Christians for their lack of freedom,

> minority aspects (e.g. freedom of thought, freedom of religion, free-
> dom for Christian political actions) seem to be systematically over-
> valued in comparison with factors that are more revolutionary because
> they affect great human masses at one extreme of the process, e.g. in
> conditions of dire poverty, ignorance, disease and death. [p. 89]

thus implicitly arguing for the sacrifice of freedom for the improvement of the material well-being of the masses.

A hundred pages later, Segundo returns to the question of violence,
and as usual, almost immediately veers off into a discussion of the relation of ends and means in Christian ethics. Totally ignoring St.
Paul's specific rejection of the view that one may do evil so that good
may come of it (Romans 3:8), he cites Christ's statement that a man
is not defiled by what comes from outside him but by what comes

from within, such as evil thoughts, deceit, and envy (Mark 7:15–23), to argue that the morality of means "stems from their relationship to an end, not from their intrinsic nature. They must be studied in the context of a given historical situation in order to determine which means represent the richest and most promising possibilities for love" (pp. 172–73). Quoting a situation ethicist that love can make stealing and murder permissible, he concludes—in a statement that was to be quoted often by the enemies of liberation theology—that "such a situation does not frighten me, nor am I disturbed by the possibility that certain situations can turn stealing and murder into licit actions." A rule ethic condemning some actions as intrinsically evil is rejected by using an unpersuasive analogy with the complexities of choosing an appropriate social policy or government. Abortion, premarital sex, and the use of violence against the police are all cited as actions that may be justified by circumstances. What circumstances? Such details do not concern Segundo, only the need to reject all dogmas because of "an absolute faith whose content is always relative, however certain it may be." It is "an act of trust and surrender that logically deserves to be called 'faith' even though it may not entail belief in God or in a specific religious tradition" (p. 117).

In the final chapter of his book Segundo returns to the question of the manipulation of the masses. Earlier (p. 55) he had spoken of Christians as requiring a "revolutionary vanguard" if they are to apply Christ's teachings on justice ad love, but in his final chapter he challenges those who see him as an elitist—as compared, for example, with the more populist orientation of Gutierrez. Arguing that "there is no politics without minorities" (p. 234), Segundo finally rejects an either/or position in favor of a "theology of the people" to be based on a "hermeneutic circle that is rich in promise" (p. 236) because it involves both listening to the wisdom of the common people and "engaging in a serious creative return" to the normative sources of the Christian message. Thus theologians "will not be able to take the easy way out that is often taken by academic theology"—that is, "setting aside the great problems of today on the pretext that they belong to other fields or disciplines. Instead it [liberation theology] forces them to confront the major problems of history, biology, evolution, social change, and so forth" (p. 237).

With this unhelpful bit of advice the book concludes, leaving unresolved the question of how those problems are to be confronted with the single methodological tool of the hermeneutic circle and ideological suspicion, plus a vague commitment to socialism and an undefined relativism about central issues of moral and social conduct, such as the role of violence, the relation of freedom and equality, and the place of democratic participation.

Segundo has continued to write on related topics, and he has now initiated a five-volume series that Deane William Ferm has said "could turn out to be one of the stunning theological achievements of the 1980's" (*Latin American Liberation Theology: An Introduction Survey,* Maryknoll, NY: Orbis Books, 1985, p. 27). On the basis of the first book in the series, *Faith and Ideologies* (Maryknoll, NY: Orbis Books, 1984), this seems unlikely. The book contains much about ideology but little about faith. It includes three chapters on aspects of Marxist thought. They support Marx's historical materialism—which Segundo views as separable from Marx's atheism— endorse the dialectical approach to truth, and hail Marx as a "master of suspicion" because of his analysis of the nature of ideological justifications. Segundo notes "that in every socialist country it has been a minority that has violently won power, and there has been an accentuation of the role of the party and of government repression" but says that "this does not go so far as to disqualify historical materialism" (p. 199). As with his other writings, the book combines long-windedness with a lack of analytical precision or systematic argument, so that to this observer, Ferm's comparison of Segundo's importance to that of Paul Tillich seems vastly exaggerated.[3]

Possibly the comparison is based simply on sheer number of pages written. In the late 1960s and early 1970s, Segundo wrote a five-volume *Theology for the Artisans of a New Humanity* (translated and published by Orbis Books, 1973–1974). While there are occasional references to liberation themes, they are more strictly theological in a post–Vatican II but still traditional sense, discussing grace, the sacraments, and the church as a community. I doubt if anyone except the graduate students who wrote theses on him have read these volumes in their entirety. This is also likely to be true of the current five-volume series with the overall title of *Jesus of Nazareth, Yesterday and Tomorrow.* The individual titles of the Orbis translations (1984–1988) are *Faith and Ideologies, The Historical Jesus of the Synoptics, The Humanist Christology of Paul, The Christ of the Ignation Exercises,* and *An Evolutionary Approach to Jesus of Nazareth.* The later volumes are more biblical in their orientation—

paralleling a general development in liberation theology in the 1980s.[4]

Whether because of his claim to have invented liberation theology before Gutierrez, because of the confused and impenetrable nature of his prose, or for other reasons, Father Segundo is not a member of the liberation theology "club." While he has taught at major American and Canadian universities, he was not invited to the twentieth anniversary celebrations at Maryknoll in July 1988, and he does not participate in international meetings of the liberationists. In Uruguay itself, he is not a public figure (in contrast to the Boffs in Brazil or Gustavo Gutierrez in Peru), and he seems to have no influence. Only *The Liberation of Theology* seems to be widely read, and its argument is derivative of earlier writers. Even the Vatican seems largely to have ignored him, preferring to single out Boff, Gutierrez, and Sobrino. (This is despite such theological eye-catchers as his statenent that the resurrection accounts "do not strictly speaking, recount any miracle at all. The presence of the eschatological is there without the need to replace or break through any natural law. . . . And the transformation of the disciples . . . can be explained perfectly well as the achievement of a deeper level in their faith in Jesus Christ" [*The Historical Jesus of the Synoptics*, p. 176].)

Theology in the Americas—Detroit, 1975

While liberation theology had been attacked and defended in a number of religious journals in the United States, there had been little opportunity for genuine dialogue between North and South American theologians. That opportunity came in August 1975 when a carefully prepared meeting on "Theology in the Americas" was held in Detroit. It was sponsored jointly by the U.S. Catholic Conference and the World Council of Churches and involved an impressive list of theologians from both continents. Preparatory background documents were sent out, including a brilliant survey of the development of liberation theology by Phillip Berryman, and reflection groups had met to discuss the implications of the new way of doing theology. The extensive preparatory documents, the results of the reflection groups and theologians' comments, and the presentation and debates at the conference have been published by Orbis (Sergio Torres and John Eagleson, eds., *Theology in the Americas*, Maryknoll, NY: Orbis Books, 1976) and give a fascinating picture of the views of the major figures in liberation theology as well as the critical reactions of important and basically sympathetic North American theologians. Each of the major writers on liberation theology made presentations, as did representatives of black theology, feminist theology, and those who were attempting to develop a liberation theology for North America in the year before the bicentennial of American independence. The nature of the political orientation of the conference organizers was clear from the opening document, which began by discussing the decline of "the American empire," "the breakdown of the American Dream," and the danger of the "international and domestic thrashing" and "racist scapegoating" that will accompany the collapse of that empire (pp. 7–10).

Yet for all its leftist rhetoric the conference also provided an opportunity to raise some serious questions about the liberation theologians in Latin America. An obvious objection that the North American feminist, black, and chicano liberationists raised was the exclusively economic and structuralist focus of the Marxist-oriented analyses of the Latin Americans. Discussions of the need for racial and sexual liberation seemed to be absent from the analyses of oppression in a continent built on exploitation of the Indian, and in which machismo was the dominant sexual ethic. Several sympathetic North American observers also criticized the vagueness and generality of the liberation critique. Phillip Berryman's paper confessed that while

> one of the most evident signs of our time is a profound crisis of Western civilization and a struggle for liberation. . . . I resist leaping from this sign of our times to erecting an overarching theory that covers all . . . history (although I am wholeheartedly for a theology that emerges from participation in the 'historic project' of our own generation).

He added that

> liberation theologians are insistent on the importance of praxis but in their own theological reflections they often remain on a very generic level. . . . It should be clear that many do devote a great deal of time and energy to specific problems of practice in their lives. However these specific problems do not enter into their theology. [pp. 72–74]

The American Jesuit John Coleman S.J. also criticized the lack of a "developed economic ethics . . . which might help us to make discriminating judgements about alternative economic and political choices with which we are faced" (p. 385), while Gregory Baum, a Canadian theologian, noted that the liberation theologians speak of "social analysis" in the singular and mean by it a "conflictual sociological model, making use of Marxist-style class analysis which brings to light the contradictions present in the social order and orients the imagination toward the transformation of the present system" (p. 407).

Baum's observation was clearly illustrated in the statement of Gustavo Gutierrez to the conference in which, after noting that theology had entered into "a crisis of rationality" that could be alleviated by adopting "a new way of thinking," he drew the following conclusion:

> The marginated nonpersons have a way of understanding history and their social situation (social sciences, Marxist analysis, socialist path) that begins to be illuminative for the thinking through of faith in our day. . . . It is impossible to situate ourselves in the situation of the nonperson and not carry forward a conflictive struggle, a conflictive theology that will allow us to understand in a true way that we love our enemies. Maybe in order to practice this part of the gospel it is necessary to have enemies. We must recognize our enemies in history; we must live our faith in this different commitment. [p. 312]

Gutierrez's continuing commitment to a socialist revolution as the solution for the problems of the Latin American poor and his continuing use of Marxist categories are even more clearly demonstrated in the articles that he wrote in this period that were published in English in 1983 as chapters of *The Power of the Poor in History*. In 1973 he wrote:

> The poor, the oppressed are members of one social class that is being subtly (or not so subtly) exploited by another social class. This exploited class, especially in its most clear sighted segment, the proletariat, is an active one. Hence, an option for the poor is an option for one social class against another. An option for the poor means a new awareness of class confrontation. It means taking sides with the dispossessed. . . . Latin American misery and injustice go too deep to be responsive to palliatives. Hence we speak of social revolution, not reform; of liberation, not development; of socialism, not modernization of the prevailing system. . . . It is an undertaking in progress based on studies of the most rigorous scientific exactitude. . . . External dependency and internal domination are the marks of the social structure of Latin America. Hence only class analysis will show what is really at stake in the opposition between oppressed lands and dominant peoples.

. . . Only by overcoming a society divided into classes, only by in-stalling a political power at the service of the great popular majorities, only by eliminating the private appropriation of the wealth created by human toil, can we build the foundation of a more just society. [*The Power of the Poor in History*, Maryknoll, NY: Orbis Books, 1983, pp. 45–46]

Four years later, in 1977, he was still using the same dependency-cum-Marxism framework. At the end of a sweeping historical review in his essay "Theology from the Underside of History," he concluded:

The theory of dependency in the social sciences has contributed in re-cent years to a new political awareness in Latin America. . . . Here in the heart of a concrete historical process and not in the peace and quiet of a library or a dialogue among intellectuals, there arises for the popular movement an encounter with the social sciences and Marxist analysis. They have their importance for understanding the mechanisms of oppression imposed by the prevailing social order. More than any-thing else it is the system itself that is being called into question by the exploited. . . . This is why the popular movement is also the locus of encounter of the social sciences and Marxist analysis with theology. . . . The project of crafting a new and different society includes the creation of new human persons as well, who must be progressively liberated from whatever enslaves them [*Power of the Poor*, p 192]

It is easy to see why these are among the most often-quoted parts of Gutierrez's many works. The opponents of liberation theology have seized upon them to demonstrate that the founder of liberation theology is an advocate of a thoroughgoing Marxist revolution. The ambiguities in the wording as to who will carry out that revolution (what is "a political power at the service of the great popular ma-jorities," and who will engage in "the creation of new human per-sons . . . who must be progressively liberated from whatever en-slaves them"?) and the simplistic equation of the poor with the proletariat and the abolition of private property with a just society did not fail to be noted by critics of liberation theology. The fact that the English translation was published only in 1983 also led to the er-roneous impression that these were the current views of Gutierrez. (See, for example, the discussion by Michael Novak in *Will It Lib-erate?* New York: Paulist Press, 1986, pp. 167–70.)

Enrique Dussel—The Dialectic of Cultures in History

The criticism at the Detroit conference that the Latin American liberation theologians do not pay sufficient attention to sexual, racial, and ethnic factors did not take into account the writings of one well-known liberation theologian, Enrique Dussel. An Argentine layman who declined to attend the 1972 meeting of the Christians for Socialism in Chile because he felt it was being politically manipulated, he was forced to leave his native land when his house was bombed in 1976. He now directs the Center for the History of the Latin American Church (CEHILA) in Mexico City. His principal contribution has been historical, but in the only work by a liberationist attempting to develop a philosophy of liberation that is independent of theological references, *A Philosophy of Liberation* (Maryknoll, NY: Orbis Books, 1985, originally written in 1976) he analyzes sexual oppression in terms of what he calls "phallocracy," domination by male sexuality. The book is not highly original, being heavily dependent on Marcuse and Freud, but it is unusual in that it focuses upon an aspect of Latin American culture and praxis that most of the theologians from that area ignore.

Dussel's major contributions are his books on the history of the Latin American church. The best-known, *A History of the Church in Latin America: Colonialism to Liberation, 1492–1979* (Grand Rapids, MI: Eerdmans, 1981—a translation of the third edition, published in Spanish in 1979) begins by describing the "genetic-erotic" and "genetic-pedagogical" bases of oppression in Latin America—that is, the sexual violence inflicted on the Indians, mestizos, mulattos, and blacks by the Spanish conqueror, and the violent conquest of native culture by alien Europeans (pp. 4–6). Much of the history of the church in Latin America is interpreted from a racial-cultural point of view—with certain church leaders taking the part of the oppressed Indians but most of the conquerors totally identified with "Hispanic messianism" (p. 69).

An elaborate system of historical periodization is employed, with the important dates after independence being 1850, the beginnings of the spread of Anglo-Saxon liberalism resulting in a "veritable transformation of the elements of the Latin American collective conscience" (*conciencia,* better translated as "consciousness"); 1930, the beginning of the model of the "New Christendom"—in other words, Catholic Action, Christian Democracy, and Catholic-influenced trade unions; and 1962, following which there was a "new beginning" and a "crisis of liberation" rejecting Christian Democracy and recognizing that the "struggle is for economic, cultural and human independence in Latin America" through a possible Latin American socialism, emerging from "a Christian existential understanding [which is] founded on a political process that unites the American and Asiatic peoples who are no longer on developmental tracks but on the way to, or in the process of liberation from the oppressor-oppressed structure" (p. 218). Theologically this was reflected in the development of liberation theology "from the prophetic commitment, that is, from existential praxis."

Dussel concludes:

> Latin America and its Church are awakening and hear more clearly the rich prophetic voice that creates the new: that which comes to move people towards their historical and eschatological future, and that which appears to put into motion the dialectic movement of the countries which suffer from the neocolonial oppression of the North American empire. All of this is a "sign of the times" and that beyond time. "Stand erect, hold your heads high, because your liberation is near at hand." [Luke 21:28]

Dussel says he is not a Marxist. However there seems rather to be a strong resemblance between his thought and that of the Left Hegelians who so much influenced the early Marx. Economics, which is central to Marx, is given very little emphasis in Dussel. It is the dialectical relationship of cultures in the history and in personal relations that is the focus of his analysis. The structural similarity of the triadic character of the dialectic to the Christian doctrine of the Trinity is specifically noted, and the dialectic between the developed countries (the oppressors) and the underdeveloped countries (the oppressed) "is transformed and superseded by the emergence of the fraternal, historical being" (p. 252). In the church too, Dussel sees a continuing interaction between the traditionalist integralist, the progressive "Europeanized or Marxist liberal" (*sic*) and the extreme populist supporter of folk Catholicism, who continue in trinitarian unity until the end of history (pp. 252–53). Put in other terms there are now three levels of "Christian commitment"—preconciliar conservatives, conciliar progressives, and "a third level composed of those who are committed to liberation not only eschatologically but also politically, economically, and culturally, because of their insight into the reality of dependence. A result of Christian reflection on this level is the 'theology of liberation' " (pp. 250–51).

Once again it should be noted that the dependence that Dussel opposes is as much cultural as economic. One important aspect of this cultural domination is the area of theology:

> The theology of the center has no relevance for the periphery [because it] has not found reasons for opposing the evils of racialism, sexism, capitalism, colonialism, and neo-colonialism. . . . It is frequently a theology of domination because it has identified itself through the model of Christendom with the dominant countries, classes, races, sexes.[5]

The economic factor is one aspect of broader cultural relations, but capitalism is by nature an intrinsic part of the system of oppression that must be overcome in the process of liberation. One of the instruments of that transformation will be the church, since Christians will engage in a reformulation of Marxism, ridding it of its atheism but using its analysis to challenge capitalist oppression (*De Medellín a Puebla,* Mexico City: Editorial Edicol, 1979, ch. 1).

José Comblin—Critique of Marxism

If the reader at this point has become impatient with the vagueness and generality of the liberation theologians' references to Marxism and socialism, he or she is justified in that attitude. Aside from evincing a common opposition to capitalism and to all structures of domination, nearly all the liberation theologians speak in such general terms that it is difficult to derive any concrete proposals of a positive nature from their writings. There is, however, one writer who is an exception to this rule—not only in the sophistication of his analysis, but in the clarity of his effort to derive a clearer notion of the implications of a Christian and humanistic notion of liberation. He is Joseph (or José) Comblin. Comblin is a Belgian who has worked in Latin America for thirty years, mainly in Chile and Brazil. Most of his forty books in many languages are on spiritual subjects (for instance, *La Résurrection,* Paris: Editions Universitaires, 1959; *Le Christ dans l'Apocalypse,* Tournai: Desclée, 1965; *Jesus of Nazareth: Meditations on His Humanity,* Maryknoll, NY: Orbis Books,

1976; *Sent from the Father: Meditations on the Fourth Gospel,*
Marknoll, NY: Orbis Books, 1979; and *The Holy Spirit and Liberation,* Maryknoll, NY: Orbis Books, 1988). As the titles imply, many
of his books attempt to develop a new Christology in the post–
Vatican II church—a concern he shares with two more liberation
theologians whom we shall discuss in the next chapter, Leonardo Boff
and Jon Sobrino. For present purposes, however, it is important to
know that he also has written in French on the subject of the theology of revolution. *Theologie de la Révolution* (Editions Universitaires, 1970) was published in Paris just as the initial meetings and
articles on liberation theology were beginning to have an impact on
Latin America. Earlier, he had published a criticism of the Catholic
Action approach to the relation on the church and the world (*Echec
de l'Action Catholique?,* Paris: Editions Universitaires, 1961), which
anticipated some of the initial themes of the liberationists. In 1974 he
published *Theologie de la Pratique Revolutionnaire* (Paris: Editions
Universitaires), which related his earlier work to the new revolutionary mood in Latin America. The book is too detailed to summarize,
but certain themes are notable. First is his profound historical knowledge of church history, both in Europe and Latin America, and the
persuasiveness of his argument that Christianity has always had both
radical and conservative implications. Second is his theological effort
to relate Christian radicalism both to the lived experience of the
Christian community (a common theme of the liberation theologians)
and to the life of Christ (a less common theme in the earlier writers
whom we have examined). "The specifically Christian element in the
praxis is the life of Christ, his actions" (translated from p. 51). The
driving force of the revolution for a Christian must be love. Here he
quotes Camilo Torres's explanation of why he joined the Colombian
guerrillas in 1966:

> The main principle in Catholicism is love of neighbor. . . . If gener-
> osity, alms, some free school, some low-cost construction—what is
> called "charity," are not sufficient to give food to the majority of the
> hungry, nor clothes to the majority of the naked, nor education to the
> majority of those who are illiterate, we must seek effective means to
> promote the well-being of the majorities. That is why revolution is not
> only permitted, but obligatory for Christians who see it as the only
> effective and long-lasting way to realize love for all men. [translated
> from p. 21]

The rest of the book is an effort to work out the implications of such a revolution for Christians.

Its most striking section is an attack on Marxist socialism (pp. 139–40), which begins: "Marxist socialism in the sense of a formal movement organized on the basis of Marxism, has no future." Comblin explains that a central element of that movement has always been the collectivization, in the sense of nationalization, of the means of production, and that collectivization has been demonstrated to be "precarious, ambiguous, and finally disappointing to the worker." Marxism can be useful only if its adherents are free to criticize the official doctrine, and except for a limited period in China this has not happened. Second, Marxism is inevitably linked to "dictatorship, the absence of individual liberties, and the repression of the opposition. The shadow of Stalinism hangs over it inevitably." It has no program of freedom except the denunciation of the merely formal character of bourgeois freedom. Finally, Marxism does not produce class consciousness among the workers but as "for example, in the tragic case of Chile," it does become a divisive factor. Citing the "socialism with a human face" of the Prague spring of 1968, Comblin argues that "a revolution can only succed if it is not Marxist. In practice Marxism only prepares the way for fascism by producing disarray, division, and frustration among the workers."

What should a new socialism contain? Comblin cites two elements—(1) democratic freedoms, especially giving workers some control over management and forcing the ruling classes to submit to the good of all rather than subordinating the common good to their own; and (2) a selectivity among goods to be produced so that instead of high technology that benefits the rich, production and societal values will be oriented to the needs of the masses. "The form of ownership is secondary and should be decided empirically on the basis of the fundamental principle" (p. 142). Comblin cites Dubçek's Czechoslovakia, Nyerere's Tanzania, Kaunda's Zambia, and possibly the Peru of the military reformers associated with the Velasco government (1968–1975) as examples of the socialism he supports.

A further indication of Comblin's thought appears in an article in vol. 6, no. 10 of the *Concilium* series (*The Mystical and Political Dimension of the Christian Faith,* edited by Claude Geffré and Gustavo Gutierrez, New York: Herder and Herder, 1974). The problem as Comblin sees it is for the Third World to avoid the path of technological nationalism that has been traced out in the "Western model."

"Freedom is the search for a new way of social relations but how is one to master these techniques if their structure and operation are controlled by centers in the dominant countries?" Yet the socialist countries are no better:

> The socialist experiment has shown that there is no such thing as innocent power. . . . A socialism built by the power of the state, whatever it may be called, is a system of domination. There is freedom only in the control and limitation of power by the citizens and by private associations. The proletarian state is a myth which serves to conceal the ascent of a new middle class and a new capitalism. [p. 103]

Of Comblin's many books, the best-known to English-speaking audiences is *The Church and the National Security State* (Maryknoll, NY: Orbis Books, 1979). As its title implies, it is an analysis of the attempt by Latin American military regimes to enlist the support of the church for the ideology of national security that they have developed to justify their hold on power. Comblin's objections to that doctrine center on its Hobbesian view of the world as organized violence and its worship of the state. In a discussion that some of his fellow liberation theologians might benefit from reading, he distinguishes between evangelization and politicization (p. 87), and argues that while it is difficult to give a definition of the Gospel message, a central element is its opposition to violence, and this means it cannot endorse either leftist guerrilla efforts or the national security doctrine of the right. While it is true that the Gospel has been spread by coercive methods in the past, only methods that are compatible with freedom are Gospel-inspired. Second, evangelization must avoid specific identification of the Gospel with a particular party or group, including both Christians for Socialism on the left, and the National Security system on the right (pp. 87–88). The church's new pastoral approach, focusing on human rights and development (p. 100), is necessary because "a political society is open to love and charity only when power is limited and there is room enough for citizens to make free commitments" (p. 113). The church must criticize economistic and technologically oriented models, which are aimed at increasing national power and favor social groups with economic potential, while ignoring human needs. Citing Archbishop Helder Camara's criticisms of the Brazilian development model, Comblin argues that the church must continue to exercise a prophetic criticism as "the voice of the voiceless" (p. 118).

The New Testament provides the liberating principles for "the shaping of a new people" which are distinct from "the materialist idealism" of the Marxists and the "spiritual idealism" of the modernization theorists. The two idealisms have similar characteristics, according to Comblin. They both begin with the promise of human freedom, individualism, and permissiveness. However, in both cases they find that the promised transformation of nature by means of science and technology is impossible without the imposition by violence of the totalitarian control that is required to carry out that transformation. Thus, "There is no difference between Marxism and Western totalitarianism. In both cases the praxis of liberation is nothing more than total mobilization of the nation whether through a militarized party or the armed forces themselves" (p. 137).

In place of the two idealisms, Comblin proposes a New Testament-based conception of liberation. He analyzes the writings of St. Paul to prove that Christian liberty involves a change of will which produces a new life based on the command "love thy neighbor as thyself, [creating] new ties of service to neighbor. The transformation process is not only a personal but a social change. . . . Freedom is the bond of mutual service among the new people. Love is the energy that creates a new people" (pp. 147–49).

We must turn to Christianity and reject the myths of East and West. Theology provides ultimate criteria for judging social issues and means. Those in Europe and Latin America who have recommended Marxism as "a correct methodology for interpreting social issues" in order later to "give a Christian judgement about a situation interpreted by means of a Marxist methodology" are in error. "Marxist categories in interpreting social issues use the whole system and cannot be separated from it" (p. 192).

According to Jesus and Paul, liberation free from sin is love of neighbor. . . . Sin is a breaking down of relationships based on friendship and agreement, and the creation of new ones based on domination, rivalry, individual selfishness, and the exploitation of others. Sin is present in everything—in all personal behavior and all social structures. The very organization of life and society is based on sin and domination. . . . [p. 160]

. . . According to the Christian definition, liberty cannot even be imagined as the individual disposition of the person alone, isolated from others; independent from any ties and commitments. Rather liberty is a new kind of common life, a mutual relationship based on equality and cooperation. . . . There is no liberty without the institutions of liberty being established as the structures of national life. There is no liberty without . . . a parliament, congress, or some form of popular representation, constitutions, courts of justice and independence from repressive or military power, etc. [pp. 160–61]

Comblin concludes the book with a discussion of revolution drawn from his earlier books. As in those works, he is careful to contrast the Marxist and Christian approaches to the subject. While Marxism has in his view exposed the ideological character of Western science, especially economics, it has not replaced it, as it claims, with a science of its own:

Marxist science is only the ideology of the party, the result of the reduction of any rationality to the voluntarism of the party, a collection of arguments to justify the pragmatic decisions of the party. . . . In practice the party finds the problem of power more important than the problem of freedom. Consequently in Marxist revolution there is not freedom for the people, only for the party. The same science that expels freedom from history and revolution expels God from humankind and history. The party is supposed to be sufficient to create a new world, but it ends by creating a new power. [pp. 219–20]

Comblin then outlines the principles for judgment of revolutionary enterprises in terms of their goals, those who are involved, the role of the state, and the cultural background, concluding that "one cannot define a social ethic without a theology of revolution—without an analysis of the pastoral approach and a strategy for the constant change and the particular events of change that make up history and the actual fate of mankind" (p. 224).

In the introduction of the book Comblin describes his background as that of a Belgian Catholic liberal who responded to the Vatican's call to go to Latin America and was radicalized by his experience there. Yet it is clear that he retains a profoundly liberal concern for individual and juridically guaranteed rights that is notably absent from the writings of the other liberation theologians of this period. He also clearly rejects the scientific pretensions of Marxism that are at least partially accepted by many of his colleagues (although he accepts the Marxist critique of ideology, using it for his own antitechnological purposes), and he shares with them a prophetic vision of an unalienated future society based on love and community that has some resemblances with the earlier writings of Marx (although not with his later more economically oriented work). Comblin refers often to the working of "the Spirit" in history, by which as a Christian presumably he means the Holy Spirit, but he does not share the faith in the historical role of Latin America in moving mankind to a higher level of human existence that Enrique Dussel, for example, expresses. Moreover, unlike other liberation theologians such as Hugo Assmann and Juan Luis Segundo, he believes that the Christian message has some specific implications for politics that can be spelled out in some detail, including the promotion of human freedom and the development of a heightened sense of community based on love.[6] Those principles are drawn specifically from Christ's liberating message as further developed in the epistles of St. Paul.

Comblin, however, is the exception to a general tendency of those who wrote in the earlier years of liberation theology to use Marxist methodologies as the most appropriate way to argue for the structuralist anticapitalism that they all shared. And this had certain important effects upon their theories. Among them I would cite the following:

1. The rejection of "development" as the "lie that it is" (Assmann) also includes a rejection of "the hoax of democracy" (Miguez Bonino). "Socialism" is favored, but aside from the important exception of Comblin, the emphasis found in the writings of many contemporary European socialists upon the importance of political democracy is absent. And this is curious since the Christian Base Communities are a form of grass-roots democracy. Yet we look in vain for a discussion of the place of democracy in the future socialist order. It seems that, as in the case of Marx himself, political institutions after the revolution are not discussed because it is assumed that economic transformation will produce the necessary changes, and that political institutions are mere epiphenomena, parts of the superstructure that are determined by the resolution of the fundamental issue of the control of the means of production.

2. This also leads (again with the exception of Comblin) to a lack of concern with the need to place limits on those in power—the question of constitutionalism. Institutional restraints can be exploited by minorities against the will of the majority, and therefore they are seen as potential obstacles to liberation. This is very strange, since the Christian belief in the continuing effects of man's sinfulness would seem to argue—as it does in the thought of Niebuhr (and of Com-

blin)—for the need for institutional limits on the exercise of political power.

3. We have noted Juan Luis Segundo's blithe dismissal of a concern for human rights. Indeed, a general theory of rights is simply absent from the writings of the liberation theologians in the 1970s—with the exception of Comblin. And this seems to be related to the dialectical nature of their approach to the world. In the theories both of liberalism and of the social teachings of the church, rights inhere in the person as such—but the liberationists see such claims as frequently ideological, and always conditioned by historical experience. It is ironic, therefore, that at the very time when the Roman Catholic Church (in *Pacem in Terris*—1963—and during and after the Second Vatican Council) had finally come to endorse human rights and the Latin American Church had become a major critic of their widespread violation throughout the continent, an important sector of its intellectual elite not only ignored them, but even took an approach undermining the theoretical basis for their teachings. If praxis and dialectical thinking are the basis of liberation theology, there are important intellectual obstacles to the development of a theory of human rights.

4. One of the attractions of Marxism for the liberation theologians was its recognition of the fact of conflict—in Marx's case—of *class* conflict in the world. However as we have seen, this created a situation in which some theologians had considerable difficulty in reconciling their conflictual approach with the Christian command to love one's neighbor. The circumlocutions and evasions that resulted when the liberationist writers spoke of how one can express one's love for the oppressor were a persuasive indication of the tension between Christian views and those of the Marxist tradition.[7]

5. Furthermore, is it true that, as Gutierrez wrote in 1973, "studies of the most rigorous scientific exactitude" reveal that "only class analysis" will show the way to overcoming exploitation and poverty? There are many types of exploitation and oppression, and it is anything but scientific to reduce them all to the exploitation of the worker—even less so, of the poor who are the liberation theologians' concern. Socialism in the sense of the abolition of private ownership of the means of production will not end other types of exploitation, and may simply replace one type of economic exploitation with another.

The problem was to make a more nuanced evaluation of the various aspects that were jumbled together in the liberation theologians' writings. That development had not brought prosperity to the poor in the 1960s did not mean it was a "lie." That democracy often operated through unresponsive elites or corrupt politicians did not mean it was a "hoax." If constitutional guarantees and the separation of powers occasionally were used by the wealthy to frustrate or distort the popular will, this did not mean that constitutionalism was a fraud. If there are large numbers in Latin America living in misery, does the fault necessarily lie with capitalist development patterns? And the fact that a number of Latin American states had been taken over by the military did not prove that capitalism inevitably produced military rule. In Venezuela, Costa Rica, and Colombia, capitalism continued to develop without military coups. The use of "Marxist tools of analysis" thus seemed to have resulted in a simplistic reductionism that did not consider what were the appropriate strategies for a praxis that could liberate the poor. This would come in the 1980s when the question began to be posed whether the exaggerated revolutionary rhetoric of the 1970s was an appropriate response to the needs of the poor in Latin America.

5

Christology and Community: The Boffs and Jon Sobrino

AN ITALIAN OBSERVER of liberation theology has argued that 1976 marked the beginning of the systematization of the movement.[1] This was the year in which the Ecumenical Association of Third World Theologians (EATWOT) held its first meeting in Tanzania. It was also the year of the last institutionalized military coup (in Argentina) and of the first signs of the possible withdrawal of the military from power in a number of countries (Peru and Ecuador). No longer could one argue that Latin America was on the eve of a continent-wide socialist revolution, but neither was it clear that the military had been successful in establishing itself permanently in power. The argument of the Latin American left that the only alternatives were socialism or fascism was no longer persuasive, but it was not evident that liberal democracy or some kind of third-position populism was the wave of the future. It was time for the liberationists to take stock of their position, to respond to the challenges that had been posed to their writings, and to develop these writings further in a more organized way.

In two areas particularly there seemed to be need for additional work. The spiritual base of the liberation movement needed more sustenance, if only to respond to those who saw liberation theology as simply one more form of Christian Marxism; and the rapidly emerging base community movement, particularly in Brazil and Central America, needed to be related more directly to liberation themes. Two Brazilians and a Basque Jesuit teaching in El Salvador emerged in this period to write and lecture on these themes—Leonardo and

Clodovis Boff, and Jon Sobrino. By their writings they succeeded in reorienting the emphasis of liberation theology toward themes that, while present in earlier writers, had not received the same degree of attention. Their writings became sufficiently well known to challenge the dominant position of Gustavo Gutierrez in the field, and to become the objects of investigations by the Vatican.

Leonardo Boff is a Brazilian Franciscan who studied theology in Petropolis (Brazil) and Germany. His doctoral thesis for the University of Munich was begun in Petropolis at the suggestion of Boaventura Kloppenburg, a Brazilian Franciscan (now auxiliary bishop of Salvador, Brazil) and one of the most outspoken critics of liberation theology. It was published in Germany as a book in a theological series at the suggestion of Professor (now Cardinal) Joseph Ratzinger, who later became prefect of the Vatican Congregation for the Doctrine of the Faith and actively opposed Boff and liberation theology. Entitled *Die Kirche als Sakrament im Horizont der Welterfahrung* (The Church as Sacrament from the Point of View of Secular Experience) and published in Paderborn in 1972, it is a 552-page technical treatise in theology, but it already hints at themes that would later be given a liberationist twist. It reviews different approaches to the church in a secular age in the light of the post–Vatican II re-evaluation of traditional approaches, and concludes that the church should liberate man from modern ideologies by promoting a vision of an absolute future—the Kingdom of God that is revolutionary and utopian, and requires that the Christian be a rebel and nonconformist (pp. 529–34).

After completing his theological studies in Germany, Boff returned to Brazil to edit the *Revista Ecclesiastica Brasileira*. In the same year that his doctoral thesis, written in the late 1960s, was published, Boff also published a book that established him as a significant writer in the field of liberation theology, *Jesus Christ Liberator* (Petropolis: Vozes, 1972; English translation, Maryknoll, NY: Orbis Books, 1978). In it, he argued for a particular set of insights into the meaning of Jesus Christ that were based on the experience of Latin America, rather than of Europe, since "the future of the Catholic church is undeniably in Latin America." The Christology of the future should emphasize the anthropological over the ecclesiastical, the utopian over the factual, the critical over the dogmatic, the social over the personal, and orthopraxis over orthodoxy (pp. 43–47). The word *orthopraxis* had already appeared in Boff's thesis, but the new book gave it wide currency, as did his call for a Latin American "re-reading" of the Christian tradition.

An example of such a rereading would be Boff's treatment of the famous distinction made by (mostly Protestant) German theologians between the "Jesus of history" and "the Christ of faith." Boff interprets Christ's message as a revolution in thought and action that involved the liberation of the "oppressed consciousness" of his time and the creation of a new man (ch. 4). By rejecting the pharisaism and legalism of his time, mixing with social outcasts (prostitutes, tax-collectors, and former guerrillas), and crossing class barriers, Boff argues, Jesus produced a social and cultural revolution without violence that became the basis of Western civilization. He interprets the theological significance of Christ's death and resurrection as the result of a radical crisis among the Apostles that produced the faith that in turn created the church (thus bridging the gap between the Jesus of history and the Christ of faith).

The Catholic Church, "because of its unbroken link with Jesus Christ" is "a special institutional articulation of Christianity," with the clearest interpretation of the mystery of God and man and their mutual interpenetration. Yet at the same time it is "a sinful and pilgrim organization far from the Father's house." Other religions have a religious and salvific value, and the church should learn from them so as to be more universal and "to see and capture the reality of God and Christ outside its own articulation and outside the sociological limits of its own reality" (pp. 257–58).

Boff also develops the themes of the theological significance of the cross and resurrection in the Geffré and Gutierrez volume of *Concilium* cited earlier. Christ represents a "liberation praxis" of love above the law that transcends class differences. The cross had been the symbol of the human will to power, but Christ transformed it into a sign of liberation by his resurrection:

> The process of liberation in order to maintain its purely Christian character, implies the acceptance in its praxis of the Paschal experience. In other words it must die to its own models and its own conquests. On the one hand, it must embrace them with great zeal because they constitute the Kingdom which is present in the ambiguities of history and on the other hand, it must die to them because they are not the whole liberation or the whole Kingdom. With its death, it makes way for the resurrection of other concrete formulations which will mediate the Kingdom. [pp. 89–90][2]

In an untranslated work on "The Theology of Captivity" (*Teologia do Cativeiro e da Libertação,* Petropolis: Vozes, 1980) Boff turned to the Old Testament for models of the Latin American church in a continent that was largely under military rule:

> We live in Egypt. The poor are suffering in Babylon. In their veins runs the blood of martyrs. But we are in a different Babylon and Egypt. The sun of justice has already appeared on the horizon. In Him is anticipated the liberation of all those in captivity. Against all despair, there is still hope—because of Jesus Christ and his resurrection. [pp. 55–56]

The causes of that captivity are outlined in "Christ's Liberation via Oppression: An Attempt at Theological Construction from the Standpoint of Latin America," an article written for an Italian anthology published in 1975 (translated in Rosino Gibellini, ed., *Frontiers of Theology in Latin America,* Maryknoll, NY: Orbis Books, 1979):

> Latin American underdevelopment is not a technical problem nor a fated historical circumstance. It is the by-product of a socio-economic system that favors a small minority with wealth while keeping the vast majority of humankind in a state of dependence on the margins of societal life. . . . We must break the ties of dependency and create new values that will allow us to structure a new form of social life for human beings. We must stop the exploitation of some people by others and get all people to bear their fair share of the social burden. [pp. 125–26]

A footnote then refers to "a significant body of scientific literature dealing with the socio-economic analysis of dependence" (p. 132), which includes Fernando Henrique Cardoso, Celso Furtado, Teotonio Dos Santos (all Brazilians), and André Gunder Frank, the four best-known writers on dependence theory.

Boff's book was first published in Spanish in Bogota in 1975. A Portuguese edition appeared in Brazil only in 1980, when the situation of captivity he had described had begun to change. In Brazil, exiles had been permitted to return, the censorship was lifted, former guerrillas published best-selling books about their experiences a decade earlier, and there was a partial opening of the political process. Meanwhile Boff had turned his attention to his original interest in church structures, and had published *Ecclesiogenesis* (*Ecclesiogenese,* Petropolis: Editora Vozes, 1977; English translation, Maryknoll, NY:

Orbis Books, 1986), a theological analysis of what Boff calls "the reinvention of the church" in the form of the growth of the Ecclesial Base Communities in Brazil. In response to the shortage of priests and the desires of local groups for a means of worship and meditation on the Scripture, the number of Base Communities had expanded rapidly in Brazil. Boff saw these groups as a return to the sense of community and the presence of the Holy Spirit that characterized the early church, but he was careful to emphasize that the Base Communities (CEBs) do not function in opposition to the institutional church but in "permanent co-existence" with it. Arguing against a "pyramidal" or hierarchical model of the church, he interprets the papacy, the bishops, and priesthood as "necessary responses" of the Christian community, because of the need for "union, universality, and bonding with the great witnesses of the apostolic past," but they should exercise their function *within* the communities and not *over* them, "integrating duties instead of accumulating them, respecting the various charisms, and leading them to the oneness of one and the same body" (p. 60).

The issue, of course, is what the maintenance of unity implies in the way of authority. Boff is certainly right that before the Second Vatican Council the Catholic church overemphasized the "top down" character of church authority, focusing too much on Christ's grant of authority to Peter (and his successors) and not enough on the collegial character of the apostles, and the community of believers. Boff, however, seems to see the hierarchy as created by the community for the sake of unity rather than established by Christ, as most Catholics have believed. Post–Vatican II ecclesiology has reasserted the role of bishops and of the church community in the constitution of the church, but Boff goes much further. "Reinventing" the church could simply mean "rediscovering" it (its Latin etymological root meaning),[3] but for Boff it seems to mean returning to a primitive decentralized church that is somehow loosely associated on a national and international basis in order to maintain historical continuity. What that means in practice was to come out more clearly in the mid-1980s when a much more radical statement of his theories involved him in extended difficulties with the Vatican.

Boff was able to cite a number of European and American writers of the post–Vatican II period in support of his views, many of them concerned to play down the differences between Catholic and Protestant views of the structure of the church in the interest of ecumenism. In the final chapters of the book, he further challenges existing Catholic practice by taking up a number of "disputed questions." He makes a case for the celebration of the Eucharist by the Christian Base Communities in the absence of an ordained priest—with the head of the community acting as "extraordinary minister" in special circumstances, although "in the absence of an ordained minister, the sacrament is incomplete" (p. 70). Boff also examines the controversial issue of the ordination of women, concluding that despite a 1976 Vatican statement to the contrary, there are no decisive theological arguments against such ordination and that it would make a positive contribution to the development of spirituality and worship within the church. Citing the criticism of the Vatican statement by the European Jesuit theologian Karl Rahner, Boff concludes: "The document constitutes a step in the discussion; it does not close the matter" (p. 97).

The role of the Ecclesiastical Base Communities is discussed further by Clodovis Boff, Leonardo's brother, in a book written after the beginnings of the political opening (*abertura*) in Brazil in 1979. *Ecclesial Base Communities and the Practices of Liberation* (Spanish edition, Bogota: Indo-American Press Service, 1981; and Brazilian edition, Petropolis: Vozes, 1980) presents a series of case studies of the political impact of Base Communities in Brazil. It recounts cases of resistance to landowners, protests against police brutality, and agitation for improved bus service—all organized by groups related to the Base Communities. It then shows how this experience had an impact on the creation of an opposition coalition in connection with the 1978 elections in Brazil. It "shared a commitment to the rights of the oppressed, and to the economic independence of Brazil" as well as a "socialist orientation, that is to say, it sought to place the economy under the control of the organized people" (p. 21). Clodovis Boff discusses the problem of the politicization of religion but argues that these efforts, while inspired by the religious groups, were not carried out directly by them except in an earlier period when political activity was forbidden and only the Base Communities offered the "social space" for such activities. Their action was that of "transformers who change an anonymous mass into an organized people" (p. 36).

In the area where Boff worked, he claims, capitalism as well as "third positionism" were rejected in favor of socialism. That socialism involved an attempt to develop a "new social alternative" that would bring a specifically Christian element to the construction of a new society by means of "the alliance of Christian faith and a socialist society" (p. 37). Boff quotes the French Marxist writer Roger Garaudy, who argues that Latin America had already made three distinctive contributions to world socialism—the pedagogy of the oppressed, the theology of liberation, and the Ecclesial Base Communities (p. 38). The short booklet concludes with a description of the ways in which the activities of the Base Communities can be understood as a preparation for liberation and socialism as a part of salvation history (pp. 40–43).

The book never directly describes a problem that was to face the liberation movement in the 1980s—the relation of its commitment to socialism to its belief in democratic grass-roots participation. That problem was not an urgent one when Latin America was dominated by the repressive national security state, but when elections began to take place and political parties began to be organized the movement, along with the rest of the Latin American left, was required to define itself in relation to the redemocratization process. It had been easy enough to see rightist oppression as the inevitable result of capitalism and imperialism when the capitalist economies of the military-dominated states of Latin America were experimenting with the models of the free market propounded by Milton Friedman and "the Chicago boys" in Chile, or their equivalents in Argentina, Uruguay, or Peru, but how were the liberation theologians to respond to popular demands for a return to democracy that did not also call for socialism? If participatory grass-roots democracy could be established but did not carry with it a demand for the overthrow of capitalism, what was to become of proposals to create a new man and a new society?

For the Boffs, it is clear how the people should act—to establish socialism and abolish capitalism. Leonardo Boff, for example, in a long meditation on *The Lord's Prayer* (Petropolis: Vozes, 1979; English translation, Maryknoll, NY: Orbis Books, 1983) rephrases the petition, "Deliver us from evil" as "Liberate us from the evil one." Today, he says, the evil one is "embodied in an elitist, exclusivist social system that has no solidarity with the great multitudes of the poor. He has a name; he is the Capitalism of private property and the Capitalism of the state. . . . This evil one slyly creeps into our minds and makes the heart insensitive to those structural inequities that he has created" (p. 119).

For Clodovis Boff as represented by the Theologian in the dialogue he presents in *Salvation and Liberation* (*Da Libertação*, Petropolis:

Vozes, 1979; English translation, Maryknoll, NY: Orbis Books, 1984), "Liberation is the social emancipation of the oppressed. Our concrete task is to replace the capitalism system and move toward a new society—a society of a socialist type" (p. 116). How do we know this? Because the theologian must be aware of "the structural character of social relationships" and "incorporate (as an extrinsically constitutive element) the new *episteme*—the sciences of the human being including the social sciences" (*Theology and Praxis*, Petropolis: Vozes, 1978; English translation, Maryknoll, NY: Orbis Books, 1987, p. 222). The analysis of poverty offered by the social sciences is either functionalist, which is the liberal bourgeois explanation with development as its solution, or dialectical, which sees poverty as a "conflictive phenomenon which can be overcome only by replacing the present social system with an alternative system. The way out of this situation is revolution, understood as the transformation of the bases of the economic and social system" (Leonardo and Clodovis Boff, *Introducing Liberation Theology*, Petropolis: Vozes, 1986; English translation, Maryknoll, NY: Orbis Books, 1987, pp. 26–27).

The functionalist-dialectical dualism is taken up again in an interview in the 1980s in which Clodovis Boff is asked about the relation of liberation to Marxism. He replies that Marxist theory is the only alternative to functionalist analysis as developed by Weber, Durkheim, and Talcott Parsons. The Christian communities make use of it because without Marxist analysis, "capitalism which is our problem with all its dehumanizing effects would not be criticized and censured." The Christian communities "have a critical and corrective relationship" to Marxism but "to prevent Christian communities and theologians from having recourse to Marxism is to remain within the capitalist system."[4]

Yet it is not clear what aspects of Marxism are to be used in this critical and corrective way. Presumably Marx's critique of ideology would be useful in "unmasking" the various justifications for power. Yet as José Comblin had written, that critique is also capable of being turned against existing alternatives to capitalism. Marx's doctrine of the class struggle would clearly have to be modified if only to place the poor in the role of the "universal class" that is exercised by the proletariat in Marx's writings. As in the case of Marx's proletariat in the last stages of capitalism, the poor are the majority in Latin America. And as in the case of Marxism, those who support them also can be identified with them. But must the Base Communities be restricted to the poor and those who support them? The Boffs are insistent that the Base Communities represent something different from more traditional ("bourgeois") church organizations such as the Christian Family Movement, or the *Cursillos* of Christianity. The issue of the relation of the poor to the church and to socialism would continue to be a problem for liberation theology in the 1980s.

Behind the oversimplifications of the functionalist-dualist dichotomy is a more fundamental distinction—between beliefs in harmonious and conflictive views of society. Underlying all the verbiage in the liberationist critique of the social doctrine of the church and of the liberal view of the world lies a fundamental option—and it is not a question of opting for the rich or the poor, as the liberationists would have it. That option is between (1) working out differences on the basis of a belief that men of good will (Christianity) or fundamentally rational human beings (the liberal Enlightenment view) can work together and compromise their differences without using force, and (2) a view of the world that is persuaded that there are fundamental differences, mainly economic, that can be resolved only by force. It is, of course, an oversimplification to identify either the Christian or the liberal tradition with the view that all differences can be resolved without force, but there are many Christians and liberals who incline to that view. Similarly there are a number of Marxists, particularly in recent years, who are willing to recognize that the combination of discussion and the threat of disorder can produce democratic results without violence. However, it is also true that both the liberal and the Christian tradition lean toward the peaceful resolution of disputes, because of a belief in the primacy of rationality or of love as motives for human action, and both Marxists and liberationists emphasize the irreducible character of socioeconomic conflict.

The latter view is, of course, present in the Christian tradition. The Holy War has a long biblical history and justification, and the God/Satan opposition as well as the belief that man is fundamentally inclined to evil and selfishness as a result of the Fall provide a Judaeo-Christian base for a conflictual view of the world. And if the emphasis is placed on good versus evil, rich versus poor, oppressor versus oppressed, and bondage versus liberation, one can see how there can be a Weberian "elective affinity" between the liberation theology and Marxism—for it too sees the world in dichotomous categories (lord and serf, bourgeois and proletarian) that are ultimately resolvable by inevitable conflict leading to a transformed society and humanity in the classless society (in the liberationist view, the Kingdom of God).

In fact, of course, the relation of force and persuasion, compromise and conflict, ideology and science, and functionalist and dialectical world views is much more complex. Conservatives and liberals, as well as traditional and reformist Christians, are aware of the role of coercion and conflict in the world, although it is not as clear that Marxists and liberationists are as aware of the potentialities of reason and of love. In any case, it is or should be a matter of degree in both cases rather than a simplistic labeling of one group as functionalist integrators or the other as violence-prone dialecticians.

By the last half of the 1970s liberation theology faced two new challenges, which have been described earlier. One was the emergence of feminist theology, and the other was the new emphasis in the Latin American church on the defense of human rights against oppressive military regimes. Leonardo Boff developed important responses in both areas.

We have already noted his support for the ordination of women, but his writing ranged much further. In 1979 he wrote *The Maternal Face of God* (Petropolis: Vozes; English translation, San Francisco: Harper and Row, 1987), a long meditation on the theological meaning of the feminine, and on the place of the Virgin Mary in the Christian religion, both as myth and symbol. He also published in 1980 *The Hail Mary,* and later gave a frank interview with Elsa Tamez, an Argentine feminist liberation theologian, in which he attacked the dominance of white, celibate males in the church and argued that Christ offers a model of the integration of the decisiveness of the male and the tenderness and compassion of the female (Elsa Tamez, ed., *Teologos de la Liberación Hablan sobre el Mujer,* San Jose: DEI, 1986, pp. 107–15).

In the area of human rights, Leonardo Boff, as well as many other liberation theologians (for instance, Juan Luis Segundo and Jon Sobrino), makes a sharp distinction between "liberal" or individualistic rights and biblically based rights of the poor. He and his brother sum it up in *Introducing Liberation Theology* as follows:

> The liberal-bourgeois tradition defends individual rights disconnected from society and from basic solidarity with all. Liberation theology has corrected and enriched this tradition by taking account of biblical

sources. These speak primarily of the rights of the poor, of outcasts, orphans and widows. . . . The rights of the poor are the rights of God. The struggle for the promotion of human dignity and defense of threatened rights must begin with the rights of the poor. They show us the need for a certain hierarchization of rights: first must come *basic* rights, the rights to life and to the means of sustaining life (food, work, basic health care, housing, literacy); then come the other human rights: freedom of expression, of conscience, of movement, and of religion. [p. 81][5]

What do the Boffs mean by *hierarchization?* Do they mean that political and personal freedoms should be sacrificed to achieve full employment, health care, literacy, and so forth? This has been the argument used by some Western liberals to defend Mao's China, Stalin's Russia, or Castro's Cuba—but later revelations in all three cases have cast some doubt on the effectiveness or the necessity of such a trade-off. If this is indeed the liberationist, biblically based theory of rights (they also cite Matthew 25 about feeding the hungry and clothing the naked—although Christ's reference to visiting prisoners is not mentioned), it is easier to explain their enthusiasm for Nicaragua, Cuba, and, in the case of Leonardo Boff, the Soviet Union (see chapter 9, p. 173).

Jon Sobrino and El Salvador

The themes of Christology and community are also central to the thinking of Jon Sobrino, a Spanish Basque by birth who studied in the United States and Germany and has been a long-time resident of El Salvador and professor at the Jesuit university in that country's capital, San Salvador. Like Leonardo Boff, he is heavily influenced by German theologians such as Juergen Moltmann and Wolfhart Pannenberg, criticizing as Boff had done the distinction between the Jesus of history and the Christ of faith. His first important work was given the English title *Christology at the Crossroads: A Latin American Approach* (Maryknoll, NY: Orbis Books, 1978), but a direct English translation of its original title as published in Mexico City in 1976 would describe it more accurately: *Christology from Latin America: An Outline Based on the Following of the Historical Jesus.* It argues that the Latin American experience of political struggle in the application of one's faith illuminates the real nature of the historical role of Jesus in ways that have been obscured by later theological discussion.

Sobrino argues against the effort to explain away "the scandal of the cross" with transcendent theories of salvation derived from Greek idealistic philosophy. Good Friday must be seen as an historical event—as the death of a suffering God who expresses his love for the miserable and oppressed by sharing it with them. In Latin America, "popular intuition" has rightly grasped the authentic element of Christian faith in Good Friday, but it has often grasped it in very passive terms. The present-day situation in Latin America has brought out a somewhat different focus, particularly among groups more deeply involved in the effort for social change. This new Christian focus on the cross of Jesus is more activist in character.

> While resurrection remains the paradigm of liberation, the cross is no longer seen simply as the symbol of suffering or as the negative dialectical moment which immediately and directly gives rise to the positive moment of liberation. People now realize that a whole process of analysis is required before the latter positive phase can be viable. . . . It is possible to verify the truth of what happened at the resurrection only through a transforming praxis based on the resurrection. The elements of misery and protest in the biblical texts can be understood only in an active process of change which transforms the present. . . . Political hermeneutics must take into account the theology of the cross, for the work of transforming reality goes on in the presence of the power wielded by evil and injustice. Christian transforming praxis is characterized by the acceptance of suffering in the face of contradiction. . . . This action is structurally akin to that of Jesus, and here we have an unvarying constant in Christian praxis. It is directed toward the public sector, toward the concrete manifestations of politics, body life, and the cosmos. . . . The following of Christ is a praxis in which one experiences the same sort of structural conflicts that Jesus did. [pp. 180, 256]

Jesus was not a Zealot but he was executed because of the subversive effects of his teaching of a love that is "political in that it seems to be real and effective in a given situation. . . . He manifests his love for the oppressed by being with them. . . . He manifests his love for oppressors by being against them" (p. 214).

"In Latin America, liberation theology has turned almost spontaneously to the figure of the historical Jesus" (p. 274). We gain access to him not through creeds and cults but through "a specific kind of praxis which the Gospels describe as the 'following of Christ' or 'discipleship' " (p. 275):

> Understanding the resurrection of Jesus today presupposes several things. One must possess a historical consciousness that sees history both as promise and as mission. And one must engage in a specific praxis that is nothing else but discipleship [which is carried out through] service to the community performed out of love. [pp. 380–81]

Only in this way is the Jesus of history united to the Christ of faith.

Is this Marxism? Despite all the talk about praxis, history, the dialectical method, and oppressors/oppressed, it seems to be a kind of Christian Hegelianism—if it is anything that can be identified in the history of European thought. More specifically it is a conscious attempt to apply the mysteries of the cross and resurrection to the contemporary Latin American situation—and to relate this to contemporary theology elsewhere.

Yet Sobrino was one of the first liberation theologians to have his writings questioned by the Vatican. He was accused of implicitly denying the divinity of Christ and transforming him into a political revolutionary. What he seems to be doing, rather, is arguing that political participation of a partisan kind inevitably follows from an effort to apply Christ's message. Sobrino's emphasis on the inevitably partisan and conflictive character of Christian political involvement runs through all his writings. It reflects the radicalization of political conflict in El Salvador in the 1970s, as well as the increasing involvement of Christians in social change in that country.

Jesus in Latin America, a later work published in El Salvador in 1983 (Universidad Centroamericana) and in English by Orbis Press in 1987, is a collection of articles many of which were written in the late 1970s before the outbreak of Salvadoran civil war in 1980. In the opening chapter Sobrino insists on his acceptance of the full humanity and full divinity of Christ as taught by the church since the Council of Chalcedon (451 AD), and denies that "liberation Christology" is guilty of "horizontal reductionism" (p. 11), as his critics had claimed. The rest of the book develops Sobrino's conception of Jesus as an historical figure who takes the side of the poor and oppressed, emphasizing the central position of the community as the method of "reappropriating" the historical Jesus. Sobrino is speaking from experience, since the Base Community movement in El Salvador grew very rapidly in the period of military repression in the late

1970s. Another element that was to become important in later discussion was Sobrino's observation that in Latin America and in the world, the poor and the outcast are a majority, and that that majority lives in misery because of socioeconomic structures. The discussion of "the logic of the grand majorities" in Central America in the 1980s was thus already anticipated in Sobrino's writings in late 1970s. And the dramatic emergence of mass organizations in many Central American countries organized under religious auspices or influence was given religious legitimation when Sobrino wrote that "Jesus' actions were designed not only to declare their dignity in the sight of God, but also to mount a radical assault on the causes of their social indignity—the material conditions of their existence and the religious concepts of their time" (p. 142).

This chapter has intended to cover the development of liberation theology in the late 1970s, so that the question of the relation of Sobrino's writings to the revolution and civil war in El Salvador after October 1979 is left to a later chapter. It seems unlikely that reading a fairly abstruse theological treatise has ever turned anyone into a revolutionary. However, along with other priest-professors and through the journals published at the Jesuit university (*Estudios Centroamericanos* and *Revista de Teologia Latinoamericana*), an atmosphere was created that encouraged activism by committed Christians in public life, contributing in a major way to the upsurge of political unrest in the 1970s.

Yet until 1979 liberation theology, while controversial, was regarded more as an intellectual curiosity—a Latin American Christian radicalism—rather than a serious challenge to the status quo. Its leaders wrote books and articles and attended meetings, but aside from vigorous efforts beginning in 1972 to undercut their influence in the bureaucracy of the Latin American Bishops Conference, they were not regarded as fundamentally influencing the future of Latin America. The change of attitude toward what they represented took place in 1979 as a result of two events—the Third General Conference of Latin American Bishops (CELAM) held in January and February in Puebla, Mexico, and the triumph of the Sandinista-led revolution in Nicaragua in July. The next two chapters will discuss the impact on these two events on the development of liberation theology.

6

The Battle of Puebla

BY THE LATE 1970s liberation theology had become a rallying cry for one part of the Latin American church, and a symbol of what had gone wrong for another. We have already discussed the effort of Bishop (now Cardinal) Alfonso Lopez Trujillo to do battle against the new theories. In his book *De Medellín a Puebla,* already alluded to, he distinguished between a true liberation, which continued the tradition of the Medellín Conference in relating it to religious themes such as sin, conversion, and reconciliation, and what he viewed as a distortion of the understanding of Medellín, which emphasized politics and conflict, associated principally with Gustavo Gutierrez, Hugo Assmann, José Comblin, and Juan Luis Segundo. The genuine theology of liberation that Medellín represented involved an effort by the whole community with specific roles for pastors and priests that proved "an evangelical presence in the struggle for justice" but not "decision-making, leadership, or structuring of solutions." Medellín recognized the "sinful situation in Latin America and proclaimed a call for conversion by announcement and denunciation, an option for liberation in the service of the poor, and reconciliation" (p. 229), but rejected the effort to fuse Marxist elements with Christian social involvement.

Lopez Trujillo recognizes that liberation theology is not itself Marxism, despite its use of Marxist tools, and that it represents an important new current in Latin American thought. He is concerned, however, that although its intentions are pastoral, "the insertion of the political-conflictual dimension by the use of Marxist analysis is an imported element which has drawn all the attention away from the genuinely valuable and relatively original Latin American elements which derive from Medellín" (p. 235). A further criticism is that while all the liberation writers agree on the necessity of abolishing private property in the means of production, "they are very vague about the content of the proposed socialism which is to replace it, and completely intolerant of any effort at reform along Christian Democratic or third position lines." Who is going to abolish private property but the state, and is there not here a danger of totalitarianism unless we discuss concrete structures to limit centralized power? And is there any evidence that socialism will work in Latin America? Peronism in Argentina and the nationalizations by the military in Peru seem far from what the liberation theologians desire. But what *do* they desire (pp. 246–47)?

The other major criticism of the liberationists made by Lopez Trujillo involves their conception of the church's role in promoting the socialist revolution. On the one hand, it appears that Christians must choose, and there is only one legitimate choice—socialism. On the other hand, Lopez Trujillo recognizes that Gustavo Gutierrez oscillates between "the use of theology as the driving impulse for the revolutionary option, and his rejection, as a conditioned reflect of the old theology, of such a legitimating function" (p. 257).

While Lopez Trujillo could take a nuanced position with regard to the content of liberation theology, once he was elected secretary-general of the Latin American Bishops Conference (CELAM) in 1972, he was determined to diminish its influence in CELAM's central administration. The liberation theologians were eliminated from the staffs of CELAM's structures or reduced in influence and replaced by more moderate churchmen. Enrique Dussel, one of the purged theologians, in a book with the same title as that of Lopez Trujillo (*De Medellín a Puebla*) and covering the same period from a very different point of view, argued that there was a conspiracy involving "Father Vekemans, the Christian Democrats of Europe and Latin America, the social democrats and conservatives or liberals in Latin America (in some cases with the aid of the Armed Forces, through their chaplaincies) and the American intelligence services"—in fact, everyone but the left had ganged up on the liberationists.[1] The issue for Dussel, as he explains in the first chapter of his book, is not Christianity against communism, but the wealthy against the poor and capitalism against socialism, and an effort of the propertied classes to prevent the church from exercising its prophetic role in moving a dependent, exploited, and oppressed Latin American toward a "sane socialism" based on a revision of Marxism that rejects its atheistic elements but accepts its opposition to money fetishism and the subordination of nature to profit. Similarly in the case of the structure of the church, the issue is not between the institutional church and an opposing popular church, but between church authorities in league with the powerful, and the poor and oppressed who are members of the church.

While liberation theologians such as Dussel spoke of the access of Vekemans and Lopez Trujillo to outside money—especially the De Rance Foundation in Milwaukee, which they viewed as a CIA conduit, and the Adveniat fund of the German bishops—the liberation theologians themselves seem also to have had considerable ability to get around the continent and to Europe and the United States for such meetings as those in Detroit in 1975 and at the Escorial in Spain in 1972. By now, the liberationists had become an influential group not only in Latin America, but also outside. In Germany a solidarity group called *Kirche und Befreiung* supported them, and their efforts were regarded favorably by well-known American and European theologians, both Catholic and Protestant, such as Harvey Cox, Robert McAfee Brown, Gregory Baum, Yves Congar, and Karl Rahner. In November 1977 a "Memorandum of German Theologians on the Campaign Against the Theology of Liberation" was published in Germany just before the church collections for Adveniat, arguing that the fund was being used to finance attacks on liberation theology and to oppose the "clear position of the Latin American bishops at Medellín in favor of the liberation of the peoples of that continent from age-old misery, dependence, and tutelage" (Dussel, *De Medellín,* p. 485). In mid-1978 an open letter signed by Congar and other well-known European theologians supported "the spirit of Medellín" and the value and usefulness "of that reflection by those Latin American colleagues who are attempting to develop a theology which arises from that land so rich in suffering and in future potential." In the United States as well, the liberal theological establishment—including Richard Shaull, Rosemary Reuther, Phillip Berryman, Harvey Cox, and James Wipfler—signed a letter supporting the liberation theologians and attacking what they called "The Theology of Conspiracy" that stated "Following the initiatives that you made in Medellín, we are discovering that the Gospel has a completely new meaning for us as well, when we read it through the eyes of the poor" (pp. 86–87). The *National Catholic Reporter,* published in Kansas City, and *Latin America Press,* published in English in Lima, also gave the position of the liberation theologians widespread publicity.

The two letters were published in connection with the preparations for the next General Meeting of the Latin American Bishops, to be held in Puebla in late 1978. That meeting, announced in 1976, was originally scheduled for the tenth anniversary of Medellín, but the death of two popes (Paul VI and John Paul I, the latter a month after his election in mid-1978) resulted in its postponement until January 1979. In preparation for the meeting, a theological team prepared a Consultative Document in late 1977 that was sent to all the bishops and to Rome. The lengthy document became a *cause célèbre* because it seemed to illustrate how far the counterrevolution had gone in the central administration of CELAM. Its critics argued that the document preached resignation to the poor and failed to focus on the social and economic causes of poverty in Latin America. Gustavo Gutierrez wrote that while "it skips along the mountaintops with broad generalizations, problems multiply on the mountainsides and in the valley," since it fails to mention

> the social costs imposed on Latin America as a result of the industrialization process . . . centered as it is in the affluent countries. . . . [It] manages to speak of industrial society without mentioning the working class, without entering the world of the underemployed and the unemployed who provide a supply of cheap labor for an industrial system that benefits multinational corporations and their local allies.[2]

For Gutierrez the text was "a counsel of resignation" and was reluctant "to deal face to face—beyond small verbal concessions—with the vast dimensions of social conflict in Latin America" (p. 116). Most fundamentally, it failed to recognize that "injustice is not an accident" and that "the possibility of significantly improving the distribution of income by correcting some aspects of the system's functioning, without altering the system itself, is no longer believable after the experience of many attempts at 'reform' in Latin America" (p. 117). Gutierrez thus reasserted the basic structuralist anticapitalism of his thinking, rejecting attempts at reform in favor of a fundamental transformation (that is, abolition) of capitalism. Gutierrez also criticized the failure of the document to discuss the *comunidades de base,* which had been mentioned at the original planning meeting for the conference.

Lopez Trujillo and others opposed to the new radical currents in the Latin American church saw the base communities as part of an effort to create a "parallel church," and to divide the Catholic church by distinguishing between the institutional hierarchical church and "the church of the people" (*iglesia popular*), or of the poor, which would be formed by a network of base communities committed to social justice and the needs of the poor.[3] The Consultative Document took note of the problem and asked the National Bishops Conferences in Latin America to evaluate theological outlooks that might give rise to "attitudes that depart from the organic character of the church or systematically oppose it." It observed that these tendencies differed from country to country, and were often actuated by a concern for the poor and for social justice, but could be influenced by "ideological currents in some cases which join to that anti-institutional attitude secularist elements and attitudes of messianism and pure utopianism" (pp. 578–81). For Lopez Trujillo and his associates, it was not just the liberation theologians who were at fault, but also the religious orders, many of them foreign, who were carrying out missionary work in Latin America. Their coordinating body, the Council of Latin American Religious (CLAR), was seen as particularly sympathetic to these views.

With the publication of the Consultative Document, the battle lines were drawn. It became the occasion for extensive debates along left-right lines within the Episcopal Conferences and in broader circles as well. Behind those debates were two world views, both claiming religious legitimacy. On the left the problem was to mobilize the majority in favor of what they saw as the spirit of Medellín, now threatened by a counterrevolution led from Bogota by Lopez Trujillo and his associates, with the sinister figure of Father Roger Vekemans in the background. This group was seen as attempting to reassert the "vertical" church, and controlling, if not discrediting, the new grass-roots movements and the demands for structural change in favor of the poor. For Penny Lernoux, *The Nation*'s correspondent for Latin America, the Document of Consultation "rejected Medellín's strong call for social justice" and the CELAM secretariat was engaged in a "German-financed smear campaign" against the liberation theologians. The Vatican was cooperating with this effort in the person of Cardinal Sebastiano Baggio, the president of the Pontifical Commission for Latin America,[4] and linked to this "theology of conspiracy" were U.S. interests, the multinationals, and the international press— as well as the wealthy and powerful of Latin America.

On the other side were those who saw the liberation theologians as seduced by "a theological and political Manicheanism" (Lopez Trujillo) that had distorted a valid commitment to the poor and to liberation by importing non-Christian (that is, Marxist) categories of analysis, and a polarized ecclesiology. The liberationists had rejected the social teaching of the church as expressed in the papal encyclicals on labor and they had subverted the teachings of the Medellín Conference. To the charges of a purge in CELAM, the critics answered that the officers elected in 1972 represented the majority opinion of the Latin American bishops who were concerned that some elements had distorted the message of Medellín. Moreover, there had been an effort to allow all currents to share in dialogue, as demonstrated by the CELAM publications that included representation of the liberation theologians' views. Lopez Trujillo also emphasized in his book *Medellín a Puebla* (pp. 283–85) that the Consultative Document had been simply a basis for discussion, and that the *Working Document* produced in the following year took account of the criticisms, and had been written by four bishops and experts named by the president of CELAM, Cardinal Aloisio Lorscheider of Brazil. (The Brazilian church had been most critical of the original Document).

Penny Lernoux's version of the same process had "tensions between the cardinal and Lopez Trujillo" resulting in Lorscheider being twice confined to his bed with a serious heart condition (p. 419).[5] Lernoux also has Lopez Trujillo and the Vatican selecting 181 delegates to the conference out of a total of 356, thus assuring conservative control of the conference. In fact, as all other sources indicate, the Vatican named twelve additional bishops to those selected by the national bishops conferences as voting members of the conference on the basis of one delegate for each five bishops, and one for every ten in cases of bishops conferences with more than one hundred members— that is, Brazil. About a hundred others were named by the Vatican as participants in various capacities but without the right to vote.

The Working Document of the Conference is described by Enrique Dussel as much superior to what went before (p. 505), but he notes that at one point (no. 183) it singles out for criticism the popular church and Marxist socialism, and criticizes conceptions of theology that "parallel" the teaching of the hierarchy (no. 47). The Mexican press, which gave extensive coverage to the preparations for the meeting, quoted Lopez Trujillo as declaring that "liberation theology, a tributary to Marxist analysis, . . . does not have citizenship papers in the thinking of our theologians" (p. 507). When the expert theologians who were to advise the bishops were announced, the liberation theologians were significant by their absence. Revealing their ignorance or prejudice against those not members of the liberationist club, two American observers wrote of the newly appointed advisers, "Most of them [were unknown] and all of them conservative" hardly a description of Renato Poblete S.J., of Chile's *Mensaje,* or Pierre Bigo S.J., of *ILADES* in Santiago.[6]

When it became known that Gustavo Gutierrez, for example, had not been invited to the conference as a *peritus* (expert), the word went out through the network of theologians and theological publications in many countries of Latin America. Progressive Jesuit magazines such as *Christus* in Mexico, *Sic* in Venezuela, and *Mensaje* in Chile, as well as CLAR, complained of Lopez Trujillo's maneuvers, and a plan was developed to bring in the liberation theologians as advisers to individual bishops who were delegates. Despite the complaints about the stacking of the delegations (Dussel [p. 509] complained that the procedures for majority voting rather than proportional representation excluded the left—an indication both of how politicized the conference had become, and of the minority status of the left in all episcopal conferences) enough "progressive" bishops were found to permit twenty-two liberation theologians and eight social scientists (including Richard Barnet, the author of an influential critique of multinational corporations, *The Global Reach,* mistakenly identified by Dussel [p. 538] as "a professor at Harvard and Yale") to come to the meeting as advisers to individual bishops.

The death of John Paul I after a month as pope had forced the postponement of the meeting, and it is indicative of the mythologies that had developed on both sides that by the time the Puebla gathering took place in late January 1979, John Paul I's death by heart attack was being attributed to arguments "with a cardinal of the curia" about the appointments of delegates to Puebla.[7]

In late January a total of 350 participants appeared in Puebla, Mexico, for the conference. Of these 175 were elected bishops from the national conferences and 12 were bishops appointed by the Vatican, the rest being accredited representatives from the religious orders, other religions, and churches in other parts of the world, as well as sixteen official theological advisers. The twenty-two liberation theologians and eight social scientists were not admitted to the heavily guarded seminary where the meetings were held, but they were in direct contact with the progressives within, and were able to react immediately to all developments with position papers that the progressives circulated within the meeting. In addition the Centro National de Comunicación Social (CENCOS) from Mexico City organized briefings, bulletins, and press conferences for the liberation theologians "outside the walls" of the seminary.

On the plane to the meeting, Pope John Paul II forecast what his position would be. Where, according to some (probably inaccurate) press reports, Lopez Trujillo wanted a blanket condemnation of liberation theology, John Paul II took a much more nuanced position. On the plane to the meeting he told the *New York Times* correspondent, "Liberation theology is a true theology. But perhaps it is also a false theology because if it starts to politicize theology, apply doctrines of political systems, ways of analysis which are not Christian, then this is no longer theology. . . . Theology of liberation but which one?" (*New York Times,* January 30, 1979).

The pope received a tumultuous reception in Mexico City, and spoke at the Shrine of Our Lady of Guadaloupe before motoring to the city of Puebla de los Angeles, about seventy-five miles away. The Mexican and international press covered the meeting extensively, and the pope's opening speech took a tone that seemed to signal the beginning of a second Battle of Puebla. (The first had been the victory of Mexico over the French invaders on May 5, 1862—commemorated by "Cinco de Mayo" streets in many Mexican cities.)

The pope's opening address, delivered on January 28, 1979, minced no words. It was aimed directly at the liberation theologians—or at least at some of them—without ever mentioning them by name. It had three main goals: to criticize excessively politicized interpretations of Christ's message and role, to reassert the organic character of the structure of the church against efforts to encourage the development of a parallel church, and to defend the social teaching of the church against the attacks that had been made upon it by the new post–Vatican II theological currents.

In the area of Christology, the pope attacked "rereadings of the gospel that are the product of theoretical speculations rather than of authentic meditation on the word of God and genuine evangelical commitment. . . . In some cases people are silent about Christ's divinity or else people purport to depict Jesus as a political activist, as a fighter against Roman domination, and even as someone involved in the class struggle." Quoting the New Testament the pope insisted that Christ "does not accept the position of those who mix the things of God with merely political attitudes. . . . He unequivocally rejects recourse to violence. He opens his message of conversion to all" (Eagleson and Scharper, pp. 59–60).

On the structure of the church, John Paul insisted on "sincere respect for the sacred *magisterium*" (the official teaching of the church) as the "authentic word of God." He criticized the view he perceived in some of the comments by the national bishops conferences that seemed to understand the Kingdom of God in a rather secularist sense—that is, that we do not arrive at the Kingdom through faith and membership in the church but rather merely by structural change and sociopolitical involvement. John Paul II quoted one of the last statements of John Paul I to the effect that "it is a mistake to state that political, economic, and social liberation coincide with salvation in Jesus Christ" (John Paul I, September 20, 1978). The pope also denounced the creation of an opposition between the institutional church and a "people's church which is born of the people and is fleshed out in the poor. These positions could contain varying and not always easily measurable degrees of familiar ideological forms of conditioning." He concluded that "the complete truth about human beings is the basis of the Church's social teaching, even as it is the basis of authentic liberation" (Eagleson and Scharper, pp. 62–64).

Signaling the approach that he would continue to take toward liberation theology, the pope argued for a "Christian conception of liberation. . . . It is a liberation that cannot be reduced simply to the restricted domain of economics, society, and culture [and] can never be sacrificed to the requirements of . . . some short-term praxis or gain" (a quote from Paul VI's encyclical of 1976, *Evangeli Nuntiandi*). The pope concluded that against those who would "try to sow doubts and lack of confidence in it" the church should study, teach, and apply the "rich and complex heritage that is [its] social doctrine" (pp. 68–69). Included in that doctrine is the church's teaching "that there is a social mortgage on all private property," which should be applied in ways that "will lead to a more just and equitable distribution of goods, not only within each nation but also in the wide world as a whole. And this will prevent the stronger countries from using their power to the detriment of the weaker ones" (p. 67). Having said this, the pope went on to reject the dependency theorists by speaking of the ties of interdependence and quoting Paul-VI's statement that "development is the new name for peace," while at the same time condemning "the ever increasing wealth of the rich at the expense of the ever increasing poverty of the poor" (p. 67).

After the pope's address, the conference then broke up into twenty-one committees to draft parts of the Final Document, which was to be voted upon by the entire conference.[8]

In the middle of the committee meetings, the leftist Mexico City daily *Uno Mas Uno* created a sensation by publishing the text of a confidential letter by Archbishop Lopez Trujillo that had remained on a cassette given to a journalist when his dictaphone tape ran out. It seemed to verify all the suspicions about the politicization of the preparations for the conference. Sent to the president of the Social Action Department of CELAM, the letter complained of the adverse influence of the Brazilians, CLAR, and the Jesuit General, Pedro Arrupe. It urged him to "prepare your airplane bombers for Puebla" and "get into training before entering the ring for a world match" (Lernoux, p. 435; Eagleson and Scharper, p. 37).

However, Lopez Trujillo's influence was undercut at the outset when the conference rejected a proposal to have the CELAM staff act as a steering committee, and elected five of its own members to take charge of the meeting. Preliminary straw votes were taken at various times over the next several weeks. In the final voting the only part not to receive the obligatory two-thirds vote was a section that referred to the "systems" in Latin America as "permanently violating human rights." It was said that 25 percent of the Final Document was affected by the activities of the liberation theologians outside of the meeting, who prepared a total of eighty-four position papers that were circulated to the members of the committees. The Mexicans reported that President Carter had ordered the CIA to carry out surveillance of the meeting in order to avoid a repetition of the Iranian debacle, leading Harvey Cox, an American Protestant observer, to organize an open letter of protest on the subject. (For the text see Dussel, pp. 583–84).

The Final Document of 1310 paragraphs included something for everyone. It did not condemn liberation theology. If this had ever been the intention of Lopez Trujillo, it was clear from Pope John's statement to the *New York Times* on the plane to Mexico that he would not be successful. However, strong statements were made on the politicization of theology and against the "popular church," and the social teaching of the church was reaffirmed. On the other hand, the conference was as critical of liberal capitalism (and of Marxism) as any earlier church document, and it added a specific condemnation of the Doctrine of National Security used to justify military rule. Most important, it made a decisive commitment to "the preferential option for the poor," which was to be as controversial in future discussions of Puebla as the reference to "institutionalized violence" had been after Medellín; and it specifically endorsed the Christian Base Communities provided that they acted within the overall structure of the church.[9]

Beginning with the sociocultural context of contemporary Latin America, the document speaks of the "hunger, chronic diseases, illiteracy, impoverishment, injustice in international relations and particularly in commercial interchanges, and situations of economic and cultural neocolonialism." It strikes the liberation theme by stating that "the Church has a duty to proclaim the liberation of millions of human beings among whom are many of the Church's own children—the duty to help bring this liberation forth in the world, to bear witness to it, and make sure that it is total" (no. 26). The document calls the growing gap between rich and poor a scandal that is "the product of specific situations and economic, social, and political structures" (no. 30). The document attacks "the free market economy," which "in its most rigid expression is still the prevailing system on our continent" because it gives preference to capital over labor and makes it possible for small groups "often tied to foreign interests" to make profits "while the vast majority of the people suffer" (no. 47). This is followed by a criticism of Marxism for sacrificing human values and using "force as a basic tool," and a specific attack on ideologies of National Security that also are based on force and violate human rights, even as they claim to profess the Christian faith (nos. 47–49). The same approach is taken about halfway through the lengthy document when it denounces "capitalist liberalism, the idolatrous worship of wealth in individualistic terms" and relates it to scandalous contrasts and dependence and oppression on both the national and international levels. While the document admits that capitalism's original historical form of expression has been attenuated by necessary forms of social legislation and specific instances of government intervention, in other countries, it says, capitalism has persisted and even retrogressed to more primitive forms (no. 542).

This is followed by a discussion of Marxism that seems to be aimed at the liberation theologians. After noting that Marxist collectivism is based on a class struggle analysis that leads to the dictatorship of the party, and has in all historical instances been carried out in a totalitarian framework, the bishops warn of "the risk of ideologization run by theological reflection when it is based on a praxis that has recourse to Marxist analysis," leading to "the total politicization of Christian existence, the disintegration of the language of faith into that of the social sciences, and the draining away of the transcendental dimension of Christian salvation" (nos. 543–45). In this section and earlier the bishops warn of the danger of the partisan political exploitation of the Gospel based on a "re-reading of the Gospel on the basis of a political option," which is a new form of traditionalist integralism uniting civil and ecclesiastical authorities in the form of "a strategic alliance between the Church and Marxism" (nos. 559–61, see also no. 91). The bishops thus seem to reassert the "third positionism" that the church had always adopted, adding the arguments of the proponents of the New International Economic Order and the Brandt Commission about the widening gap between the rich and poor nations. Indeed, at the end of the document they specifically endorse an international code of conduct regulating multinational enterprises, internationalization of the sea bed, and "a new international order . . . grounded on legitimate human social needs" (nos. 1277–80).

In the chapter on "The Ecclesial Reality in Latin America," the bishops make their oft-quoted reference to "the cry of a suffering people who demand justice, freedom, and respect for the basic rights of human beings and peoples" (no. 87), and follow this with a specific endorsement of the emerging Christian Base Communities, which had been established since the Medellín meeting in 1968. Yet even here there is a word of warning that "in some areas, clearly political interests try to manipulate [the CEBs] and to sever them from authentic communion with their bishops" (no. 98). Later in the document, when the CEBs are mentioned again they are endorsed as giving a dynamic vitality on the grass-roots level, but a warning is given against "the danger of organizational anarchy or narrow-minded sectarian elitism" (no. 261). This is followed by a denunciation of the theories of "the People's Church, born of the people in opposition to an 'alienating' official or institutional church" (no. 263).

During the conference debate there had been specific discussion of the writings of Jon Sobrino on Christology. Those discussions were reflected in the section about Christ warning that "We cannot distort, factionalize, or ideologize the person of Jesus Christ. That can be done in one of two ways: either by turning him into a politician, a leader, a revolutionary, or a simple prophet on the one hand; or on the other hand, by restricting him, the Lord of History, to the merely private realm" (no. 178).

When the bishops turned to a discussion of Christian liberation, which they described as "the creative search for approaches free of ambiguity and reductionism and fully faithful to the Word of God" (no. 488), they expressed themselves on the controversial issue of the role of the clergy in politics. The Puebla meeting argued that the Church is involved in politics in the broad sense, since it spells out the fundamental values, ethics, and the means of social relationships. However, the specific application of those values to political action is the realm of lay people while priests and deacons should be concerned with unity and the promotion of fundamental values (nos. 521–30). Violence is rejected as a means because criminal acts can in no way be justified as the way to liberation. "Violence inexorably engenders new forms of oppression and bondage which usually prove to be more serious than the ones the people are allegedly being liberated from" (nos. 531–32).

The most significant single section of the Puebla Document is Part Four, much of which is devoted to the "preferential option for the poor." The bishops observe that the majority of Latin Americans are poor, indigenous peoples, peasants, manual laborers, and marginalized urban dwellers. Claiming to be following the precedent of the 1968 Medellín Conference, the bishops say, "Despite the distortions and interpretations of some, who vitiate the spirit of Medellín, and despite the disregard and even hostility of others, we affirm the need for conversion on the part of the whole church to a preferential option for the poor, an option aimed at their integral liberation" (no. 1134).

Linking the various interpretations of liberation, and rejecting by implication any interpretation of that option as expressing a choice of the poor over the rich or a class struggle approach, the bishops state that "service to the poor is the privileged, although not the exclusive, gauge of our following of Christ. The best service to our fellows is evangelization, which disposes them to fulfill themselves as children of God, liberates them from injustice, and fosters their integral advancement" (no. 1145). The focus on the poor is then followed by a discussion of the need for a similar preferential option for the young.

Archbishop Lopez Trujillo's commentary on this section in his book takes pains to underline the "nonexclusive" character of the church's commitment to the poor. He refers specifically to Gustavo Gutierrez's *Theology of Liberation*, which speaks of converting the church to the service of the class struggle, so that "the authentic unity of the church necessarily implies the option for the oppressed and exploited of this world." (The quotation appears on p. 277 of the English translation of *A Theology of Liberation*.) He then links this view with Gutierrez's rejection of reformism and development in favor of revolution and liberation to argue that Gutierrez's interpretation is equivalent to the "people's church" approach that the bishops had condemned, and insists that the word "nonexclusive" was used at Puebla when the bishops endorsed the preferential option for the poor, in order to give it an evangelizing rather than political interpretation.

Lopez Trujillo claimed that some would read Puebla along polarized lines of interpretation—an error in his view. Jon Sobrino's commentary on the Final Document seems to fit this description. In his view the headline-capturing references by the pope and the bishops to misinterpretation of Medellín, reductionism in Christology, and the people's church came from those who had neither read nor understood the liberation writings (Eagleson and Scharper, p. 291). For Sobrino the document as a whole represented an affirmation of the "real church" over ecclesiastical figures who at first were more interested in offering opinions about reality than in talking from within the heart of that reality. Those ecclesiastical figures had conservative tendencies for the most part, "particularly in the way that they were invited to the conference" (p. 296). Sobrino also noted that the conference did not "condemn liberation theology nor the church of the poor. Indeed strictly speaking there was not even a condemnation of Marxist analysis, though Puebla did criticize its overall ideology" (p. 304). Even the insistence on the nonexclusive character of the option for the poor is reinterpreted to mean that "no one should feel excluded from the church that has made such an option" (p. 308), which of course was not what the bishops said in their document.

The world press had covered the Puebla meeting because it was the first public appearance outside of Italy of the new pope. There was another reason, however—the increasing interest in the subject of the relation between religion and politics. In the United States, the rise of the religious right with a conservative political agenda was demonstrating that what had appeared to be a very secular society had deep religious commitments that could be significant for politics. In the same year, 1979, the Iranian Revolution, which brought Islamic fundamentalism to power headed by the Ayotollah, also showed how significant religion could be in Third World politics. But for our story the most important example of the influence of religion on politics was the new role of Christianity, especially Roman Catholicism, in the politics of Central America. It was an important factor contributing to the two important changes in that area in 1979—the overthrow of Anastasio Somoza in July, and the turmoil in El Salvador that began in October. In both countries, groups influenced by liberation theology played a significant role.

7

El Salvador and Nicaragua: Test Cases of Liberation?

THE NICARAGUAN REVOLUTION provided another case study in the application of the liberation theologians' writings—and as attitudes toward the Sandinista government became more polarized over time, the interpretations of the appropriate role of Christians in the revolution also became increasingly controversial. The civil war that developed in El Salvador in 1980 and the aid that the Nicaraguans provided to the Salvadoran rebels, particularly in late 1980, led to deeper U.S. involvement in Central America. The United States sent arms and advisers to El Salvador and in 1982 began to support and arm anti-Sandinista *contras* on the Honduran-Nicaraguan border. In analyzing the causes of the revolutions in Central America, many observers cited the changing role of the Catholic church following Vatican II and the Medellín Conference. It is thus useful to examine that role, and in particular, to attempt to relate it to the theory and praxis of the liberation theologians.

Archbishop (later Cardinal) Obando y Bravo of Managua did not attend the Puebla meeting, but was represented by the president of the Nicaraguan Bishops Conference, Manuel Salazar, Bishop of León. Oscar Romero, the Archbishop of El Salvador, was not elected by his fellow bishops but was nominated by the Vatican as a member of the Pontifical Commission for Latin America. The Nicaraguan and Salvadoran bishops spoke of the repression of the church in their respective countries, and while those countries were not singled out by name in the Final Document, open letters were initiated by the liberation theology caucus and signed by many of the participants expressing support and solidarity with their persecuted churches. The persecution of the two churches by authoritarian regimes in power was typical of the increasing conflict between a reform-minded church and the military regimes that were in power in most Latin American countries during the 1970s. The violence with which the governments reacted to even the slightest hint of reform radicalized many churchmen and church-influenced groups, making them more sympathetic to the arguments of the liberation theologians.

El Salvador

In El Salvador, church-influenced groups such as the Christian Democratic Party under the progressive mayor of San Salvador, José Napoleon Duarte, and the Christian Federation of Salvadoran Peasants (FECCAS) proposed an agrarian reform program that would respond to the desperate land hunger of an overpopulated country in which most of the land was in the hands of a small, wealthy oligarchy ("the fourteen families"). Duarte ran for the presidency in 1972, but when it appeared that he was winning, the vote count was suspended and after several days of delay it was announced that the military candidate had won. Duarte was subsequently arrested, tortured, and expelled from the country.

During this same period, the church had become active in establishing Christian Base Communities in the rural areas, building on earlier efforts to establish peasant cooperatives. One of the first signs of the violence to come was the 1970 kidnapping and beating of the archdiocesan delegate to the first agrarian reform congress, Father José Inocencio Alas. The Jesuit school in San Salvador, which had educated the children of the upper class, now began to take an active social role. Students went to the countryside to help Jesuit teams evangelize the peasantry using the new participatory methods, which included the election of Delegates of the Word to lead the Christian Base Communities. One of the most active Jesuits was Father Rutilio Grande S.J., whose work in the rural parish of Aguilares between 1972 and 1976 finally led to his assassination by a death squad. He was one of fifteen priests to be killed by Salvadoran death squads in the middle and late 1970s as opposition to their efforts by the military and the landowners increased. The Central American university, run

by the Jesuits, was attacked for promoting reform, and Ignacio Ellacuria, the editor of its journal and a liberation theologian, was accused of leftist sympathies.

Like the other well-known Jesuit theologian in El Salvador, Jon
Sobrino, Ellacuria was a Spaniard—more specifically a Basque—but
he had then lived in El Salvador for more than 25 years. He has written many articles in Spanish, but only one book has been published
in English, *Freedom Made Flesh* (Maryknoll, NY: Orbis Books,
1976), a translation of his *Teologia Politica,* which was published
in El Salvador in 1972—just as things were beginning to heat up politically. The book was published in Spanish by the Social Secretariat
of the Salvadoran Bishops, and as its title implies, it attempts to analyze the relation of theology and politics. For Ellacuria the aim of
theology "should be to be a critical and creative consciousness at
work in the service of the community" (p. 9). Jesus was the latest
and greatest of a long line of Hebrew prophets who attacked "the oppression exercised by religion in the name of God" (p. 30). Christ's
denunciations undermined the power of the priestly class, and focused attention on the theological implications of poverty. In the specific situation of Israel of his time, Ellacuria asserts, Jesus saw the
poor as the "preferred locus of God's revelation" (p. 35). The pov-
erty-wealth theme has "nothing to do with the class struggle" but it
reveals "a dialectical relationship in which wealth causes and produces poverty, so that one is forced to choose between being with
the oppressor or being with the oppressed" (p. 35). Jesus was not a
guerrilla revolutionary (Zealot) himself, but he was crucified with
them and his crime was that he claimed to be a king. Judas Iscariot
may have had that name because he carried a dagger (*sicarius*) as
did the Zealots, and Simon Peter's other name, Barjona, may mean
"terrorist" (p. 50). His followers were armed when the Romans
came to get Jesus in the Garden, and he advised the man who did
not have a sword to sell his cloak and buy one (Luke 22:36).

Much of the rest of the book is devoted to a theological analysis
of violence—the central theme of which is that there are two kinds
of violence, that of "the unjust oppressor which is the original ag-
gressive violence" (p. 196), and the "violence performed on behalf
of the oppressed, the violence with which God punishes the unjust
oppressor on this earth." Ellacuria describes the latter as "good violence" involving not only "moral denunciation" but "the elements of
chastisement, punishment, and the rehabilitation of the order that

has been put out of kilter by the abuses of the unjust people in power."

Ellacuria seems to argue for a holy war against injustice but when he treats specifics, as in his comparison of the approaches to violence of Charles Foucault, Martin Luther King, and Father Camilo Torres, he admits that

> The kind of solution exemplified by Camilo Torres does not necessarily deny basic Christian values, although it runs the risk of doing precisely that. There is a temptation here, but it is not a sin. . . . People who have defended the legitimacy of war should not be scandalized by solutions akin to the one chosen by Camilo Torres. . . . This combative action must keep in mind two points of utmost importance: 1) Not everything in the existing structures is evil, neither as structure nor as personal achievement; 2) The Christian message demands that we move out of the whole schema of violence versus resistance to violence by the use of force, as quickly as possible. [p. 226]

Ellacuria concludes his book by arguing that "Christian liberation is not to be interpreted solely in terms of sociopolitical and economic oppression," recommending that authentic Christian liberation is to be found through divine revelation, which is heard in the church, "i.e. the ecclesial community brought together by God's word" (p. 235).

Ellacuria's book was probably not widely read in El Salvador but it reflected the currents of thinking among Catholic intellectuals and students at the Jesuit university. The careful—and not so careful—distinctions that he makes were forgotten, but the basic message that in extreme situations (and few would deny that contemporary El Salvador was an extreme situation) violence is justified against the current violent and oppressive system was accepted by many of the young people and professionals of El Salvador during the 1970s, and that acceptance was at least partially related to the influence of liberation theology. As priests and religious workers were arrested, beaten, exiled, and killed by the military government it was difficult not to associate the situation with the "institutionalized violence" cited by the Medellín Conference, and to argue that the situation was so extreme that violence was justified in an effort to change it. That "institutionalized violence" is seen by Ellacuria as directly related to the capitalist system, and in opposing it

> it is necessary to run the risks that are necessary to end this system of injustice and violence. . . . The part of the church that holds this

point of view takes a sympathetic view of revolutionary movements as the principal opponents of the dominant capitalism. It does not agree with their ideology or with many of their practices, but they appear more representative of a possible project of the people, and more open to correction than their opponents now in power. [*Diakonia,* Managua (26), June 1983]

(Despite his critical attitude toward the Marxist Left, Father Ellacuria was later accused by the Salvadoran Right of being the "intellectual author" of the Salvadoran revolution. On November 16, 1989, he and five other Jesuit priests were dragged from their dormitory by armed men in uniform and murdered.)

As the spiral of mutual assassinations in El Salvador rose in the middle of the decade, an election was held for the presidency in 1977, and when the government party won by a 2-to-1 margin, it was clear that there had been massive fraud. In the same month Archbishop Chavez of San Salvador retired and was replaced by Bishop Oscar Romero of the Santiago diocese, who was widely regarded to be a conservative in his political outlook. As he took office, the repression was escalating. In January and February three priests were tortured, one was kidnapped, and two were expelled from the country. On February 28, the army attacked an open-air Mass in the plaza and 100 people were killed. The bishops met and, alluding to Medellín, condemned the uninvestigated murders, the expulsion of the priests, and the repression of the peasants. A week later, Father Rutilio Grande was ambushed on his way to say Mass and assassinated. Archbishop Romero closed the Catholic schools for three weeks, suspended Masses except in the cathedral, and announced that he would attend no public functions until Father Grande's death was investigated. In April, the foreign minister was kidnapped by one of the leftist guerrilla movements and his body was found two weeks later. A right-wing organization, the White Warriors Union, blamed the Jesuits and "Communist priests" for the rise of the left and vowed to carry out killings in retaliation. When the foreign minister's body was found two weeks later, the White Warriors killed Father Alfonso Navarro and began to circulate handbills reading, "Be a Patriot, Kill a Priest." In June they announced that all Jesuits must leave the country within thirty days or they would be killed.

Along with three other Latin American countries, El Salvador had rejected U.S. military aid because of the human rights restrictions placed on it by the new American administration of President Jimmy

Carter. Guerrilla groups continued to kidnap businessmen, several more priests were killed, and Archbishop Romero gave sermons and wrote pastoral letters that often included analyses of the question of violence and nonviolence.[1]

In his Fourth Pastoral Letter, published August 6, 1979, Romero distinguishes among (1) "institutionalized violence" which he identifies as "the unjust distribution of wealth and property, especially landownership"; (2) the arbitrary violence of the state that responds to "any dissent against the present form of capitalism" with torture, murder, or disappearance"; (3) the violence of the extreme right in defense of an unjust social order; (4) "terrorist" violence "by politico-military groups or individuals when they intentionally victimize innocent persons, or when the damage they do is disproportionate to the positive effect they wish to achieve"; (5) insurrectional violence (and here he quotes Pope Paul on the need for "exceptional circumstances of an evident prolonged tyranny that seriously works against fundamental human rights"; and (6) the violence of legitimate self-defense. Romero follows this conditional approval for revolution with an analysis of Marxism that warns of its dangers but distinguishes, as liberation theolgians had done so often, between its anti-Christian ideology and its use as a "scientific analysis of the economic and social order." In the latter case, Romero warns that there are dangers of the use of unethical means, the "absolutization of popular political organizations," and attempts to cut off adherents from the church. Having said this, he concludes that "in concrete terms, capitalism is in fact what is most unjust and unChristian about the society in which we live" (translated in *Voice of the Voiceless,* pp. 143–46).

That this sounds like a mixture of recent church teachings with elements drawn from liberation theology should not be surprising, since it was widely believed in San Salvador at the time that Ignacio Ellacuria had played a major role in drafting Archbishop Romero's statements. He was also close to Jon Sobrino and Sobrino wrote the introduction to *Voice of the Voiceless,* the collection of his pastoral letters, and refers to Ellacuria often in his writings.[2]

After the overthrow of Somoza in July 1979, it was clear that El Salvador was on the verge of civil war. On October 15, 1979, 400 officers of the Salvadoran army arrested their commanders, overthrew the government, and established a joint military-civilian junta, several of the members of which were from the Jesuit-run Universidad Centroamericana. The junta announced its intention to carry out an agrarian reform, grant amnesty to political prisoners, and abolish the major right-wing terrorist group. When the repression continued and the right wing of the army seemed to have reasserted itself, the initial junta resigned and was replaced in January by a new junta, which included two Christian Democrats. One of them resigned two months later in favor of the 1972 presidential candidate of the Christian Democrats, José Napoleon Duarte, who had returned from seven years in exile in Venezuela. When the education minister of the first junta appeared on television with a machine gun to announce that he was joining the guerrillas, Archbishop Romero was quoted as saying that those really responsible for the violence in the country were the oligarchy and "idolizers of wealth, who closed off peaceful solutions to problems." Romero also wrote a letter to President Carter asking him not to send military aid until the repression had stopped and quoting the Puebla Conference in favor of "self-determination of peoples." At the end of March in his broadcast weekly sermon at Sunday Mass he appealed to the military to stop the killing, stating that "no soldier is obliged to obey an order against God's law. . . . In the name of God, and in the name of this suffering people whose laments rise up to heaven each day in greater numbers, I implore you, I beg you, I order you—stop the repression." The next day he was murdered while saying an anniversary Requiem Mass in the chapel of a local hospital.

Some ten thousand people gathered in the plaza for the funeral Mass on the following Sunday. Shooting broke out, at least two bombs exploded, and twenty-six people were killed in the ensuing hysteria. After Romero's death, his words were recalled, "As a Christian I do not believe in death without resurrection. If they kill me I will rise again in the Salvadoran people."

Following the resignation of the first junta and the murder of the archbishop, some Christian Democrats joined the guerrillas, and others announced the formation of the Popular Social Christian Movement (MPSC), affiliated with the newly formed Democratic Revolutionary Front (FDR) headed by a social democrat, Guillermo Ungo, who had been a member of the first junta. A National Council of the People's Church (CONIP) was established in June linking together a number of Base Christian Communities and dedicated to supporting "the liberation project of the Salvadoran people." The beginning stages of the promised agrarian reform were implemented by the second junta, but the Christian Democratic Party was split between a majority who supported Duarte, their former standard bearer and now a junta member, and some of its younger members, mostly associated with the Jesuit university, who cast their lot with the FDR or with one of the five guerrilla organizations that made up the Farabundo Marti National Liberation Front (FMLN), with which the FDR allied itself after its head was murdered by a death squad in November 1980.

The United States began to send "nonlethal" military aid to the junta but this was cut off in December 1980 after three Maryknoll nuns and a lay religious worker were murdered near the airport. Two U.S. labor advisers were also killed at the beginning of January, but when it became apparent that the left had initiated a "final offensive" to overthrow the government before Ronald Reagan would take office on January 20, 1981, President Carter ordered resumption of aid. Carter also approved sending U.S. military advisers, which seemed to herald a deepening involvement of the United States in the struggle. The attempt by the now united FDR-FMLN to carry out an insurrection was a failure, but the country was deeply involved in civil war. The church attempted to maintain a neutral stance, supporting human rights and legal aid offices to assist the victims on both sides (most were victims of the right). The church opposed all foreign intervention, and the U.S. Catholic Conference, representing the American bishops, testified in opposition to American military aid, but the U.S. Congress adopted an aid program conditioned on presidential certification every six months of Salvadoran progress in holding free elections, combatting terrorism and repression, and implementing the agrarian reform program.

Initially only the first and fourth of the planned stages of the agrarian reform were carried out, but elections were announced for March 1982. The guerrillas and the left were invited to participate but refused to do so, citing the lack of personal security for their candidates. In addition, they threatened to disrupt the election and to kill those who voted. Nevertheless a record number of voters turned out to elect a constituent assembly that was to write a constitution and elect a provisional president. The Christian Democrats received 40 percent of the votes but the four right-wing parties elected former Major Roberto d'Aubuisson (who was reported to have been involved in the murder of Archbishop Romero) as president of the Assembly. He might have been elected provisional president of the country but for U.S. support of a neutral businessman, Alvaro Magaña, who took office in May.

In March and May 1984, a two-round presidential election was held and José Napoleon Duarte won the second round with an absolute majority against Major d'Aubuisson. The FMLN announced its policy as "No to the electoral farce, yes to the popular war," but despite its campaign of sabotage, 80 percent of the population turned out to vote. The Assembly blocked President Duarte's efforts to expand the agrarian reform, but he was successful in persuading the armed forces to dismiss or transfer officers linked to the death squads, and the number of political killings dropped from 1259 in 1983 to 220 in 1984. Talks were held in October 1985 between the government and the guerrilla leadership under the auspices of the church, now led by Archbishop Arturo Rivera y Damas. They resulted in the appointment of a Peace Commission but there was no real progress toward settling the war.

Following the negotiations, and suffering military losses, the guerrillas announced a change in strategy from holding territory in the countryside to a revival of urban terrorism and murder of right-wing leaders as well as the kidnapping and murder of the mayors of the municipalities.

In March 1985, the fourth election to be held in three years took place to choose members of the Legislative Assembly as well as municipal councils. The Christian Democrats won an upset victory, securing 33 out of the 60 seats in the Assembly and winning control of 156 of 262 municipal councils. The new Assembly removed a conservative Attorney General and replaced him with a Christian Democrat who began to take a more vigorous role in investigating and prosecuting the right-wing death squads. The murderers of the three nuns (although not the murderers' more highly placed backers) were successfully prosecuted and convicted, as were those who had killed the U.S. labor advisers. The economy was in deep recession, with almost half the population unemployed, but democracy had been restored, some reforms of landholding had been carried out, and the immediate threat from the guerrillas had been blunted.

The relative success of the Christian Democrats in El Salvador (they lost their legislative majority in March 1988 but remained the largest party) despite strong, indeed lethal, opposition from both left and right suggested some problems for the simple left-right dichotomous thinking of the liberation theologians. Their teaching legitimated the entrance into the guerrillas, or the affiliation with allied organizations, of talented Christian Democrats such as Ruben Zamora, who could have assisted in promoting democratic reform in the country. Particularly as the FMLN turned to urban terrorism, lawyers and university professors felt increasingly uncomfortable about their support for the guerrillas—and perhaps began to realize that a more viable partnership would have been with the Christian Democrats so as to give more legitimacy and votes to the reformists against the conservatives.[3] Especially once the United States had decided to support the Salvadoran government there was no chance that it would be overthrown by force, but the decision had been made, and the former Christian Democrats along with their social democratic allies were left without influence either on the guerrilla left or on the central government. If one wished to espouse the option for the poor and the oppressed, it was clear from the behavior of the poor that what they wanted was not socialism but democracy, social peace, and an end to violence—and the Christian Democrats, who were the special object of scorn of the liberation theologians, had made genuine progress in those directions, although there still was a very long distance to go. Moreover the church leadership, especially Archbishop Rivera y Damas, was still a viable interlocutor between the government and the guerrillas precisely because it had not identified itself with one political solution or the other, as the liberation theologians insisted it was obliged to do, but had maintained a position above politics but in favor of human rights and basic moral and religious values.

Nicaragua

It was much more difficult for the church to maintain such a position in Nicaragua, both before and after the 1979 national uprising that overthrew the dictator Anastasio Somoza. Nicaragua differed in important respects from El Salvador. First, it was not overpopulated, being about five times the size of El Salvador with little more than half its population. And second, in contrast with El Salvador there had been strong American interest in Nicaragua ever since the middle of the nineteenth century, when it was seen as a possible location for an interoceanic canal. That interest took the form of an invasion by an American soldier of fortune, William Walker, in the 1850s, and military intervention in the twentieth century as a contingent of U.S. marines occupied the capital from 1912 to 1925 and again from 1926 until 1933. The second occupation was opposed by a guerrilla leader, Augusto César Sandino, who successfully eluded American efforts to capture him throughout the period. After the American withdrawal Sandino was killed by the American-trained head of the Nicaraguan constabulary, Anastasio Somoza, and Somoza followed this with the ouster of the president who had been elected before the Americans left. Sandino's name, but not his nationalist anti-Marxist ideology, was adopted by the Sandinista National Liberation Front when it was formed in the early 1960s. The Sandinistas' goal was to end the Somoza family dictatorship (Anastasio Somoza had been assassinated in 1956 and was succeeded by his son, Luis, who died in 1967, to be followed by another son, Anastasio Jr.). Although at times brutally repressive, especially in the last years of the dictatorship, the Somoza government maintained a facade of elective democracy, and permitted the opposition Democratic Conservative Party to participate in elections and sit in the congress. The Somozas relied on U.S. support as well, and cooperated with the United States in such ventures as the Bay of Pigs invasion of Cuba in 1961. Rebellions such as that led by Pedro Joaquín Chamorro, the editor of the opposition newspaper, *La Prensa,* in 1954 were brutally repressed, and the American-trained Nicaraguan National Guard was a personal force in the service of the dictator and the Somoza family. Much of Nicaragua's land and important businesses was owned by the Somozas, and the dictator's personal fortune was estimated to be $500–$600 million at the time of his overthrow.

The Sandinista National Liberation Front (FSLN), founded in 1961, was made up of former student activists who had been imprisoned and in some cases tortured by Somoza for opposition activities. The group was Marxist from the beginning but named itself after the nationalist antiimperialist hero Sandino. Two of its founders, Carlos Fonseca and Tomas Borge, had been members of the Nicaraguan Communist Party (PSN), but had broken with that party after the Cuban Revolution seemed to demonstrate a better road to revolution. The Sandinistas conducted sporadic guerrilla actions during the 1960s and formed an underground student affiliate, the Student Revolutionary Front (FRE), but did not extend their base of support much beyond the middle- and upper-class students and former students who had originally established it. In 1969 the FSLN published its program, which included "freedom of expression and organization in the interests of the people, a revolutionary government that would promote direct popular participation, [and] respect for religious beliefs and support for clerics who support the working people."⁴

In the mid-1960s Ernesto Cardenal, a young Nicaraguan who had studied at the Trappist monastery in Gethsemane, Kentucky, under Thomas Merton, established a contemplative community on the island of Solentiname in Lake Nicaragua. The members of the community gradually became involved with local fishermen and farmers in Socratic-type discussions relating the Gospel to their day-to-day concerns in ways not unlike those employed later in the Christian Base Communities. Initially focusing on local concerns, these discussions became more specifically political in the early 1970s after Father Cardenal had returned from a visit to Cuba very much impressed with what he had seen there. (See his book *In Cuba*, New York: New Directions, 1974.) Four volumes of the Solentiname discussions in the 1971–1976 period have been translated by Orbis Books (1976–1982); they illustrate the way in which the Gospel was applied to national and international politics. As Berryman notes in the selections that he quotes, "Underlying it all seems to be a basic change in attitude from one of accepting the world as it is to one aiming at transforming it"—but the change went further than this in many cases. In a way that became increasingly common as the liberation theology movement developed, Cuba was seen as the embodiment of liberation and even of the Gospel message in the contemporary world. (It should be noted that the highly political and revolutionary character of the discussions is not necessarily typical of all Christian Base Community meditations on the Gospel. This rather reflected the pre-revolutionary situation of Nicaragua in the early 1970s, and Ernesto Cardenal's uncritical admiration for what he had recently seen in Cuba.)

In the group's meditation on the birth of Christ, for example, one participant claims that:

Christ came to liberate the poor. He wasn't coming to liberate the rich. [Vol. I, p. 53]

Another says [that] the rich need to be liberated from their money (and a woman says that when the poor are liberated it will be) like in Cuba, where all the children are healthy. They're all taken care of when they're sick. If you're old, they take care of you. They give you everything you need and you're healthy and eager to work. [Vol. I, p. 54]

Fernando Cardenal, Ernesto's Jesuit brother, asserts, "I don't understand how you can read the Gospels and get spiritual lessons for your life out of it and not get involved in the Revolution" (Vol. I, p. 85). When asked whether Christ's command to love your enemies included love for class enemies, Ernesto replies,

In the class struggle we are struggling to put an end to classes. As long as we are divided into classes, with opposed interests, we have to have class enemies. But if we struggle to unite with them and to form all together a humanity united in the classless society, then we are struggling for love. . . . We Christians have always said, "We must hate sin and love the sinner." I have the impression that Che [Guevara] never fought because of hatred of another people but because of hatred of injustice. [Vol. II, pp. 110–11]

When another participant interpreted the saying "Do unto others as you would have them do unto you" to mean "Just as the rich want us to work for them, so they also should work for us," Cardenal replies, "This system is called socialism. Everyone works for everyone. . . . Christ is really planning a new society for us" (Vol. II, p. 118).

The discussion of Christ's statement that "the kingdom of heaven suffers violence, and the violent take it by force" (Matthew 11:12) leads to a lengthy discussion of when violence is justified, as well as the claim that "Christianity has been conquered by force for two thousand years. Not counting the two or three hundred years of primitive Christianity . . . the rulers of the world [of weapons, money, and of culture] . . . have opposed Christ's plan to establish justice" (Vol. III, p. 227). A few pages later, the same speaker makes a sophisticated argument as to why the poor are unable to respond to the call for revolution until,

through a particularly violent reality they are able to hear. The ones that can't hear, they never do, until the revolution comes and tells them: here's your food, here's your doctor, here's your school, here's your house, here's your job, here's your whole life. That's what happened in Cuba. The Cuban people did not make the revolution; it was made by the part of the people that could hear. And the ones that couldn't hear because they didn't have ears, they got ears when the revolution was won and they saw the deeds, they saw the reality. [Vol. III, pp. 234–35]

Cuba is cited again in the next volume in the discussion of Christ's reward at the Last Judgment for those who feed the hungry, clothe the naked, and visit the sick (Matthew 25). One participant states that "in Cuba everybody's been fed and given clothing, adequate housing, medical care, education. I think that when Christ spoke of these things, which are a person's basic necessities . . . he was thinking more than of traditional charity, of revolutionary charity" (Vol. IV, p. 52). (There is no mention of Christ's commendation of those who visit prisoners, which presumably might also have had some relevance to Cuba, which had an estimated 20,000 political prisoners at the time.)

Ernesto Cardenal also makes some startling claims in the discussion of Christ's crucifixion and resurrection. Interpreting Mary's statement in the poem the Magnificat, "the powerful will be put down from their thrones, and the humble will be exalted" (Luke 1:52), Cardenal asserts:

> Mary was a revolutionary and a Communist before Jesus was born. Those ideas she had received from the prophets of the Bible. [Vol. IV, p. 234]
>
> When he died, people thought he had failed as has also been thought about revolutionaries that have died for the people: Che, Camilo Torres, Allende, and they don't know that that's their victory. [Vol. IV, p. 239]

The equation by a Catholic priest of Christ's resurrection with that of the more recent revolutionaries becomes more comprehensible a few pages later when Cardenal says, "Christ talks a lot about 'eternal life' but we now know that that does not mean a life beyond this world but a life without death. Many modern theologians say there is no other world than this one. . . . I simply believe . . . that the tombs of all those who have loved their fellow human beings are empty" (Vol. IV, p. 256).

In October 1977 the National Guard raided and destroyed the community at Solentiname because its members had attacked a Guard unit, and Ernesto Cardenal went into exile in Costa Rica. From there he announced that he had joined the FSLN, and he justified those who had taken up arms against the dictator, arguing that the armed resistance of his community was carried out for only one reason:

For their love for the kingdom of God, for the ardent desire that a just society be implanted, a real and concrete kingdom of God here on earth. . . . Some day there will be no more war in Nicaragua. . . . Instead there will be an abundance of schools, hospitals, and clinics for everyone, food adequate for everyone, art and entertainment. But most important there will be love among all. [Vol. IV, pp. 274–75]

Ernesto Cardenal is a poet, and his direct identification of Cuba and the Nicaraguan revolution with the kingdom of God on earth is not typical, but he was not the only clergyman who was enthusiastic about the Sandinistas and Marxism. His brother, Fernando, who participated in some of the dialogues, was a professor at the National University and became a member of the FSLN in 1974. A Franciscan priest, Father Uriel Molina, organized a Base Community in a poor parish of Managua in 1971 and returned from the Christians for Socialism meeting in Chile convinced of the importance of Marxist-Christian cooperation against the dictatorship. He read *A Theology of Liberation* and it was discussed by the Base Community. Tomas Borge, who had been his high school classmate, contacted him clandestinely and urged him to involve Christians in the struggle. Molina and Fernando Cardenal formed the Christian Revolutionary Movement (MCR), which, he said, applied Christianity to revolutionary action "using Marxism as a method, thus deepening our faith and political commitment."[5]

By 1977, when the *Tercerista* faction of the FSLN was dominant, the Sandinistas had adopted a strategy of alliances not only with Christians but with middle-class intellectuals and social democrats. In 1977 a group of prominent intellectuals including Father Fernando Castillo and a Maryknoll priest, Miguel d'Escoto, announced their support for the FSLN and gave it the appearance of a broad national coalition. Ernesto Cardenal was not included, in his view "because I had been regularly proclaiming myself as a Marxist and they were choosing a group of persons that would not awake, let us say, provoke, American aggression."[6]

By 1977 the opposition to Somoza had expanded to include nearly the whole of Nicaraguan society. The escalation of opposition can be dated from the 1972 earthquake which leveled the center of Managua, and the subsequent corruption and greed exhibited by Somoza in handling the relief funds that flowed in. A Committee for Aid and Development (CEPAD) brought the various Protestant sects together, and tensions rose between Somoza and the Catholic church, headed since 1970 by a progressive archbishop, Miguel Obando y Bravo. In 1974 the bishops wrote against the use of "repressive force" and in defense of the "right of dissent." By 1977 the bishops were speaking of a "state of terror" in Nicaragua, leading to denunciations by the supporters of Somoza of "priests in a red cassock" and of Archbishop Obando as "a supporter of Communist revolution with his inflammatory pastoral letters" (Berryman, pp. 73–74). The letter in question had actually criticized the Sandinistas by implication when it equated the government's actions with "those other movements which call themselves liberating but which cause passions to overflow and lead to personal revenge with the sole result that the new masters run public affairs with no gain for human freedoms" (quoted in Berryman, pp. 73–75). In that same year Gaspar Garcia Laviana, a Spanish missionary, joined the Sandinistas and announced that he had done so because *"Somocismo* is sin" and "I have decided to join this war as the humblest soldier of the Sandinista Front because it is a just war" (Berryman, p. 76). (Father Garcia was killed a year later. His name has been given to one of the publications of the Central American Historical Institute in Managua.)

In January 1978 the murder of Pedro Joaquín Chamorro mobilized the entire population and a general strike was organized by business groups. In July the Broad Opposition Front, which included opposition parties, unions, and business groups, organized a one-day strike. In August the Sandinistas staged a dramatic raid on the National Palace, holding two thousand people hostage. It was led by Edén Pastora (Comandante Zero), who thus became a hero of the Revolution. (In 1982 he joined the contras.) The archbishop acted as a mediator in securing Somoza's acceptance of the FSLN conditions for the release of the prisoners. In the fall of 1978 a mediation team of the Organization of American States (OAS) attempted unsuccessfully to arrange for free elections and the departure of Somoza. In June 1979, after heavy fighting in which many lives were lost and it began to be evident the National Guard was losing the war, the Sandinistas promised that the revolutionary government would be based on a mixed economy, political pluralism, and international nonalignment. The bishops' conference issued a pastoral letter that legitimated revolution "in the case of evident and prolonged tyranny that gravely threatens the fundamental rights of the person and the common good of the country" (a quotation from

Populorum Progressio of Pope Paul VI). In July, Somoza was forced to flee—partly as a result of American pressure—and the Sandinistas entered Managua in triumph on July 19, 1979, to the acclaim of the entire population, including many priests and nuns who had actively participated in the revolution.

After the Revolution

What followed was a process of increasing estrangement between the Sandinistas and the Catholic bishops, which has been subject to differing interpretations. For Berryman the process paralleled the heightening tensions between the Sandinistas and the country's business community (p. 243), while for Humberto Belli it was the result of increasing pressures by a Marxist-Leninist leadership determined to subordinate the Church as an independent center of criticism (ch. 13, "The Sandinistas vs. the Church"). On July 31, 1979, in their first letter after the Sandinista victory, the bishops called for respect for basic human rights and warned that *"concientización* does not mean imposing something alien." Fernando and Ernesto Cardenal criticized the letter, and the Central American Historical Institute (HCA) now became a major center promoting Christian support of the Sandinista government. In November, the bishops published a more positive letter that, while critical of abuses such as arbitrary executions and mistreatment of prisoners, spoke favorably of "the revolutionary process" and supported agrarian reform, the projected literacy campaign, and "a socialism that would be participatory, equalitarian, and democratic, that respects religious beliefs and the rights of parents to educate their children according to their convictions" (that is, in religious schools). The revolutionary process should be "original, creative, deeply national and in no way imitative," moving toward a society that is "authentically Nicaraguan, neither capitalist, nor dependent, nor totalitarian." The bishops spoke of Christ's message as one of liberation and justice, and viewed the present moment as a crucial opportunity to make concrete "the preferential option for the poor."[7]

This was perhaps the high point of support by the bishops for the Sandinistas. In the ensuing months, they became less enthusiastic about what they saw as attempts to indoctrinate the young with Marxism in the literacy campaign, and especially the use of the armed services (the *Sandinista* army, and the *Sandinista* police) to indoctrinate recruits with the FSLN ideology. (I can attest to listening to what sounded like a sermon on Sandinismo over the loudspeakers at the army base next to the major hotel in Managua on a Sunday morning in 1981.) In April 1980 the two non-Sandinista members of the junta, Alfonso Robelo and Violeta Chamorro (the widow of the murdered newspaper editor) resigned from the Council of State after the Sandinistas enlarged it to ensure absolute control through their affiliated organizations. The church became more polarized as the Antonio Valdivieso Center (CAV) and the Central American Historical Institute (IHCA) attempted to place Christian symbols at the service of the revolution. There were charges that the feasts of the Immaculate Conception (*La Purisima*) and Christmas were being politicized, and a book published by the Central American Historical Institute showed a guerrilla fighter with a gun with his hands upraised, superimposed on an image of Christ crucified. A pamphlet published by Father Alvaro Arguello's Central American Historical Institute criticized Christians who feared Communism (*Socialismo, Marxismo, Comunismo, Yo Le Tengo Miedo y Vos?*) and quoted "Padre Comandante" Gaspar Garcia Laviana that "the liberation of an oppressed people is an integral part of the total redemption of Christ" (p. 21). Father Juan Hernandez Pico S.J. wrote in an institute publication, "There is no other way for a Christian to show his faith in the kindom than by committing himself to a contingent project," while Father Arguello put it more bluntly: "Christians should realize very clearly that they do not have more than two alternatives left: either they are with the revolutionary process . . . or else they are unavoidably against such a process, regardless of how holy or humanitarian their intentions may be."[8]

The question of the relation of religion and the Sandinista revolution became increasingly intense. In response to the debate, the FSLN issued a communique on October 7, 1980, that attempted to answer those who accused the Sandinistas of being opposed to religion. They cited the "Christian patriots and revolutionaries" who had been "an integral part of the Popular Sandinista Revolution, not just now but for many years past," including the Catholic priest who had been killed in the guerrilla movement in 1978. They praised the "valiant participation of Archbishop Obando y Bravo and Bishop Salazar of Leon," and said that "Christians have been an integral part of our revolutionary history to a degree unprecedented in any other revolutionary movement in Latin America," asserting that "the right to profess a religious faith is an inalienable right of the people that the Revolutionary Government fully guarantees." They added that "our experience shows us that one can be a believer and at the same time a consistent revolutionary and that there is no insurmountable contradiction between the two. There are members of distinctive religious beliefs and no beliefs in the Sandinista Front." They denied that the FSLN was "trying to divide the Church or exploiting religious celebrations." (This was a reference to a confidential FSLN memo written in 1979 and published by *La Prensa* on how to make the Christian celebrations useful to the FSLN.) The letter concluded with an argument that priests and religious leaders had a right as citizens to continue to participate in the government. (Four priests, including the Cardenal brothers and Father d'Escoto, were cabinet members, and the question was being actively discussed of the applicability of the canon law provisions and the statements at Puebla against partisan political activity by priests.[9])

The bishops replied that there was ideological indoctrination and pressure against religious beliefs as well as "atheist proselytism by state institutions [which] seek to use the church as a tool. . . . They accept for strategic reasons the desirability of gaining the church's participation, but only as an instrument to consecrate and bless the movement towards a monolithic and absolutist system." On the participation of the four priests the bishops replied, "It is one thing to call a priest to exercise his ministry and a very different thing for him to insert himself into a system in order to justify it or give it religious legitimacy," and they quoted the Puebla statement on the need to put aside all partisan political ideologies that may condition their attitudes and judgments.[10]

It was just this possibility of transcending partisanship on the part of the church that the liberation theologians and revolutionary Christians had denied. As Gustavo Gutierrez had put it in the early 1970s,

> To opt for the poor is to opt for one social class over another.
> . . . Poor and oppressed people are members of a social class which is overtly or covertly exploited by another social class. The proletariat is simply the most belligerent and clear-cut segment of this exploited social class. . . . It comes down to taking a socialist and revolutionary stand, thereby shouldering the tasks of politics from a very different perspective.[11]

In late 1980, the head of the Private Enterprise Council, COSEP, was ambushed and killed by the state security agency, and in March 1981, an opposition rally led by Alfonso Robelo, a former member of the junta, was broken up by mobs, and the organizer's home was set on fire. Archbishop Obando, however, still maintained when he traveled abroad that there was pluralism in Nicaragua, since the Catholic schools were still functioning, the opposition newspaper *La Prensa* was publishing, and opposition trade unions and parties were carrying on despite occasional harassment by state security or Sandinista mobs.

However, the polarization of opinion was encouraged by the FSLN, which was using a "he who is not with me is against me" approach in order to broaden what before 1978 had been a small popular base, and to discredit its rivals for power. Elections, which had been promised at the time of the overthrow of Somoza, were postponed until 1985 (they were held in November 1984), and youth, women's, and trade union groups as well as the expanded armed forces were used to build up support for the FSLN. Among these groups were the revolutionary Christians of "the popular church"—who were given wide publicity by *Barricada* and *Diario Nuevo,* the two newspapers that were sympathetic to the government.

A more direct confrontation between the church and the government began in June 1981 when the bishops first asked the priests involved in government to return to their pastoral work and then permitted them to remain at their posts as a special exception provided that they voluntarily ceased to say Mass and hear confessions. Base Communities sympathetic to the revolutionary Christians launched rallies and protests against the bishops. In July the government suspended the televised Sunday Mass and sermon by the archbishop that had been telecast for many years. At the end of the year the first reports of U.S. support for anti-Sandinista forces in Honduras began to produce further divisions in Nicaragua. On the religious side, those divisions tended to be between, on one hand, the bishops and the native diocesan clergy, who were increasingly opposed to the government, and on the other, the order priests and nuns, many of them foreign-born or foreign-educated, who favored critical (or more often than not, uncritical) support of the Sandinistas as representing the current Nicaraguan embodiment of the preferential option for the poor.

In early 1982, the bishops issued a communiqué condemning the violation of human rights by the government in relocating the Miskito

Indians on the coast, citing forced marches, destruction of homes and property, and murder. (Americas Watch, the human rights group, reported in 1982 that 130 Miskitos had been tortured or forced to sign confessions at gunpoint, and in 1986 their report noted that the Nicaraguan government was paying compensation to 99 families of Miskitos who had been murdered or "disappeared" in 1981–1982.) A month later, a state of emergency was declared and the censorship of *La Prensa* was intensified. In July a papal letter criticizing the popular church in Nicaragua for opposing the bishops and for "the infiltration of strongly ideological connotations" (*Origins,* XII, 11, August 26, 1982) was not allowed to be published. In August, what appears to have been a government "frame-up" involving a meeting between a woman with many Sandinista connections and Father Bismarck Carballo, the spokesman for the archdiocese, led to televised and printed pictures of a naked priest being dragged from a house in front of a large crowd. A defector later reported that the whole scene had been orchestrated by the Interior Minister, Tomas Borge, and the Managua Chief of Police, Lenin Cerna.

The world learned of the conflicts within the Nicaraguan church when the pope visited Nicaragua in March 1983. On his arrival, he publicly scolded Ernesto Cardenal in front of the television cameras, urging him to regularize his relations with the hierarchy. There is continuing controversy about what took place at the open-air Mass that afternoon. The mothers of those who had died as a result of the attacks by the CIA-funded contras in the north demanded that the pope make a statement on the subject, and access to the loudspeakers was facilitated for them. The Mass ended with raised fists and the singing of the Sandinista hymn—which includes the line branding "the Yankees" as "the enemy of the human race." Following the pope's visit Father Juan Hernandez Pico S.J. published a book on it that included an open letter by the liberation theologians to the pope accusing him of having "frustrated the petition of the people for peace and for the honorable remembrance of their fallen ones."[12] The liberation theologians spoke of their identification with the church of the poor in Nicaragua, yet it was clear to most observers during the visit that the pope and the archbishop had much wider support among the poor than did the revolutionary Christians.

The split between the hierarchy and the regime became more pronounced in August 1983 when the bishops criticized the new draft law (*Servicio Patriotico Militar*) on the grounds that the Nicaraguan armed forces were now organized around the ideology of a specific party that was opposed to the religious convictions of many of those who were being drafted. The military draft was to go into effect at the end of September and the Sandinistas denounced what they called "the Obando document" as treasonous. They continued to press the archbishop and the bishops' conference for a specific denunciation of U.S. aid to the contras—a highly controversial issue in the U.S. Congress, where the Democratic-controlled House of Representatives was increasingly critical of the "covert" aid to the contras. In April 1984 the Pastoral Letter on Reconciliation of the Nicaraguan bishops' conference criticized "foreign powers" that take "advantage of our situation to promote economic and ideological exploitation," and stated that "any form of assistance regardless of the source which causes the destruction, suffering and death of our families, or which sows hatred and discord among the Nicaraguan people is reprehensible"—which could be interpreted as opposing both U.S. and Soviet-Cuban aid and propaganda. The letter also attacked those who "claim at times to accept Christ and his doctrine but reject the church, succumbing to the temptation to create 'churches' outside the foundation of the Apostles and their successors, the legitimate bishops." It accused "a part, although a small part, of our church" of abandoning the unity of the church and "submitting themselves to the guidance of a materialist philosophy." The bishops called for a dialogue among all Nicaraguans "whether in or outside of the country without discrimination of ideology, class, or party position," including those "Nicaraguans who have taken arms against the government."[13]

The Sandinistas continued to oppose any dialogue with "the mercenaries," whose number had now swelled beyond ten thousand. They rejected any comparison to the dialogue in El Salvador between the Duarte government and the FMLN guerrillas (whose numbers—about six thousand—were considerably less in a country with twice the population) because, they claimed, the FMLN spoke for "the people," while the contras were Somocistas paid by the CIA.

In April 1985 Archbishop Obando was made a cardinal, and after receiving his red hat he returned via Miami, where he said Mass for the Nicaraguan exiles including the contra leaders Adolfo Calero and Eden Pastora. In July, Foreign Minister Miguel d'Escoto began a month-long fast for peace in which many Base Communities participated, describing it as an "evangelical insurrection." In October the government closed the new church publication *Iglesia* and seized its printing press. This was followed by the silencing of the church radio on the specious grounds that it had broken the law by not broadcasting the whole of a speech by President Ortega. In February 1986 Father d'Escoto made a two-week Way of the Cross for peace with fourteen stations between the Honduran border and Managua. In April 1986 the church bulletin was confiscated, and Obando's Sunday sermon as well as the bishops' pastoral letter were censored from *La Prensa*. When Cardinal Obando was asked why he did not take a public stand against U.S. aid to the contras he stated that the Sandinista's "real objective is not to seek moral guidance but rather to use our statements to manipulate opinion," and compared the question to the Pharisees' question to Jesus about paying taxes to the Roman emperor. He stated that the contras could use the same arguments the Sandinistas had used in seeking aid from other countries— namely, to oppose a nondemocratic government—and quoted the bishops' condemnation of material and ideological interference by both sides (*Washington Post,* May 12, 1986). In July the Sandinistas expelled five Catholic priests and nuns, including Father Carballo, and refused to allow Bishop Pablo Antonio Vega to return to Nicaragua.

The issue of priests in government continued without resolution. Fernando Cardenal defended his continued participation in the cabinet by arguing that he had a higher duty to his fellow citizens and to God than to the church authorities. He asserted that the Vatican's policy against priests' participation in government coincided with that of President Reagan "in trying to weaken the revolution." When he refused to resign, his Jesuit superiors in Rome expelled him for disobedience although the local Jesuit community supported him and he continued to live at the Jesuit residence. Father Miguel d'Escoto, on the other hand, had no action taken against him by the Maryknoll order, but in January he and Ernesto Cardenal (who is a diocesan priest) were suspended from their priestly functions by their bishops. Edgardo Parrales, the fourth priest in the government, requested laicization.

After the pope's visit, Blaise Bonpane, a former Maryknoll missionary who had been expelled from Guatemala in 1967 because of his contacts with the guerrillas, wrote an open letter to the pope.

> To the scandal of the faithful, you publicly chastised a prominent hero of the Sandinista revolution, Father Ernesto Cardenal. History will not

forget your attack on one of Latin America's best known literary figures, on the Minister of Culture of Nicaragua, on a saintly priest, a
poet and a model for the faithful. . . . You did not chastise any of
the officials of the United States who plan and carry out murder every
day. . . . Your Holiness, I believe your vision has been clouded by
the poison of atheistic capitalism. The poor of the earth are simply not
going to tolerate this institutionalized violence any longer. . . . Your
Holiness, you met the future in Nicaragua and you failed to recognize it.[14]

In the midst of the controversies, the Central American Historical
Institute published *A History of the Church of the Poor in Nicaragua*
(December 8, 1983), which was popularly written and illustrated,
and deeply committed in the current struggle. It began with the Spanish conquest, giving special attention to Antonio Valdivieso, the six-
teenth-century bishop of Managua who denounced the enslavement
of the Indians to the king and was murdered for doing so:[15] "With
the blood of his martyrdom, was born the church of the poor in Nicaragua" (p. 15). In the discussion of the nineteenth century, special
attention is given to the "gringo pirate" William Walker, who established a slave republic in Nicaragua and proclaimed himself president
in 1855. The book asserts that some bishops and priests supported
Walker, and one even gave him silver from the shrine of Our Lady of
Granada so that it could be melted down and made into bullets.
"From that time on the church in Nicaragua to be faithful to the gospels had to carry out the struggle against American domination"
(p. 37). The book concludes with quotes from the 1979 bishops'
statement favorable to the revolution and from the 1980 Sandinista
declaration on religion. It argues that there are two models of the
church, one that participates in the literacy campaign, the agrarian
reform, and the defense of the country against American imperialism,
and the other that distrusts the Christian Base Communities, opposes military service, and supports the counterrevolution. "We need
a new theology, a new liturgy, and new pastoral action. . . . The
God of the poor present in history, lives and acts in this crisis" (pp.
61–63).

The Jesuit and Maryknoll orders in Nicaragua continue to support the Sandinista government. The position of the Jesuits has been
described by César Jerez, the former head of the Central American
province and the rector of the Jesuit-run Universidad Centroamericana in Managua (*The Church and the Nicaraguan Revolution,* Lon-

don: Catholic Institute for International Relations, 1985). They believe that a Christian presence in the revolution is possible.

> It is worth the risks involved in order to evangelize the new Nicaragua.
> They do not overlook the Marxist elements involved in building the
> new Nicaragua. Such elements, however, do not mean that the San-
> dinistas are pursuing a rigid Marxist strategy to establish a socialist
> regime. They do not see the Sandinistas as systematically hostile to the
> religion or to the church. They are willing to risk being a critical pres-
> ence inside the revolution.

Father Jerez notes that the members of this group had called themselves "the church of the people" but had stopped using the name
because of its ambiguity and the opposition of right-wing groups.
They believe that the church should be understood primarily as "the
people of God, whose first citizens are the poor" but they do not reject the hierarchy, as an embodiment of the "charism" of pastors and
guides.

> The structures of the church include not only discipline and obedience,
> but above all a listening to the Word and an obedience to the Spirit
> which is reflected in the adult charismatic and prophetic ecclesial com-
> munity. The few cases of priests who temporarily or permanently have
> undertaken delicate tasks in politics proper . . . would be treated as
> exceptions, borderline cases. . . . [There have been instances] of sub-
> mission to political plans and directives and dubious identifications
> between revolutionary processes and the kingdom of God [but this
> phenomenon, which is] infrequent and certainly not deliberately or
> theologically sustained should not be used to attack a larger sector in
> the church made up of those who stand fast by the church of the
> poor. [pp. 13–15]

By 1986, the official church hierarchy was clearly aligned against
the Sandinistas. The Easter Pastoral Letter of the Bishops' Conference accused the "popular church" of "manipulating the fundamental
truths of our faith" by "injecting into it Marxist concepts such as the
class struggle." The Vatican transferred the Papal Nuncio, who had
been acting as a mediator between Cardinal Obando and the government, reportedly at the request of Obando, and the Sandinistas began
to call seminary students for the draft.

In 1987, however, the relations between the government and the
church began to improve. The conversations between representatives
of both groups, which had been suspended in November 1986, were

taken up again. In August, when the Central American presidents signed the Arias Peace Plan, with a provision for a Reconciliation Commission in each country that was to include a representative of the church, Cardinal Obando was chosen by his fellow churchmen, and the government surprised many observers by naming him as chairman. Priests who had been expelled were allowed to return, and Radio Catolica was able to begin broadcasting although it was forbidden to broadcast news. When indirect negotiations began between the Sandinistas and the contras, Cardinal Obando acted as the intermediary, ending this role when face-to-face negotiations began in early 1988. The church throughout Central America has supported the peace process, and there are some indications that the deep divisions of the earlier period are beginning to be overcome, although the rejection of Christian-inspired reformism, especially as represented by the Christian Democratic parties of the area, remains an obstacle to closer cooperation between the reformers and radical Christians.[16] In mid-1988, relations between the Sandinistas and the church soured again, as opposition members were arrested, and Radio Catolica was closed down once again. The bishops also expressed their "disagreement with a form of education that is materialistic and atheistic and that imposes the ideology of a minority on the children and youth of Nicaragua" (Pastoral Letter, June 29, 1988).

It is possible to exaggerate the direct political influence of liberation theology in Latin America. However, in small countries such as those in Central America, which are unstable and uncertain of their future, the conversion of a relatively small group of students, intellectuals, and labor and peasant leaders can have a significant influence on the future. The ideas of the liberation theologians had and have a strong impact on the professors at the Jesuit universities in Managua and San Salvador; they recruited many churchmen and churchwomen to the revolutionary struggle against Somoza in Nicaragua and against a repressive military in El Salvador, and they legitimated cooperation with (some would say, cooptation by) Marxist movements in both countries. The question for the future is whether they will help or hinder the development of peaceful, democratic, and just societies in Central America.

8

American Responses
to Liberation Theology

So FAR, our attention has been concentrated on Latin America, with some attention to the Vatican as well. With the exception of a reference to the 1975 meeting in Detroit of liberation theologians from Latin America with a number of sympathetic American theologians, we have not yet reviewed the ways in which American theologians and analysts responded to the new movement in Latin America. That response was considerably influenced by the personal political outlook of those who responded, but it was also affected by theological outlooks that were sometimes different from political ideology. Thus, it is possible for a theological conservative to hold political views that would classify him or her as being on the left. (Pope John Paul II would be an example of this on such issues as nuclear disarmament and the disparities in the world economy.) On the whole, however, the two world views tend to be in harmony. Liberation theologians take a radical view both of theology and of politics, and their conservative opponents tend to hold conservative views on theology as well.

The proceedings of the Detroit conference illustrate this well. (See Sergio Torres and John Eagleson, eds., *Theology in the Americas,* Maryknoll, NY: Orbis Books, 1976.) They are sprinkled with references to the "American empire," the evils of the multinational corporation, and the "bankruptcy" of liberalism, and, while critical of Marxism, they call for a new form of socialism to replace exploitative capitalism. Those invited to the conference tended to be aligned with the left politically (Phillip Berryman, Rosemary Ruether, Gregory Baum, Robert McAfee Brown) and were generally uncritical of liberation theology,[1] except for drawing the attention of the Latin Americans to the need for discussion of racism and sexism.

American Catholic Critics

The one exception in the Torres-Eagleson volume would be Avery Dulles S.J., who in a series of insightful questions in a written commentary focused on important issues that the other participants had ignored, that is,

> Can the church be at home with a theology of conflict and class struggle rather than a theology of reconciliation? . . . Are sin and grace inevitably bound up with social structures? . . . Can a theology that is fully committed to revolutionary praxis be genuinely self-critical? etc. [p. 95]

Monika Hellwig of Georgetown University attempted to respond to the first question posed by Father Dulles by arguing (not altogether convincingly) that the liberation theologians tended to be sympathetic to nonviolent forms of resistance of the kind advocated and practiced by Gandhi, Martin Luther King, and César Chavez. However she admitted that she had difficulty "coming to grips with the substance of liberation theology, because all the literature with which I am acquainted is a critique of the available systematic theology, and none of it really amounts to a new systematic theology" (p. 101).

Another American Catholic (Anglo-Catholic at the time, later a convert to Roman Catholicism) critic in the 1970s was Dale Vree, who accused

> dialogical Christians [of engaging] in a monologue whereby Marxism assimilated Christianity into the dominant chorus of the times . . . a purely one-way process; there is no question of contemporary thought adapting itself to the Gospel. The Gospel must come into line entirely with contemporary thought. [*On Synthesizing Marxism and Christianity,* New York: John Wiley, 1976, p. 22]

Vree accused the liberationists of the heresy of Pelagianism—denying the doctrine of original sin and believing that man could become godlike. For enthusiasts of liberation theology in America such as the

Protestant theologian Harvey Cox, salvation "is not an eternal life beyond death but the full liberation of mankind by which he means a society where people no longer crave power and property, and no longer seek to manipulate people" (p. 77). To those who attempt to downplay Marx's atheism, Vree quotes Marx's endorsement of Prometheus' defiant words, "I shall never exchange my fetters for slavish servility. 'Tis better to be chained to the rock than bound to the service of Zeus" (p. 125).

A more balanced assessment by a North American Catholic appears in the chapter on liberation theology in Arthur McGovern S.J., *Marxism, An American-Christian Perspective* (Maryknoll, NY: Orbis Press, 1980).[2] McGovern tends to downplay the Marxist elements in the liberation theologians' analyses, although he admits that the class struggle has a very important place and that socialism is a "preferential option." He adds that "how qualified or unqualified this option should be, remains an issue" but he does not give specific evidence on the subject. (As we will see in the concluding chapter, this continues to be an important problem for liberation theology since all liberation theologians seem to believe in some form of socialism.) Gutierrez's *A Theology of Liberation* speaks of a theoretical and practical diversity in approaches to socialism (p. 90) and calls for "cautious language and careful distinctions," but the actual writing by liberation theologians on the subject of socialism is notoriously weak on details—perhaps because of their own theory that the reality of *praxis* will determine the nature of the society of the future.

McGovern is critical of liberation theologians such as Juan Luis Segundo, who put the question in either/or terms, particularly when Segundo defines socialism as handing over "the means of production to higher institutions whose main concern is the common good." McGovern notes that this would give control and profits to a small government elite, while the very notion of praxis, he says, should rule out such an either/or decision made in advance. McGovern focuses on an issue that is central to an evaluation of liberation theology. Is it a method, a way of doing theology and politics without a predefined goal other than, in most general terms, the absence of oppression, or is it something more specific, involving the abolition of capitalism, the ending of economic relations of dependency, and the triumph of socialism? And this distinction in turn is related to the tension between what we have identified as two central thrusts of liberation theology—the populist and unstructured grass-roots approach typified in the Basic Christian Communities, and the anticapitalist structuralism that reduces all of Latin America's problems to dependency, imperialism, and exploitation.

The American responses thus tended to follow the familiar conservative, liberal, and radical division. Those who attended the Detroit Conference supported the liberationist analysis and urged its extension to the United States and to the problems of racism and sexism. Vree and other religious conservatives rejected liberationism as a form of a "dialogical" Christianity that amounted to acceptance of the Marxist message, while liberals such as McGovern attempted to give the liberation theologians a sympathetic hearing but criticized the vagueness or inadequacy of its political prescriptions.

Evangelical Critics

One example of an evangelical Protestant critique of liberation theology was written even before that theology received its name from Gutierrez's book. In 1970, C. Peter Wagner, an evangelical missionary in Bolivia, published *Latin American Theology, Radical or Evangelical?* (Grand Rapids, MI: Wm. B. Eerdmans, 1970), criticizing major themes in the thinking of several Protestant representatives of what was to become liberation theology. Examining the writings of Richard Shaull, José Miguez Bonino, and Rubem Alves, Wagner concludes that "it would be safe to say that a Marxist-oriented ideology has at least as much influence on some of them as the Bible" (p. 59). He accuses them of preaching a kind of "syncretism" that is far removed from the church's primary mission—to reconcile men to God through Christ. Christians have a duty of social service to mankind as an expression of Christian love, but this service may involve capitalism or it may involve socialism. It may imply gradual evolution or violent revolution. The radical left in Latin America is correct in criticizing evangelical Protestants for their lack of social involvement, but such involvement should always remain secondary to the specifically religious goals of the church. Wagner thus concludes with a conception of the relation of the church to society, that emphasizes a distinction between the church and the world that the liberation theologians specifically reject.

Further critical works were published by evangelicals after the major works of liberation theology were published. In 1979 Schubert

Ogden published *Faith and Freedom: Towards a Theology of Liberation* (Nashville: Abingdon), which turned upon the liberationists their critique of the ideological quality of neoorthodox and liberal theology, by maintaining that they were making

> one more proposal for the bondage of theology . . . the rationalization of certain positions instead of critical reflection on their meaning and truth. . . . If theology otherwise is open to the charge of ideology, this charge is hardly rendered groundless simply because the positions theology rationalizes are those of the oppressed instead of the oppressors. . . . The one-sided method it recommends could no more be accepted by an adequate Christian theology than the one-sided method it opposes. [pp. 120–21]

Ogden proposes an alternative liberation theology that is not "homocentric" but is based on the unity of man and nature in dependence on God, and encourages critical reflection on all experience (including that of oppression) in the light of "human existence as such in its profound exigency for the truth that alone can make us free" (p. 123).

J. Andrew Kirk, another evangelical, also criticizes the implicit ethical assumptions involved in the liberation theologians' use of Marxism (*Liberation Theology, An Evangelical View from the Third World*, Atlanta: John Knox Press, 1979, pp. 164ff.). Challenging the liberation theologians' claim that they are using Marxism only as a "tool of analysis," Kirk argues that while the Marxist critique makes us aware of the ideological element in empirical expressions of the Christian faith, the liberation theologians use it for something more—as a revolutionary theory about how and why to change reality, and a theory of oppression that is derived from "an inadequate analysis of evil" that is "but one more example of the modern tendency towards philosophical monism." The Bible places the center of man's alienation elsewhere—"in his desire to be autonomous with regard to his Creator"—and it defines man's freedom "only in terms of the recognition that he is a creature absolutely held to account by God for the way he pursues his relationships" and that his Son is "the only one sent by God to take away the sin of the world" (p. 192).

A more analytic and radical rejection of liberation theology from the evangelical point of view is Gerard Berghoef and Lester Dekoster, *Liberation Theology, The Church's Future Shock* (Grand Rapids, MI: Christian's Library Press, 1984). The two authors single out four central elements of Marxism—the class struggle, the rejection of private ownership of the means of production, the promotion of revolution, and the belief in redemption through the development of "the new man"—and locate all four in the writings of the liberation theologians. Indeed, they are identified as "the four pillars of liberation theology," which is also accused of denying the fall, the atonement, the last judgment, and Christian love. The liberation theologians "masquerade a concern for the poor and the oppressed which, after the debris of rebellion is cleared away, multiplies murder, intensifies slavery, and mounts a more systematic exploitation of the many by the few than mankind has known in centuries" (p. 180).

The Niebuhrian Critique

The basic criticism the evangelicals make is that the concept of liberation at the root of the new movement is not biblical but depends heavily on a particular variety of Marxist-influenced sociology, anthropology, and hermeneutics. In particular, they all note the lack of awareness of the effects of original sin on the way man conducts himself both individually and socially. That critique is carried further, with more depth and perceptiveness, by a Protestant and a Catholic both deeply influenced by the thinking of a Protestant theologian who analyzed the effects of sin on society, politics, and international relations in ways that were profoundly influential in Western thought, but almost unknown in Latin America: Reinhold Niebuhr. (Only *Moral Man and Immoral Society* and *The Irony of American History* have been translated into Spanish, the former in Buenos Aires and the latter in Madrid.)

We have already referred to the criticism of liberation theology from a Niebuhrian point of view published by Thomas Sanders in *Christianity and Crisis* in 1973, shortly after Gustavo Gutierrez's book was first published in English. It accused the liberation theologians of "moralism" that amounted to a "soft utopianism" not unlike that of the proponents of the Social Gospel in early twentieth-century American Protestantism. Sanders, who had spent many years in Latin America as a representative of the American Universities Field Staff, described the movement as a reaction to the conservatism and legalism of traditional Latin American Catholicism, and advised the liberation theologians to become more aware of the realities of power as a factor in national and international relations (*Christianity and Crisis*, September 1973, pp. 167–73).

The most thoroughgoing and persuasive attempt to relate Niebuhr to liberation theology and, besides the chapter in McGovern's book, the only work critical of liberation theology among the 300-plus books published by Orbis Books on the topic is Dennis McCann's *Christian Realism and Liberation Theology* (Maryknoll, NY: Orbis Books, 1981). McCann first gives an account of Niebuhr's own intellectual development, including his early encounters with the social gospel, with socialism, and with Marxism, and then attempts to relate Niebuhr's theory of Christian realism to the writings of the liberation theologians. In terms of the specific analysis of Latin America's problems, McCann concludes that while both theologies emerged from a pastoral ministry, Niebuhr believed in reform rather than revolution—a position that the liberation theologians specifically rejected. He concludes,

> The major issue separating them boils down to this: Is American neo-colonialism really the primary cause of the misery among the oppressed peoples of Latin America, or is it not? If it is, then the paradigm of dependence/liberation is probably the most suitable framework for analyzing the problems of the area. If it is not, then some other paradigm—not necessarily the one designated by "developmentalism"—will have to be adopted. [p. 153]

McCann, however, is not as interested in the factual question as in a theoretical analysis of the approach taken by the liberation theologians. He is fascinated by the process of *concientização* developed by Paulo Freire, especially its approach to "demythologization" through the use of the dialectical method. For McCann the dialectical vision "is incompatible with the religious vision of Christianity in general, and Catholicism in particular" (p. 166). It "sees history as a struggle for freedom without defining the content of that freedom, save as overcoming all possible limit-situations" (p. 170). While this provides a rationale for the work of Ecclesial Base Communities, it also challenges any attempt at evangelization—that is, to spread the Christian message—because *there is no message*. "Theology itself will be liberated, its myths decoded, leaving little more than a rhetorical invitation to share in the dialectical vision and its praxis" (p. 174).

For McCann therefore the proposal of "Gutierrez for a conscientizing [*sic*] evangelism is a contradiction in terms. Liberation is either a method or a content. If it is a method, it has no content. If it is a content, it cannot apply the method to that content—whether it is the Gospel or Marxism."

McCann sums up the differences between Niebuhr's approach and that described in Juan Luis Segundo's *The Liberation of Theology*:

> Although both thinkers respond to the problem of modern theology by distinguishing faith from ideology in the historical consciousness of Christians, the one insists that Christian faith has substantive meaning, the other implies that it is purely formal. Assuming that meaning, Niebuhr's mythical method seems to interpret it, even as Segundo's total conscientization of liberation theology decodes it. [p. 230]

McCann's book has been attacked by an American liberation theologian Matthew Lamb (*Solidarity with Victims: Toward a Theology of Social Transformation*, New York: Crossroad, 1982). Lamb accuses McCann of imputing an exaggerated version of Freire's effort to remove "limit-situations" to liberation theologians such as Gutierrez and Segundo who make little or no use of Freire's work. He also notes that McCann tends to imply that Gutierrez equates salvation and liberation, and a utopian vision and the Kingdom of God, when in fact he and the other liberation theologians distinguish between them quite clearly. The broader issue that McCann raises, however, is still a problem for liberation theology. How far should a critical method be taken? Does the dialectical critique also apply to the content of liberation theologians' own teaching? Does it extend to the basic biblical message as well—as seems to be the case in the writings of Segundo? While McCann may have overstated the negative aspects of the dialectical approach, the question remains—how far should it be taken? The issue of the relationship of method and content that we raised at the beginning of this book is also the issue that McCann discusses, and the "paradoxical" vision of Niebuhr does provide an alternative Christian vision to the "epiphanic" view of the liberation theologians. The difference between the two approaches is as much psychological as it is logical. The Niebuhrians are just as committed to social reform as the liberationists, but they subject themselves and those allied with them to continual criticism, constantly aware of the human capacity for self-deception and self-interest, while the liberationists, at least as indicated in their writings, tend to be very certain of the absolute evil of those they oppose and the absolute virtue of those to whom they are committed (that is, the poor and the powerless). In international relations as well, there tends to be a selective vision as to the source of evil in the world— it is capitalism and imperialism, rather than sin. Social sin is identi- fied with the existing system, and the capacity for sin of alternative systems, especially socialist systems, is not discussed, nor are institu- tional safeguards against abuse suggested.

It should be noted, however, that the criticisms of McCann, like other critiques written in the late 1970s, were aimed at the body of liberationist literature that had emerged in the early part of the decade, which was characterized by a naive faith in revolution that has now been tempered by experience. The very distinction that McCann makes is one that can be used in favor of liberation theol- ogy. If one distinguishes between the method and its original content, one can argue that the same method (praxis, learning from the ex- perience of the oppressed, the dialectic between Scripture and experi- ence) can produce a different content in altered circumstances.

The Neo-Conservative Critique—Schall, Quade, and Novak

Before the 1980s most of the discussion of liberation theology had been confined to theological or religious circles. However, the con- frontation at the Puebla Meeting of CELAM in January–February 1979 and even more, the overthrow of the Somoza dictatorship by a mass uprising headed by Marxist-Leninists but also including several priests among its leadership focused attention on the revolutionary possibilities of Christian radicalism in Latin America. When this was followed by the overthrow of the Shah of Iran by a religiously moti- vated radical Moslem leader, and a coup followed by civil war in El Salvador, as well as rebel activity in Guatemala, in both cases involv- ing alliances of Christians and Marxists, it became apparent that the Catholic left was a force to be reckoned with in Latin America. At the same time in the United States there was a reaction to the overexten- sion of the welfare state and to what appeared to be a weakening of U.S. influence in the contemporary world, which ultimately brought Ronald Reagan to the White House. Part of that movement involved the conversion of some significant intellectuals to conservatism and the opening of new avenues of publicity to conservative writers. One of the targets of those writers was liberation theology.

The first attack by the neoconservatives (whom a wag once defined as "a liberal who has been mugged in the subway") took place in *Commentary* magazine in June 1979, with the publication of "Liberation Theology and the Pope" by Michael Novak. Novak was a former seminarian who later studied philosophy at Harvard, attended the Second Vatican Council (which he wrote about with enthusiasm in *The Open Church*), and endorsed the efforts of student revolutionaries on American campuses in the 1960s. Indeed, he gave the radicalism of the young a theological backing in his 1969 book *A Theology for Radical Politics* (New York: Herder and Herder, 1969) for their opposition to "an ugly and brutal intervention in a nationalist civil war in Vietnam [and their awareness of] their own complicity in evil, evil on a mass scale never known in history. Every dollar they spend—even on a fountain pen—might somewhere under a different sense of priorities, be saving the life of a child" (p. 23). Novak's discussion of the dilemmas of the use of violence resembles the writings of the liberation theologians in Latin America during the same period. Novak recognized that some of the student revolutionaries had committed themselves to armed violence because

> every social arrangement involves them in violence and even in murder. [p. 75]
> [As long as] the tyrannical and indifferent majority controls the destiny of America, it appears, the nation will remain militarist, racist, and counterrevolutionary [and] the wretched of the earth will suffer more. [p. 79]
> However [despite] the moral sickness of the democratic majority . . . the moment has clearly not arrived for armed revolution . . . if we proceed with coolness and skill, the revolution will not be a step backward; if we are blessed, it may be a long step ahead. [p. 80]

Ten years later, Novak had abandoned the revolutionary fervor of the New Left. After writing books celebrating the "unmeltable ethnics" and the joys of baseball, he was invited to join the American Enterprise Institute, a moderate pro-business think-tank in Washington, as scholar in residence with a special interest in the relation of economics and theology. An early concern was the strong anticapitalist bias of the Latin American theologians. In "Liberation Theology and the Pope," Novak quoted John Paul II's criticisms at Puebla of "rereadings" of the Gospel that make Christ a revolutionary and reduce the Christian message to social and political action. Citing anticapitalist statements by Juan Luis Segundo, Gustavo Gutierrez, and Miguel d'Escoto (the last was identified as "director of communications at Maryknoll"—the article was published just before d'Escoto became foreign minister of the new Sandinista-dominated government of Nicaragua), Novak argued that when the liberation theologians endorse the class struggle they are thinking of the quasi-feudal opposition of landholder and peasant, rather than Marx's struggle between the proletariat and bourgeoisie. Nevertheless the Latin American bishops had legitimated the liberationist rhetoric by their "bald use of Marxist categories at the 1968 Medellín conference," and even if the liberationists are "populist Marxists" their commitment to Marxist "praxis" is as uncritical of the realities of world Marxism as it is critical of capitalism. Striking a theme that he would reiterate often in subsequent publications, he advised the liberation theologians to look to the way in which other cultures—for example, those on the rim of Asia—had overcome poverty not through Marxism but through capitalism. He praised the pope for criticizing the "unthinking fantasies of theologians bent on the creation of totalitarian processes whose consequences they do not allow themselves to foresee and whose dynamics they cannot control."

The Novak attack was followed by two other publications by American conservatives. Despite the reputation of the Jesuits in parts of Latin America, especially in Central America, for endorsing radicalism, James V. Schall S.J., a Jesuit who teaches at Georgetown and the University of San Francisco, launched a frontal attack upon liberation theology in a collection of critical essays, *Liberation Theology* (San Francisco: Ignatius Press, 1982). In a 126-page introduction Schall asserted (rather than argued, since his statements were not part of a systematic argument) that liberation theology's "eventual growth and success would institutionalize in Latin America a life of low-level socialist poverty enforced by a rigid party-military discipline in control of economic enterprise and the movement of peoples" (p. 67). No effort was made to support this claim either by logic or by reference to the writings of liberation theologians, nor to make a case for the assertion that "liberation theology is itself a major cause of underdevelopment because it deflects energy and intelligence from the real causes and the best means to aid the poor, not merely in their poverty but in their total persons" (p. 103). Unaware of the ideological character of his own thinking, Schall endorsed the "non-Marxist, free, productive, and innovative development that comes from the pragmatic rejection of the ideologies of our time" (p. 103).

Another collection of critical essays published in the same year, Quentin L. Quade, ed., *The Pope and Revolution: John Paul II Confronts Liberation Theology* (Washington, DC: Ethics and Public Policy Center, 1982), at least included an essay by Gustavo Gutierrez before printing attacks on him by Dale Vree, Novak, and Schall, as well as a number of the pope's addresses on related subjects. Quade's introduction spoke of "a drift away from the Catholic mainstream" that began with the publication of Paul VI's encyclical *Populorum Progressio* in 1967 and was continued with the Bishops' Synod of 1971. The synod's references to "integral salvation or the complete liberation of man and of peoples" could be used by liberation theologians to justify their positions, despite the fact that "liberation theology and its cousins are not religion but politics." Quade concluded that after the recent papal statements, "whatever authority the Catholic liberationist may claim for his theology, it cannot be the authority of the Church of the Pope" (p. 11).

Both the Schall and Quade collections contained the Novak *Commentary* article, and he continued to develop the argument he made at that time. In "Why Latin America Is Poor" (*Atlantic Monthly*, March 1982), Novak argued that the Latin Americans were wrong to blame other nations for their underdevelopment, quoting the Peruvian bishops' statement of 1969, "We are victims of systems that exploit our natural resources, control our political decisions, and impose on us the cultural domination of their values and consumer civilization." It was not dependency that accounted for Latin American underdevelopment, as Gutierrez and others claimed, but a lack of entrepreneurial spirit resulting from the Hispanic value system that is "an ethos better suited to aristocrats, monks, and peasants who lack respect for commerce and industrial life and the moral views on which these depend" (p. 71). It is not private property that has produced underdevelopment, as Gutierrez claims, but "the concentration of economic and political power in the hands of a few" (p. 73). Latin America is developing rapidly but that development is not being distributed because of an unequal social system.

Such an argument would seem to imply some kind of public action to break up large estates and to redistribute property, but this is not what Novak has in mind. The system he recommends is outlined in an important book published in the same year that devotes several chapters to the problems of Latin America—*The Spirit of Democratic Capitalism* (New York: Simon and Schuster, 1982). There he argues for the mutually reinforcing character of a market economy, political democracy, and religious and cultural pluralism. A socialist system, he argues, tends to economic inefficiency and stagnation and cultural uniformity, all of which undermine political democracy, while a free market and the encouragement of cultural and religious diversity enrich it. Elimination of state-granted monopolies, extension of credit, and removal of legal barriers to entrepreneurial activity will aid the poor far more effectively than state-imposed socialism.

The problem suggested by this typology but not discussed by Novak is the nature and extent of the area to be regulated by political democracy. Specifically, in Latin America, do political democracy and economic freedom depend on a redistribution of assets through tax programs and agrarian reform? Or are the effects of such programs so negative for economic growth that they become counter-productive?

In any case, in Novak's view the problems of economic growth, innovation, and investment are ignored by the Catholic left in Latin America, and the blame is placed principally upon the region's dependence on the United States although, in fact, its economic relations with that country have benefited Latin America by promoting economic growth, and the naive socialism proposed by the liberation theologians would hurt it (pp. 70–73).

Novak's most influential writing on the subject was an article in the *New York Times Magazine* entitled "The Case Against Liberation Theology" (October 21, 1984). The article repeated his arguments about the inadequacies of dependency theory, on which the liberation theologians placed such heavy reliance. While Novak admitted that "most" liberation theologians "do not reduce Christianity to the class struggle or to the commitment to socialism" (do *any* do so?), he argued that "the Marxist vulgate of so much Latin American intellectual life obliges them to think in terms of Marxist analysis" (p. 88). He criticized the liberation theologians for their naive utopianism about human nature and the state, for their ignorance of the importance of wealth creation ("My poverty is *ipso facto* someone else's fault, and its cure is the expropriation of the expropriators"), and for their "uncommon trust in political elites to whom they intend to confide all economic [and other] decisions," despite the dismal record of socialist experiments since 1945 and "abundant evidence that the world's freest communities with the strongest (albeit flawed) institutions in human history have relatively free economies" (p. 94).

He concludes that because of its lack of concern with the political and economic institutions to be established after the revolution, "liberation theology promises a mirror-image of the Latin American authoritarian societies of the past, but this time of the left rather than of the right." He suggests that liberation theologians look to the "liberal, pluralistic, communitarian, public-spirited, dynamic, and inventive" liberal society for a model of genuine liberation, because "there are more liberation theologies in this world, committed to practice trial and error, and to self-reform, than the liberation theologians of South America have yet to dream of" (p. 95).

Almost totally absent in *The New York Times* article is mention of what I have called the "populist" side of liberationist thinking—its emphasis on the importance of grass-roots organization and learning from the experience of the poor and oppressed. That aspect receives attention in the chapter on liberation theology in Novak's *Freedom with Justice: Catholic Social Thought and Liberal Institutions* (New York: Harper and Row, 1984, ch. 10). Much of the chapter repeats the criticism of dependency theory and of Latin America's disdain for "savings, investment, entrepreneurship, invention, and the virtues of commercial industrial life" that Novak believes is reflected in the thinking of the liberation theologians (p. 194). New, however, is his critique of the liberation theologians' claim to be responding to the "cry of the poor." While granting that it is important for theologians to listen to the poor, since theologians are likely by their class background not to be in touch with the poor, and since the poor are more likely to have genuine grievances, Novak questions the liberation theologians' claim to speak for them. "Whether liberation theologians actually do speak for a majority of the poor . . . is far from certain; and even if they did, majoritarian opinion is by no means a warrant for truth." If the poor overwhelmingly supported Hitler in Germany, or the Moslem poor overwhelmingly support the annihilation of Israel, this does not make them correct. Opinion surveys in Latin America suggest that the liberation theologians have no more right to speak for the moral majority than do those in the United States who claim a similar warrant (pp. 184–85).

Will It Liberate? Questions about Liberation Theology (New York: Paulist Press, 1986) is the most comprehensive statement of the Novak criticism of liberation theology. It combines and integrates his early writings into a sustained line of questioning not so much about the religious aspects of liberation writers as on their political and economic thought. Novak is critical of the Marxist elements in their thinking (although he admits that they do not accept the atheism, totalitarianism, and belief in the vanguard party, and in the proletariat as the agent of history that characterize Marxism-Leninism). He criticizes their affirmation of the class struggle (in this case, poor against rich), their suspicion of private property, their utopianism, and above all, the opposition to capitalism on the part of all the liberation writers, even those who claim to be opposed to Marxism, and their desire to replace it with socialism.

Will It Liberate? attacks socialism as statist, inefficient, and opposed to freedom. Those avowed socialists who are committed to personal freedom and a mixed economy, he defines as democratic capitalists because "there is no principle in socialism defending the individual. Once such a principle enters socialist thought, socialism becomes a type of democratic capitalism" (p. 192). He disagrees with the democratic socialist argument "for more substantive political controls over economic activity . . . because of [their] excessive reliance on politics and the state, to the neglect of economic activism" (pp. 177–78).

In order to make his attack stick on the Marxist elements in liberation thought, Novak quotes from the writings of the 1970s, ignoring the liberationists' more recent thinking in the redemocratization phase of the mid-1980s. Gutierrez's thought is analyzed by quoting from *A Theology of Liberation,* first published in 1971, and from *The Power of the Poor in History,* which was published in Spanish in 1979 and is made up of articles written in the mid-1970s. It is true that in the introduction and the epilogue (apparently the parts written after a trip to Latin America, and extended discussions with Hugo Assman), Novak recognizes that liberation theologians have been forced by events to be more concerned about democracy and human rights. However, their basic anticapitalism remains, and they have no practical suggestions for the economic betterment of the poor. The liberation theologians are accused of basing their endorsement of socialism on "blind hope without much specificity about the specific structures and economic institutions that will embody their socialism," and of misunderstanding "the spiritual resources and economic dynamism of liberal societies." Since Novak views the conflict as one between those who share a common faith, but differ over its application, he attempts to outline an alternative "theology of creation" and to link it with John Paul II's writings and speeches. But it is in their economics, not in their theological commitment to the poor, that the liberationists, in Novak's view, fail to offer much hope to the poor.[3]

Novak continued his battle against liberation theology in the religious press. In 1972 he had published an article in *Commentary* that was one of the first signs of his conversion from the New Left to neo-conservatism. Entitled "Needing Niebuhr Again," it argued against the enthusiastic sectarianism of the religious radicals, and endorsed Niebuhr's critical realism in politics. Niebuhr was cited again in a debate with Robert McAfee Brown in *The Christian Century* (January 27, 1986). Brown maintained that Niebuhr's views of "social sin" in *Moral Man and Immoral Society* and his use of Scripture to denounce injustice and American imperialism anticipated the approach of the liberation theologians. For Novak, on the contrary, Niebuhr's biblical realism was fundamentally opposed to the utopianism of the liberationists who "give pitifully little thought to the institutions, habits, and associations that will provide checks and balances against the ineradicable evils of the human heart" (p. 70). "Does the current Christian left," Novak asks, "as consistently criticize the left as Niebuhr did?" and are they aware, as Niebuhr put it, of "the limitations of the human imagination, the easy subservience of reason to prejudice and passion, and the consequent persistence of irrational egoism, particularly in group behavior, [that] make social conflict an inevitability in human history, probably to its very end" (*Moral Man and Immoral Society*, p. xx).

Yet the same criticism could be leveled at Novak himself. In his writings he seems no more willing to engage in criticism of capitalism than the liberation theologians are of socialism. He allows for political regulation of the economy and admits that the American system of "political economy" is neither purely capitalist nor purely socialist, and he calls the resulting mixture "democratic capitalism." Yet there is much more discussion of the virtues of capitalism than of the appropriate area for democratic restraints upon it, and when democracy is discussed it is usually in terms of the voluntary associations ("mediating structures") that he, along with De Tocqueville (and Ronald Reagan), find the distinctive and laudable feature of the American system. In *Freedom with Justice* he states that "it is difficult to draw exact lines in any purely theoretical way marking off the precise limits of the political system and of the economic system" (p. 200). Yet the question of "politics and markets" is crucial for the debate with the liberation theologians. They are deeply suspicious of the market, and see it as just one more instrument of domination, while Novak sees it as the instrument by which mankind can be liberated from poverty. For the liberation theologians, that liberation is to be carried out by the action of the poor and through a fundamental restructuring of the national and international economy. It is not enough to point to the "magic of the market" to reply to the liberationist criticisms. Some recognition of the problems of structural unemployment and of the concentration of landholding is required along with alternatives to the approaches proposed by the liberation theologians for dealing with these problems.

A second problem with Novak's attack is the frequent identification of liberation theology with Marxism,[4] and even with Marxism-Leninism. It is true that the infatuation with revolution and with Marxist categories of thought on the part of some of the liberation theologians in the period between 1968 and 1975 lends itself to such an argument. It is important, however, to view the writings of the liberationists in their historical context, and in particular, to be aware of the recent development in the thinking of the school's leading writers. Gustavo Gutierrez's recently translated book, *We Drink from Our Own Wells* (Maryknoll, NY: Orbis Books, 1984), would be difficult to relate in any way to the Marxist tradition. It is an extended meditation on "the spirituality of liberation"—a development of a subject to which he had devoted only a few pages in *A Theology of Liberation*. Relying almost exclusively on biblical sources he argues that the central message of Christ is opposed to a narrow individualism and spiritualism. Citing biblical descriptions of "the way" practiced by the early Christians, he argues that "walking according to the Spirit is an activity undertaken in community, a people on the move" (p. 89). Man is a unified whole, a "body possessing life," not the soul imprisoned within the shell of the body of Greek dualism. Conversion is a process that involves solidarity with the community, but that solidarity must first be preceded by the experience of "the gratuitousness of God's love. . . . Our relationship with God is a precondition for encounter and true communion with others. . . . Jesus Christ who is God and man is our way to the Father but he is also our way to recognition of others" (pp. 109–12).

We Drink from Our Own Wells does not abandon the critical stance of liberation theology. It relates opposition to unjust social structures to the Christian message and the current teachings of the church, especially the bishops' statements at Medellín and Puebla. When the book mentions specifics it refers to Central America, especially to the sermons of the martyred Archbishop of San Salvador, Oscar Romero, and to the period just before and after the Nicaraguan revolution (including excerpts from the letters of Christian guerrillas in the anti-Somoza effort). Missing completely from the discussion are references to Marx or even to the class struggle.

A similar spiritual and biblical focus characterizes Gutierrez's *On Job* (Maryknoll, NY: Orbis Books, 1987). It is an extended meditation on the Book of Job that seeks to explain the love of God in situations in which the innocent suffer. Gutierrez chooses Job because Job went from a comfortable life to sharing the sufferings of the poor and understanding their special relationship with God. He concludes, "If we are to receive from God the tender consolation promised by the prophet [Isaiah] we must make our own the needs of the oppressed" (p. 103).

Richard Neuhaus, a prolific Lutheran pastor who is now identified with the neoconservatives, has also written a criticism of liberation theology, *The Catholic Moment* (San Francisco: Harper and Row, 1987). He too concentrates on the early writings, but in his case the focus is on Juan Luis Segundo's multivolume *Theology for Artisans of a New Humanity*. He correctly observes that Segundo regularly contradicts himself, and calls the resulting confusion dialectical thinking. Neuhaus's main criticism, however, is that as represented by Segundo, liberation theology represents a kind of "monism" that reduces the transcendent dimension of religion to political commitment and social involvement. He calls the result "unbridled Pelagianism," referring to the fourth-century Christian heresy that denied the necessity of grace. He also accuses liberation theology of borrowing most of its major ideas from the Europeans ("North American understanding of it is based on bad English translations of bad Spanish translations of bad German ideas"—p. 177), and of advocating a partisan church and a partisan notion of the truth. Support from these accusations is not hard to find in the morass that is Segundo's multivolume work—and this without even looking at his more recent writings.

None of the American critics pay much attention to the relation of liberation theology and the Ecclesial Base Communities (CEBs). Numbering, according to various estimates, between fifty thousand and one hundred thousand with as many as 4 million members, they are most significant in Brazil, where they are strongly supported by a large segment of the hierarchy.[5] At least one thousand such communities are said to be operating in Chile, while in Colombia the church has simply renamed existing groups in many cases as CEBs. In Central America they have become very controversial in the diocese of Managua, while in other areas of Nicaragua, such as the Atlantic Coast, they function in harmony with the local bishops.

The Christian Base Communities began before the emergence of liberation theology, but they are seen as important examples of the kind of grass-roots activism that the liberation theologians support. They are often located in poor areas and vary in their politics—although they tend to be to the left—and much seems to depend at the outset on the initial leadership.

Groups of twenty to thirty heads of family meet to meditate on the Bible, and to apply its texts to their daily lives. This may lead to specific actions on the needs of the membership or the community, it may have political or economic implications as the membership becomes involved in political parties or trade unions, or it may remain a mutually supportive group without a wider impact. In nearly all cases it is linked directly to the church hierarchy (in Managua the CEBs are involved in a "popular church" that opposes Cardinal Obando, and in El Salvador CONIP, an organization of "popular" Base Communities, has been repeatedly criticized by Archbishop Rivera y Damas) and an effort is made, not always successfully, to distinguish between the religious activities of the group and direct political involvement in partisan politics. Despite the claims made by some critics of the "elitism" or "Leninism" of the liberation theologians, the Base Communities demonstrate a kind of grass-roots democracy that has not been common in Latin America in the past. Anyone who is interested in the future of democracy in Latin America should be interested in the Base Communities experience.[6]

The neoconservative criticisms were part of a general effort (1) to move the church closer to what was seen as the central tradition of Catholic social thought, from which it departed in the mid-1960s with the ultimate result of encouraging alliances with Marxism (Quade), and (2) to make it rethink and perhaps modify its criticisms of capitalism in a way analogous to its modification of its earlier hostility to "bourgeois" democracy (Novak). Yet there were serious obstacles to the unconditional acceptance of capitalism by Catholic social thinkers. While the church had always endorsed the right to private property, that right had been limited by its contribution to the common good, and Catholic social thought, for all its opposition to collectivism, had always possessed a communitarian (in earlier versions, organic) element that opposed unrestricted individual rights. And in the last twenty years, the content of the common good had been refocused in the direction of a specific concern for the poor and for the less developed countries. This was what had made the emergence of liberation theology within the church possible, but the problem that liberation theology now faced was how it was to be related to the mainstream of Catholic teaching. There were influential elements in Europe and Latin America that wished to exclude and condemn it—but there was also powerful support in certain hierarchies (notably Brazil) and among prestigious intellectuals (e.g., Karl Rahner) and elements in church teaching that it effectively invoked. By definition, the church was to be catholic—that is, universal—in its appeal, and earlier experience with condemnation and anathemas argued that these were not very effective ways to deal with new theological currents. The Puebla Conference had demonstrated that Pope John Paul II, with his repeated visits to the area, was determined to give special attention to Latin America as the area with the largest concentration of believers in the world, and he did not wish to see Marxist influence grow in that region. Thus liberation theology became a major concern during his pontificate. To the story of the confrontation between the liberation theologians and the Vatican—and of its resolution—we now turn.

9

The Vatican and Liberation Theology: Confrontation and Compromise

MUCH OF THE worldwide attention that liberation theology has received in recent years is the result of a number of highly publicized confrontations between the Vatican and liberation theology. Two important documents on the subject have been published by the Vatican Congregation for the Doctrine of the Faith, and the orthodoxy of both Gustavo Gutierrez and Leonardo Boff has been the object of Vatican investigations. In the charges and countercharges from each side, however, there has been a process of compromise, and finally what appears to be a resolution of the conflict.

The orthodoxy of Leonardo Boff had already been investigated in 1976 and 1980, but during most of the 1970s the Vatican had been content to leave the question of the orthodoxy of individual theologians to the Latin Americans. In February 1982, however, Boff sent the Congregation for the Doctrine of the Faith his reply to an investigation by the Doctrinal Commission of the archdiocese of Rio de Janeiro, headed by the conservative Cardinal Eugenio Sales, of his book *Church, Charism, and Power,* which had been published in 1981 (English translation, New York: Crossroad, 1985). The book was a further development of ideas expressed in Boff's doctoral thesis and in *Ecclesiogenesis.* Its principal focus was on ecclesiology, the study of the structure of the church. The book argued that the hierarchy had taken its form only after Christ's death, and had come to reflect "Roman and feudal" structures of authority in society around it. (At one point—p. 74 in the English translation—it cited in support of the first claim a book by Joseph Ratzinger, soon to be appointed head of the Congregation that would investigate the orthodoxy of the book.) It called for a return to an earlier "fraternal and circular" collegial structure that would still retain the hierarchy, not as source of all authority and absolute power, but as the office exercising the "charism, one among many but of prime importance, which is that of being responsible for harmony among the many and diverse charisms" (p. 163). It spoke of the violation of human rights in the church, used such terms as *pathology* to describe the exercise of church authority, and described the church as "structurally unbalanced" and "often the legitimating religious ideology for the imperial social order" (p. 113). Its most famous sentence, and the one that alone would have produced problems with church authorities, asserted that "there has been a gradual expropriation of the spiritual means of production from the Christian people by the clergy" (p. 112).

The Vatican Congregation for the Doctrine of the Faith had been established at the end of the Second Vatican Council in December 1965 as a more positively oriented theological body to replace the Holy Office, which itself had been created in 1908 to take over the functions of the Sacred Congregation of the Universal Inquisition, founded in 1542 to combat heresy. New procedures for informing those charged with deviations from the faith were established, and the Congregation began to hold conferences and organize theological study groups, a significant departure from earlier practice.

In January 1982, Cardinal Joseph Ratzinger was appointed prefect, or chairman, of the Congregation. Ratzinger was a well-known theologian who had been an adviser to Cardinal Frings of Cologne, one of the leading liberals at the Second Vatican Council. Thereafter he had taught theology at the University of Tübingen—teaching there at the time (1969) that the student radicals took over the university in the names of Karl Marx and Herbert Marcuse. In 1977 he was made Archbishop of Munich and later cardinal. His published works on theology in English include *Theology of History; Dogma and Preaching; Eschatology, Death, and Eternal Life;* and *The God of Jesus Christ.*

Ratzinger was an activist in his new position. With the support of Pope John Paul II he dedicated himself to limiting what he saw to be the theological excesses that had resulted from the opening initiated by Vatican II. In early 1983, the Italian conservative Catholic magazine *30 Giorni* published a set of "preliminary notes" that Ratzinger had written on the subject of liberation theology.[1] While the *Notes* begin with the admission that there is a whole spectrum of positions identified with liberation theology, from the concern with the poor expressed by the Latin American bishops at Medellín and Puebla to radically Marxist positions, Ratzinger claims to be analyzing only those who "have embraced the Marxist fundamental option." However, he then describes "the phenomenon of liberation theology" as "a fundamental threat to the Faith of the church." He argues that it constitutes a new way of interpreting the Bible that is based on the historicist reinterpretations of scripture of the German Protestant theologian Rudolf Bultmann, and he relates its "effort to recast the whole Christian reality in the categories of political-social liberation praxis" to neo-Marxism and "the new philosophical climate of the late sixties." The Vatican II discussion of the historical role of the "People of God" is transformed into a Marxist myth, and history is interpreted as a "process of progressive liberation . . . and the real interpreter of the Bible."

As published in English, the *Notes* do not mention any specific theologian, but there is a quote from Gutierrez's statement that "the class struggle is a fact" and a paraphrase of Jon Sobrino's interpretation of the Crucifixion as the sufferings of the poor in history. Ratzinger concludes that the answer to the challenge posed by liberation theology is to manifest "the concrete force of a better answer attested in living experience. . . . Theology alone is insufficient. Church authority alone is insufficient."

Nevertheless, Ratzinger took steps to see to it that church authority had a role to play. In March 1983 he sent the Peruvian bishops a list of ten "observations" on the writings of Gutierrez that accused him of a "selective rereading of the Bible" making the poor of the Bible into the exploited victims of the capitalist system, regarding "the theologian as the 'organic intellectual' of the historic bloc of the proletariat [Gramsci]," and viewing the class struggle as "a necessity for Christians" (Spanish translation, *Tierra Nueva,* Bogota, no. 51, October 1984, pp. 94–96). The ensuing discussion among Peru's fifty-two bishops lasted for more than a year. It led Gutierrez to publish a reply to Ratzinger that was an important new statement of his views on the relation of liberation theology and Marxism.

"Theology and the Social Sciences" was the final published version combining two essays that Gutierrez identifies in a footnote as "a reply to certain observations which have been received concerning the place of social analysis in theological reflection. This is the reason for the frequent quotations from our own writings."[2] The essay has been widely reprinted in Latin America, and substantial extracts have been translated as Appendix II to this book.

Gutierrez begins by asserting that the utilization of the social sciences by theology is "only in its first stages." He argues that a scientific approach to the hypotheses put forward by social science will subject them to continuing discussion and criticism. This is also true of liberation movements, which, like all human actions, are ambiguous "whether they occur in Vietnam, Brazil, New York, or Prague" (a quote from *A Theology of Liberation*). The struggle for liberty can be repressed both in capitalist systems and "in what today is called 'real socialism.' " History has demonstrated how illusory is the belief that a concrete historical system will eliminate all evils.

Gutierrez then argues that the dependence theory he used in his early writings was different from and opposed to Marxism because it rejected Marx's linear progressivism, which saw Europe as the image of the future development of other parts of the world. "Dependence" was mentioned by the bishops at Medellín, but there is no reason for theology to accept it uncritically or permanently. (Gutierrez was aware of the criticisms of *dependencia* theory by Latin American social scientists.) Marxism's atheism, totalitarianism, and "some interpretations of its materialism" are unacceptable to Christians, but theology, when it concerns itself with poverty and marginalization, must engage in an encounter—not with Marxism but with the social sciences, which in the Latin American context may include some Marxist elements. While the class struggle—or in broader terms, social conflict— exists in history, especially in Latin America, it is neither the motor that drives history forward nor a fundamental explanation or law of historical development. Christian charity demands that no person be excluded, but in extreme cases such as nazism, Christianity admits of only a single option. Finally, on the question of violence, Gutierrez proclaims his adherence to the traditional "just war" doctrine of St. Thomas Aquinas, and expresses his reservations concerning the European theories of a theology of revolution that appear to "baptize" violence.

Gutierrez repeatedly quotes his earlier writings, but they are quoted selectively, and it is only necessary to compare the two articles, dated 1970 and 1984 and published as appendixes to this book, to see how his views have changed. In the latter article he takes a much more critical attitude to Marxism and dependence theory, and argues that theology's use of social science should be subject to continual reevaluation and reassessment. It seems that the experience (*praxis*) of Latin America and the criticisms from the Vatican and from other theologians in many countries—especially the United States, where he is a frequent visiting lecturer—resulted in a movement away from his earlier flirtation with Marxist categories. So far, however, they have not resulted in any major shift in the anticapitalism of Gutierrez and the other liberation theologians.[3]

Gutierrez seems to have satisfied enough of the Peruvian bishops with his explanations that the Peruvian Conference of Bishops decided not to take a stand against liberation theology. They were also reported to have been influenced by a strong defense of Gutierrez sent by the distinguished European Jesuit theologian, Karl Rahner.

Ratzinger did not cease to press his case against liberation theology, however. In December 1983, the Archbishop of Medellín, Alfonso Lopez Trujillo, a long-time opponent of the liberationists, was named cardinal, and he became a member of the Congregation for the Doctrine of the Faith. The International Theological Commission, which advises the Congregation, already had among its members the Brazilian Franciscan Boaventura Kloppenburg, who had published two books attacking liberation theology as well as critical reviews of the writings of Leonardo Boff. In March 1984, Cardinal Ratzinger called the Doctrinal Commissions of the national Bishops Conferences of Latin America to a meeting in Bogota at which he denounced the "Marxist affinities" of liberation theology. He added to his criticisms a second important theme, the ecclesiological errors of which it was guilty—apparently a result of his studying the case of Leonardo Boff to whom he sent a letter in May criticizing his "ecclesiological relativism" and his "sociological" analysis of the church as an institution engaged in production and consumption. Reportedly at the suggestion of the pope, Ratzinger invited Boff to come to Rome for a "conversation" on the subject of his writings.

Ratzinger's letter accused Boff of "not paying sufficient attention to the doctrine and teaching (*magisterium*) of the Church"; using language that is "polemic, defamatory, and pamphleteering, absolutely inappropriate for a theologian"; drawing on "ideological principles of a certain neo-Marxist inspiration"; and proposing a "certain revolutionary utopia which is foreign to the church" and a "relativizing conception" of church structure and dogma. Boff replied with a fifty-page document (part of which he read to the cardinal at their interview) that cited his writings and church documents to demonstrate his orthodoxy and his acceptance of "the hierarchical constitution of the church by divine institution," while insisting that he wrote only to right the balance in the direction of the experience of the laity, the poor, and the contributions of the social sciences. He concluded, "Of one thing I am sure: I prefer to walk with the Church than go it alone with my theology. The church is a reality of Faith that I assume. Theology is a product of reason that I discuss."[4]

During his summer vacation in the German-speaking area of Italy, Ratzinger consented to a lengthy interview with an Italian journalist concerning his views on theology and the structure of the church (published in the United States as *The Ratzinger Report*). In the interview he expressed his profound pessimism about developments in the church since the Second Vatican Council. He described the contemporary crisis within the church as a result of cultural revolutions and social convulsions that the Fathers of the Council could not foresee. He criticized the view that Vatican II marked a break with what went before, and argued for a return to the "true Council" as distinct from "the self-styled 'spirit of the Council' that holds that everything that is new is always better than what has been or what is." Ratzinger was also critical of the increasing importance of National Bishops Conferences in the church, since they had no warrant in the Bible or church tradition. However, he agreed that it was wrong for the Vatican to centralize all decisions "although we preserve the right, by statute, to intervene everywhere in the Church" (p. 68). He preferred that the local bishops and religious superiors engage in dialogue with authors whose orthodoxy was questioned. Rome would intervene only if "things are not successfully clarified in this way or when the problem goes beyond local borders or assumes international dimensions."

Cardinal Ratzinger seems to have considered the case of Leonardo Boff in this category. His summons to Rome produced an outpouring of support from the Brazilian laity and hierarchy. Boff took to Rome declarations of support signed by fifty-thousand Brazilians (including, he claimed, eighty-seven prostitutes) and he was accompanied by two Brazilian cardinals (both fellow Franciscans), Alois Lorscheider of Fortaleza and Evaristo Arns of São Paulo. The Vatican communiqué on the conversations noted that Cardinal Ratzinger received his fellow cardinals "in another place" but Boff claims that they entered and discussed the case with Ratzinger two hours after the colloquy had been under way—much of it devoted to varying interpretations of Vatican II ecclesiology. (See Boff's accounts in *Der Spiegel*, September 17, 1984, and in Leonardo and Clodovis Boff, *Liberation Theology: From Dialogue to Confrontation*, New York: Harper & Row, 1986, pp. 84–88.)

In March 1985, the Congregation for the Doctrine of the Faith sent Boff a "Notification" stating that his book was guilty of at least three errors. In its conception of the institutional structure of the church it argued that the church had evolved as an institution after Christ's resurrection as a "part of the process of deeschatologization"—that is, adjustment to the fact that Christ's Second Coming was not imminent—and that in the process the church had adopted societal characteristics borrowed from contemporary Roman and later feudal society. The Congregation called this "ecclesiological relativism." The Congregation also criticized Boff's "relativistic interpretation of dogma as only good for a specific time and specific circumstances," as well as his call to the church "to be fundamentally open to everything without exception." The "Notification" also called his charge that the clergy had "expropriated the spiritual means of production from the laity" a subversion of religious reality, concluding, "The options of L. Boff analyzed here endanger the sound doctrine of the Faith which this congregation has the task of promoting and safeguarding." Although Cardinal Ratzinger signed the document, it indicated that it had been formally approved by the pope.

The "Notification" did not specifically allude to Marxism or liberation theology, being concerned primarily with Boff's conception of church structure and dogma. However, in its introduction it analyzed the relation of universal and particular churches by referring to "praxis and experience" while noting that 'praxis neither replaces the truth, but remains at the service of the truth consigned to us by the Lord.'[5]

In April Boff's Franciscan superiors were requested to impose an "obedient [*obsequium*] silence for a convenient time" on the friar. He was not to preach, give interviews, or continue as editor of the *Revista Ecclesiastica Brasileira,* and his writings were to be subject to prior censorship. He was not asked to recant his views on the structure of the church.

Boff accepted the decision, declaring, "I am not a Marxist. As a Christian and a Franciscan I am in favor of the freedoms and rights of religion and of the noble struggle for justice and for a new society. . . . I am convinced of the need to continue moving forward, in communion with the magisterium of the church, in the creation of an authentic theology of liberation" ("Theology of Liberation," *New LADOC Keyhole Series,* Lima, no. 1, 1985, p. 50). Despite the prohibition on public statements, Boff went to Nicaragua in September and declared that "God is there, fighting alongside the poor" (*Washington Post,* December 5, 1985). On March 29, 1986, less than a year after it was imposed, the sentence was lifted.

At the time of the interview with Boff, Ratzinger had just launched a frontal attack on liberation theology with the publication of *The Instruction on Certain Aspects of the "Theology of Liberation"* (*Libertatis Nuntius*), which was dated August 6, 1984, but was actually published on September 4. The *Instruction* announces at the outset that its purpose is to warn against the "risks of deviation, damaging to the faith and Christian living, that are brought about by certain forms of liberation theology which use, in an insufficiently critical manner, concepts borrowed from various currents of Marxist thought" (Introduction). Like the earlier Ratzinger memorandum, the *Instruction* admits that there are many different varieties of liberation theology so that one might better speak of "theologies of liberation," and it claims to be speaking only of those that propose "a novel interpretation of the content of faith and of Christian existence" by using "concepts uncritically borrowed from Marxist ideology and recourse to a biblical hermeneutic marked by rationalism" leading to a "new interpretation which is corrupting whatever was authentic in the generous initial commitment on behalf of the poor" (VI, 8–10). Among the "fundamental tenets [of Marxism] which are not compatible with the Christian concept of humanity and society" are "the class struggle, atheism, the denial of human rights, and a partisan conception of truth" based on the belief that society is founded on violence (VII, VIII). The *Instruction* asserts that the theory of the class struggle as the fundamental law of history is used by the liberation theologians to politicize the faith, transform and subordinate it to history, and confuse the poor of the Scripture with the proletariat of Marx. The liberationists also are said to propound a conception of the church of the people, set in opposition to the hierarchy and the teaching office (*magisterium*) of the church who are viewed as representatives of the ruling class (IX, 11–13). This leads to a political reading of the Bible, advocacy of violence, and a temporal messianism that secularizes the kingdom of god and absorbs it into human history so that the Exodus, the Magnificat, and Christ's death and resurrection are all seen in relation to the political liberation of the people. The *Instruction* concludes by urging pastors to present the full message of salvation and to develop and expand the social teaching of the church.

The *Instruction* denounces the shocking inequality among and within nations, and the domination exercised in certain parts of Latin America by oligarchs, the military, and foreign corporations, but it warns that the appropriate response is not to adopt "such an all-embracing conception of reality as the thought of Karl Marx." It quotes Paul VI's warning against accepting "elements of the Marxist analysis without recognizing its connections with the ideology, [and entering] into the practice of the class struggle and of its Marxist interpretation while failing to see the kind of totalitarian society to which this process slowly leads" (VIII, 8).

Like the earlier Ratzinger memo, the *Instruction* after initially speaking of "theologies" of liberation in the plural, then proceeds to discuss *the* theology of liberation for the rest of the document. Like it too, the *Instruction* never names names or cites actual texts, although it seems to be aimed mainly at Gutierrez's statements about the class struggle and the proletariat, and at Sobrino's identification of Christ's crucifixion and the resurrection with the struggles of the poor. The reference to the popular church may also reflect a concern about the polarization that was currently taking place in Nicaragua between the hierarchy and the pro-Sandinista church of the people.

The response of the liberation theologians to the *Instruction* was to deny that they were guilty of the reductionism of which it spoke, and to insist on the spiritual and biblical inspiration of their concern for the poor, especially in the Ecclesial Base Communities. Boff accused what he called the "Roman document" of a "Central European perspective" that failed to understand how the liberation theologians were attempting to relate the Bible to the experience of poverty and oppression. To the charge of reductionism, he answered that no liberation theologian denies "the divinity of Christ, the redemptive value of his death, nor the Mass as a way of 'actualizing' the sacrifice of the Lord and his eucharistic presence." Sobrino too insisted that his theological understanding of Christ was thoroughly orthodox and he called for a dialogue with Cardnal Ratzinger's Congregation. Others such as the Chileans Pablo Richard and Ronaldo Muñoz insisted that they accepted the hierarchy, tradition, and teaching of the church, but were working to bring it into closer contact with the "spiritual experience and liberating practice of the ecclesial communities." In his usual long-winded manner, Juan Luis Segundo wrote a whole book as a reply to the *Instruction,* which was billed as not only a reply to Cardinal Ratzinger but a "warning to the whole church." Segundo denied that any liberation theologians were guilty of the reductionism described in the *Instruction* and noted his own criticism of Marxism. More fundamentally, however, Segundo went on the offensive and argued that the *Instruction* involved a more general attack on Enlightenment humanism and modern thought, which was aimed at reestablishing an other-worldly and transcendentalist religion that is outside of history or the contemporary world, constituting a total reversal of the accomplishments of the Second Vatican Council.[6]

Thus, the reaction of the liberation theologians was to deny that they were guilty of the politicization of the Gospel or opposition to the hierarchy that the *Instruction* had denounced. And if one were to look at their current writing, as opposed to some of their more extravagant statements of the early 1970s, they were right. Except in Nicaragua, where the situation had become polarized institutionally and theologically, it was not a question of either/or (the hierarchy or the church of the people, liberating praxis versus the traditional social teaching of the church), but of both (the hierarchy in communion with the people endorsing the preferential option for the poor—the Bible applied to the experience of the oppressed).

Yet as the Nicaraguan situation demonstrated, liberation theology could be used to support what Castro had called a "strategic alliance" between Christians and Marxists, and the Marxists were aware of this. The secret documents discovered in Grenada after the American invasion in 1983 included a 1982 Cuban memorandum on the religious situation in Grenada recommending that the New Jewel Movement "promote contacts between clergymen and members of the laity from Nicaragua and other Latin American circles linked to the theology of liberation and, in general, to the idea of a church committed to revolutionary positions, and the Christian sectors in Grenada."[7] Cuban interest in liberation theology had been spurred by Castro's experience in Nicaragua. His interest in promoting better relations with "progressive" Catholics in Latin America now led him to grant twenty-three hours of interviews with Frei Betto, a young Dominican liberation theologian. The resulting book, a transcription of the interviews along with enthusiastic commentaries by Betto, was published in Cuba in 1986 and became a best-seller there and in Brazil.[8] (Frei Betto's real name is Alberto Libanio Christo, and as a leader of the leftist Young Christian Students he was briefly imprisoned after the 1964 Brazilian coup.)

In the interview Castro describes his education by the Christian Brothers and Jesuits in Santiago de Cuba and Havana, and expresses his admiration for the self-discipline and high moral commitment of the conservative Spanish Jesuits who taught him at the prestigious Colegio del Belén in Havana. Indeed Castro argues for cooperation between Christians and Communists on grounds of the similarity of their moral commitments. Both are against greed, egoism, and exploitation, and both call for respect for the family, self-sacrifice, and austerity. At one point, Castro even says that if Che Guevara had been a Christian, one would have called him a saint. He compares the Marxist message to the oppressed with the commitment to the poor contained in the Sermon on the Mount, and cites Christ's denunciation of the rich.

Betto dedicated his book to "Leonardo Boff, priest, doctor, and above all, prophet" and Castro mentions that he has collected the writings of Boff, Gutierrez, and others but has not evaluated their use of Marxism as an instrument of social analysis. His main concern is to encourage "the alliance, indeed the unity, of Christians and Marxists, as in Nicaragua" (p. 297).

Betto is enthusiastic about what he has seen in Cuba, particularly in the areas of education, health, and the ending of poverty—areas in which he feels Brazil is far behind. However, he criticizes the discrimination against Christians in Cuba in employment, education, and admission to the Communist party. On the last point, Castro replies that the Nicaraguan experience has demonstrated that "it is perfectly possible to be a Marxist without ceasing to be a Christian, to work together with Marxist Communists to transform the world" but that "conditions are not ripe" for the elimination of the "subtle discrimination" against Christians in Cuba. Religion, says Castro, is not necessarily an opiate, although it can be so used by exploiters and oppressors. Betto replies that the Latin American left has made a mistake in stressing atheism in its approach to the Latin American masses, and argues that it is more effective to build on religiously based concepts of equality, fraternity, and solidarity, as the liberation theologians have done.

The issue of discrimination against Christians was raised again subsequently in three public dialogues between the Cuban government and the Catholic bishops, and at the National Congress of the Church held in February 1986. It was also discussed at the Cuban Communist Party Congress held later in February, the working papers of which called on the Communists to honor "the moral integrity of believers" and to avoid any practice that could "wound religious sentiments" since "within the party's policy of encouraging national unity, there is no room for discrimination against believers."[9]

The Cuban effort to promote Nicaraguan-style cooperation between Communists and leftist Catholics gave renewed intensity to the efforts of the more conservative Catholic leaders to combat liberation theology. Since 1972 an Italian-based Catholic renewal group with a similar name, but very different purposes, *Communione e Liberazione,* had been attacking such cooperation in its journal and through its theologians. By the mid-1980s *Communione* had journals and organizations in many other countries, including the United States and Chile. In July 1985, the publishers of the Chilean edition of the magazine of the movement sponsored what it described as an international congress of theologians in the small Chilean town of Los Andes, one hundred miles north of Santiago, in order to discuss liberation theology. At the end of the meeting, which included among its participants Cardinal Alfonso Lopez Trujillo, the congress issued a *Declaration of Los Andes,* which praised the Vatican *Instruction* and attacked liberation theology because "The presentation of the truth as identified with praxis, and the practical equivalence between Christian salvation and socio-political liberation, imply an historical monism from which are derived anthropological reductionism and political totalitarianism, this last being made worse when it is sacralized." The Chilean Bishops Conference disavowed the statement, since it had not been asked about or invited to the meeting, and it had not taken a stand with reference to the Vatican *Instruction.* Ronaldo Muñoz, the Chilean liberation theologian, wrote an open letter to Cardinal Lopez Trujillo arguing that in countries such as Chile the *Declaration*'s identification of liberation theology with Marxism "constitutes a virtual incitement to repression, even criminal repression."[10]

The Andes Declaration had concluded with the assertion that a genuine liberation theology would be based on "the reality of the reconciliation of man with God, with himself, with others, and with all that is created," and it appealed for "dialogue in the service of the unity of the Church." The critics of its authors saw in that statement, as well as an earlier *Papal Exhortation on Reconciliation and Penitence* (1984), an effort to develop "a theology of reconciliation" as an answer to liberation theology, promoting a social ethic based on love and reconciliation that was said to be more faithful to the Christian message than liberation theology's conflict, contradiction, and dichotomy between oppressor and oppressed. (This seemed to be confirmed when the Los Andes meeting was followed by an International Congress on Liberation and Reconciliation in January 1987, which was attended by bishops from ten Latin American countries.)

These efforts were linked to a broader conservative program that was believed to be spearheaded by Cardinal Ratzinger and confirmed by the consistent Vatican preference for conservatives in its appointment of bishops and cardinals. The press picked up the issue in connection with the Extraordinary Synod of Bishops held at the Vatican in December 1985, the twentieth anniversary of the end of the Second Vatican Council.

The Synod was attended by twenty-eight Latin American bishops, twenty-two of them the heads of the national bishops conferences. Knowing that the Latin American representatives differed on liberation theology, the journalists at the synod press conference pressed Bishop Dario Castrillon Hoyos, secretary general of CELAM (the Latin American Bishops Conference) for his views and received the strong statement against "a church with a machine gun" that is quoted at the beginning of the introduction to this book. The sessions of the synod were not open, but summaries of the speeches indicated that on December 1 there were discussions of liberation theology by Cardinal Lorscheider and his cousin, Bishop José Lorscheiter, President of the Brazilian Bishops Conference. The latter strongly endorsed the movement as "a spiritual experience . . . the experience of God who is encountered in the poor" (*Vatican Press Bulletin,* December 2, 1985).

Despite the press interest, liberation theology was not a central concern of the synod. It focused more on the consolidation and reinterpretation of the Second Vatican Council's decrees on the nature and structure of the church. Discussion in the synod focused on issues of centralization and decentralization, the role of national bishops conferences, whether to authorize a universal catechism, and the church as "mystery" versus the church as an institution. However, the Brazilian bishops' statements reflected the strong interest of a majority of the 300 Brazilian bishops in the Vatican's adopting a more positive attitude on the subject. That interest focused on a second *Instruction* relating to liberation theology that had been promised in the 1984 *Instruction*. That document, originally scheduled for publication in 1985, had been delayed due, press reports had it, to Pope John Paul's dissatisfaction with it as not sufficiently positive about the Christian Base Communities and insufficiently biblical in its orientation (*National Catholic Reporter*, February 20, 1986), Another reason for the delay may have been concern about the reaction of the Brazilian church. In July 1985, a two-day meeting had been held of the members of the Steering Committee and the Doctrinal Commission of the Brazilian Bishops Conference with the Congregation for the Doctrine of the Faith. It discussed the Boff case, and especially the forthcoming *Instruction*. In March 1986, the pope also called the five Brazilian cardinals, the officers of the Brazilian Bishops Conference, and the chairmen of its regional secretariats to Rome for "an informal meeting to deepen the life and activity of the church." The meetings were not public but the participants were reported to have discussed the topic of liberation theology and the need to relate the Christian message to the problems of social justice, human rights, and world peace. The results of those discussions would become clear in April.

First, however, came the publication of the *Instruction on Christian Freedom and Liberation* (*Libertatis Conscientia*) on April 5, 1986. While it referred at the outset to the first *Instruction*'s warnings of the "risk of deviation damaging to the faith and to Christian living" it generally took a more positive attitude to the theme of liberation. It described sin as the cause of human alienation and oppression, but it accepted aspects of the structuralism of the liberation writers when it referred to the "poverty caused by industrial society" (par. 13) and "structures of exploitation and slavery" (par. 42)—although "only in a derived and secondary sense, can one speak of social sin" and one must "work simultaneously for the conversion of hearts and for the improvements of structures" (par. 75). It committed the universal church to the "love of preference for the poor" (thus avoiding the partisan overtones of the term *option*. When the latter word was used later, the *Instruction* added, "The option excludes no one"). Most significantly for liberation theology, the *Instruction* specifically endorsed the new Base Communities "if they really live in unity with the local church and with the universal church" and it supported theological reflection based on experience. "But in order that this reflection may be truly a reading of the Scripture and not a projection onto the Word of God of a meaning which it does not contain, the theologian will be careful to interpret the experience from which he begins in the light of the experience of the Church herself" (par. 70).

Warning that "the salvific dimension of liberation cannot be reduced to the socio-ethical dimension which is a consequence of it," the *Instruction* argued (par. 73) that the fundamental principles of a "Christian practice of liberation" are against individualism (*solidarity*) and collectivism (*subsidiarity*). On the issue of violence, while it denounced those who propagate "the myth of revolution," the *Instruction* admitted (quoting Pope Paul VI) that armed struggle might be resorted to "as a last resort to put an end to an obvious and prolonged tyranny" (par. 78–79). It ended as it had begun with a mixture of negative and positive comments, warning that "it would be criminal to take the energies of popular piety and misdirect them toward a purely earthly plan of liberation, which would soon be revealed as . . . a cause of new forms of slavery," and calling for a "civilization of love" to "bring into being new forms of solidarity" (par. 99).

A still more positive endorsement of liberation theology came in a letter that the pope sent to the national meeting of the Brazilian bishops on April 12th—a week after the publication of the second *Instruction*. In that letter he referred to his discussions with their representatives in March and warned of the danger of "ecclesiologies that distance themselves from that of the Second Vatican Council." However, the pope went on to discuss Brazil's social problems, reiterating the church's commitment to human rights and to its "love that is neither exclusive nor excluding but rather preferential" for "the poor, the suffering, those without influence, resources, and assistance." Then, referring to the two *Instructions*, published "with my explicit approval," he urged the bishops to find responses that are

> consistent and coherent with the teachings of the Gospel, of the living tradition, and the ongoing *magisterium* of the Church. As long as this is observed, we are convinced, we and you, that the theology of liberation is not only timely but useful and necessary. It should constitute a new stage—in close connection with former ones—of the theological reflection initiated with the apostolic tradition and continued by the

great fathers and doctors, by the ordinary and extraordinary magisterium, and in more recent years by the rich patrimony of the church's social doctrine.

Denouncing the "fatal orientations and tendencies of unbridled capitalism and of collectivism or state capitalism," he urged them to develop a "correct and necessary theology of liberation . . . in full fidelity to church doctrine, attentive to the preferential but not excluding or exclusive love for the poor" (text from *Origins,* Washington, DC, May 1986, pp. 12–15).

The second *Instruction* and the letter to the Brazilian bishops were received with enthusiasm by the liberation theologians in Latin America. Gutierrez said the second *Instruction* "closes a chapter, [and] a new more positive period is beginning." He praised its positive tone, the endorsement of Ecclesial Base Communities, and its reaffirmation of preferential love for the poor. Gutierrez proposed that the "new stage" referred to by the pope should involve a genuine dialogue between the Europeans and the Latin Americans that would make clearer than the documents do the distinction between liberty and liberation. A similar comment was made by Ignacio Ellacuria, who noted that the Vatican was attempting to universalize a "certain form of liberty (civil or bourgeois liberty)" cherished by Europeans and North Americans but that the Third World, especially Latin America, was concerned with liberation based on its historical experience, and new approaches to Christology and spirituality based on the experience of the Base Communities. Leonardo Boff saw the two documents as legitimating twenty years of innovative pastoral and theological activity in Brazil and as a recognition by the pope of the new epistemological status of sociology for the theologian and a mandate to the church to become involved in social change. Only Jon Sobrino was critical, accusing the *Instruction* of being nonhistorical, formalistic rather than processual in its approach to truth, and using an excessively simple scheme to relate the personal and spiritual to the social and material, subordinating the latter to the former.[11]

Gutierrez cited the two *Instructions* in his book *La Verdad los Hara Libres* [The Truth Shall Make You Free], published in 1986.[12] He endorsed the 1984 Instruction's call for "a critical examination of the methods of analysis which are taken from other disciplines" (VII, 10) but argued that if the church was concerned with poverty it should make use of analyses and interpretations drawn from the so-

cial sciences that could give it a better knowledge of the social reality
of Latin America (pp. 22–23). The appeal to the social sciences of
liberation theology, while it might draw "a certain number of elements from Marxist analysis," in no way involved the identification
of the social sciences with Marxism. However, it did mean that the
church should be concerned with "the premature and unjust death of
the great majorities in the subcontinent," which both Medellín and
Puebla had described as a "sinful situation." In using the social sciences to determine the causes of poverty there may be "notions that
come from the Marxist analysis (and of course other sources as
well): but liberation theology does not claim to have exclusive and
integral use of Marxist analysis, much less a kind of synthesis of faith
and Marxism" (pp. 54–55). Yet later in the book, Gutierrez reas-
serts what I have called his structural radicalism when he insists that
"radical change in a socio-economic order that creates poverty in
Latin America is a human and Christian requirement." This new society, however, must be characterized by "liberty for all." Gutierrez
insists that "personal liberty is the necessary condition for an authentic political liberation," and he quotes with approval the second
Instruction's insistence that "a liberation that does not take into
account the personal liberty of those who fight for it is already condemned to failure" (pp. 190–92).

He describes the two requirements of a human society as "justice
and liberty" adding, in what appears to depart from his early statements on private ownership, "In that area, many think that a healthy
equilibrium between private property, social property, and state property would be a good way to keep those two requirements present
and applicable" (p. 221). (The reference to social property probably
was influenced by the efforts of the reformist military government of
General Juan Velasco in Peru during the early 1970s to establish
worker-owned firms, and create industrial communities in which the
workers and investors shared ownership and management decisions.)

A further modification of Gutierrez's thinking resulted from the
continuing tragic experience in Peru with the Sendero Liminoso guerrilla movement. In an article published in mid-1986,[13] Gutierrez denounces "the terrorist violence" of Sendero as well as the "repressive
violence" used by the Peruvian army to combat it. In his earlier writings, he had distinguished institutionalized violence, repressive violence, and the counterviolence of the oppressed. Now he does not
speak of counterviolence but condemns terrorist violence, concluding,

"It is necessary to defend democratic life, however imperfect and fragile, which makes it possible to propose and discuss alternative formulas for the construction of a different kind of society. It cost us all, particularly the popular sectors, so much to achieve this possibility that we cannot allow it to be frustrated" (pp. 4–5).

In 1988 the Archbishop of Callao, Peru, Ricardo Durand S.J., who had already written one book critical of liberation theology, published *La Utopia de la Liberación,* which took note of the changes in Gutierrez's position as reflected in *La Verdad* and his essay "Theology and the Social Sciences," also reproduced in that book. He argued that Gutierrez described the changes in his thinking as "clarifications" but that what was really needed, particularly in view of the fact that his early writings were clearly the target of the first *Instruction,* was a formal retraction, rather than "lending continuing validity to what was said in the earlier books" (p. 61).

Without admitting that he was doing so, Gutierrez continued to modify his approach and to emphasize the agreement between his version of liberation theology and the social teaching of the church. He was assisted by the continuing criticism of capitalism in the recent encyclicals of the pope. In 1981, John Paul II had published *Laborem Exercens* [Human Work] to commemorate the fiftieth anniversary of *Quadragesimo Anno,* Pius XI's encyclical on the rights of labor. While rejecting the class struggle doctrine and the dictatorship of the proletariat, it had accepted the existence of a conflict of interest between capital and labor, argued that the church had always taught the priority of labor over capital (ch. 12), and accused capitalism of treating man as "an instrument of production" (ch. 7). The pope stated directly that "the right to private property is subordinated to the right to common use" and that the only legitimate title to the means of production "whether in the form of public or collective ownership is that they should serve labor and make possible the right to common use" (ch. 14).

In 1988 John Paul II observed the twentieth anniversary of Paul VI's encyclical, *Populorum Progressio,* by writing another encyclical on development, *Sollicitudo Rei Socialis* [*On Social Concerns*], which again emphasized the "social mortgage" on property and stated that "each of the two blocs harbors in its own way a tendency towards imperialism" (par. 22). Perhaps for the first time in papal documents, the encyclical listed among the human rights that everyone should be guaranteed "the right of economic initiative . . . which is important not only for the individual, but for the common good," but it balanced this with a denunciation of "economic, financial, and social mechanisms . . . maneuvered directly or indirectly by the more developed countries . . . accentuating the situation of wealth for some and poverty for the rest" (par. 15). Especially toward the end of the encyclical it stressed liberation themes. The pope denied that the church was espousing a third position between "liberal capitalism and Marxist collectivism" but asserted that it was presenting the results of "careful reflection on the complex realities of human existence" from the point of view of moral theology (par. 41). He singled out "the option or love of preference for the poor," applying it to world poverty and recalling the principle of Christian social doctrine that "the goods of this world are originally meant for all" (par. 42). (At the end of the paragraph, the balancing act was continued with a reference to "that special form of poverty which consists of being deprived of fundamental human rights, in particular the right to religious freedom and also the right of freedom of economic initiative.") The encyclical concluded by observing that since Pope Paul's 1968 encyclical,

> a new way of confronting poverty and underdevelopment has spread in some areas of the world, especially in Latin America. This approach makes liberation the fundamental category and the first principle of action. The positive values as well as the deviations and risks of deviations which are damaging to the faith and are connected with this form of theological reflection and method have been appropriately pointed out. . . . The aspiration to freedom from all forms of slavery affecting the individual and society is something noble and legitimate. This is in fact the purpose of development, or rather liberation and development, taking into account the intimate connection between the two. [par. 46][14]

Gutierrez hailed the new encyclical as a confirmation of what he had been saying. He noted the encyclical's references to liberation and to unjust social structures, and said that a central point of the encyclical was the need to change sinful structures that allow "groups, sectors, or countries to keep most of the world's resources for themselves" (*Latinamerica Press,* May 5, 1988). Shortly after Gutierrez's endorsement, however, the pope, on a two-day visit to Peru in mid-May, reasserted his criticisms of the liberationists without naming them, when, referring to the two *Instructions,* he said that "persistent error" still led some to treat their warnings "as if they were addressed to others" (*Latinamerica Press,* May 26, 1988). Vatican appointments to Latin American bishoprics also appeared to be consistently motivated by a desire to increase the influence of theological conservatives.

That the pope may have had reason to be concerned about the continuing attraction of Marxist systems for at least some liberationists was confirmed in the published reactions of Leonardo Boff to a visit to the Soviet Union in June and July of 1987. Along with his brother, Clodovis, Frei Betto, a Protestant minister, and a professor of Sociology from Rio de Janeiro, he visited seven cities in the Soviet Union at the invitation of the Russian Orthodox Church. On his return he described to the *Folha de Sao Paulo* (July 10, 1987) his enthusiasm for the Soviet Union as a "clean, healthy society" in which there was great interest in liberation theology as a variety of religion which was not the opium of the people but a factor for the liberation of the oppressed: "They are interested in our effort to create a synthesis of Christian faith and Marxist social analysis, and believe that it is a very promising development." In what one might describe as the Brazilian house organ of liberation theology, *Vozes* (December 1987), Boff went still further. In the Soviet Union the means of life-work, food, health, education, housing, transport, and basic services are guaranteed to all, although religion is restricted in its public expression and is the object of suspicion, and even at times of persecution. Socialism, because it places the social at the center of everything, "is more capable than any other system of revealing God in communion in history" (p. 690). "The 1917 socialist revolution was a new stage in the history of humanity. . . . The Kingdom should be thought of dialectically. . . . In the real socialism of the Soviet Union we find both the Kingdom and the anti-Kingdom," the latter in the domination of the state, the Leninist party, and the repression of dissenters. However, "the social organization of the Soviet Union when compared with our dependent and exclusive capitalism avoids the eroticization and commercialization of everything and maintains a basic healthiness of human and social relations, offering the objective possibility of living more easily in the spirit of the Gospels and of observing the Ten Commandments" (p. 692). For Boff, the visit suggested the possibility of a different society, "more social and less unequal and based on a popular democracy in which the organized people will be the grand historic subject of the construction of society. . . . The visit to the Soviet Union helped us think of the ways of the Kingdom of God in history, a society very different from our own" (p. 698).

What would that popular democracy look like? Evidently the social guarantees that he admired in the Soviet Union would take priority over "liberal" rights of the individual. He and his brother had written a year earlier,

> The so-called modern liberties . . . such as freedom of expression, conscience, organization, religion, have benefited privileged groups in society, leaving the great mass of the people hoping for liberation from hunger, unemployment, lack of housing and education. It is starting from these fundamental liberties that the other liberties must be integrated and achieved by all. [*Paginas,* vol. xi, no. 79, September 1986, supplement, p. 4]

Does this mean that one must wait until everyone has housing, education, health, and a job, before basic freedoms of conscience and expression will be permitted? The Boffs do not tell us.

Other liberation theologians, however, are more clearly committed to the revival of democracy in Latin America. In 1986, a journal edited by Michael Novak published a paper by Hugo Assmann, often regarded as one of the most extreme of the liberation theologians on the question of the necessity of revolution. He now expressed his preference for democratic institutions as the way to achieve liberation. Asserting that the members of the Latin American left recognize that they "must now reestablish their organic relation to the popular majorities which never understood their abstract revolutionism," and that Latin America is dominated by "an absolutely savage and inhuman form of socialism . . . no socialism exists presently or around the corner," Assmann insisted that "Real revolutionaries have learned to value democratic participation and the authentically popular movements [and they] are no longer interested in chaotic social explosions." Instead of the Manichean dualism of "certain leftist circles" that "engage" in "divinization or demonization," it is time to develop "a spirit of openness to negotiate minimal consensus."[15]

Assmann thus seems to be both retaining the structuralism of which we have spoken and adding a commitment to democracy and individual freedom, as well as a willingness to develop a minimal consensus in support of democracy, rather than continually looking for what he calls "guilt agents."

A similar commitment to democracy is evident in the Final Document of the Latin American Theologians presented at the Second General Assembly of the Ecumenical Association of Third World Theologians, held in Mexico in December 1986. The beginning of the document describes as the first current challenge for liberation theologians "forging a new democracy with the participation of the majorities," and it notes that there is now a new positive evaluation of democracy on the part of the popular sectors "considered as a space in which they can carry out [*conjugar*] various popular projects" (*Revista Latinoamericana de Teologia,* San Salvador, September–December 1986, p. 305). The new democracy is to have a "prophetic" character, and will be different from "the bourgeois order of the representative and liberal type," although in what way is not clear except that it will be characterized by much broader popular participation and a greater focus on the needs of the poor.

What seems to have happened in the case of nearly all the liberation theologians is that as a result both of the attacks to which they have been subjected by their critics, and of the changes in the historical context in which they are writing in Latin America and elsewhere (for example, Poland, Afghanistan, and China), they are now adopting a more open attitude toward the possibilities of establishing an effective democracy in Latin America. They have also left behind much of the Marxist baggage with which the movement was encumbered in the early 1970s. While hardly more favorable to capitalism than they were at that time, they are willing to make use of the mechanisms of political democracy to moderate and restrain its excesses. Participation by the Ecclesial Base Communities has replaced the abstract call for abolition of capitalism and denunciations of bourgeois democracy of the earlier period, because, in Assmann's words, "Democratic values are revolutionary values."[16]

Liberation theology does seem to have reached a new stage. It has abandoned most of the revolutionary rhetoric of the earlier period, concentrating on biblical and participatory themes, and appealing to what is now a mainstream element in official social teaching of the church—the preferential love for the poor. Even in the area of ecclesiology, the liberation theologians continue to insist on the importance of remaining in communion with the church hierarchy, although they criticize its pretensions to total control. The notion that the liberation theologians are *The Heralds of a New Reformation in Latin America* (the title of a book by Richard Shaull, published by Orbis Books in 1984) is an exaggeration.

10

After Twenty Years: Liberation Theology Today

IN A SENSE, liberation theology is a product of the 1960s. It emerged in 1968—the year of the Medellín Bishops Conference—which was also the year of the Prague Spring, student quasi-revolutions in Paris and Mexico City, the siege of the Chicago Democratic Convention, the emergence of the New Left and Black Power movements, and takeovers of Columbia and other universities in the United States, Europe, and Latin America. But unlike most of the other movements of that era liberation theology has survived—and even flourished over the last two decades. One of the reasons for its survival was that it responded to deeply felt and widely accepted needs of the Latin American church. Another, however, was its ability to grow and creatively adapt to new circumstances. In this concluding chapter I would like to review that growth and adaptation, and to make what I hope will be positive criticisms and suggestions for its future development. I do this because I think liberation theology in one form or another will continue to be an important theological approach to the world, and because I share some—although not all—of its goals and purposes.

Changes in Liberation Theology since 1968

Gustavo Gutierrez, who more than anyone else has influenced the growth and changes in liberation theology, is ready to admit development but not fundamental shifts in his thinking. When he is making a new point it is often confirmed by a selected quotation from his first book, *A Theology of Liberation*. That his thinking has changed in important ways is apparent, however, when one compares the two articles, published respectively in 1970 and 1984, that follow as appendixes. Among those changes I would cite the following:

1. The most obvious change is from an infatuation with socialist revolution to a recognition that the poor are not going to be liberated by cataclysmic political transformations, but by organizational and personal activities in Base Communities. Accompanying this change has been an altered attitude toward the possibility and desirability of violence in the pursuit of social justice. The costs and likely consequences of revolution require, as Gutierrez and others recognize, a careful consideration of what the moral theologians call "proportionality," the relation of means to ends and good and bad effects in ways that the early liberationists were unwilling to admit. One no longer hears from the liberation theologians the easy justifications of the necessity of "counterviolence" against the presumed "institutionalized violence" of contemporary institutions. Gustavo Gutierrez may be overstating the traditionalism of the liberation theologians when he says that they simply accept and apply the teaching of St. Thomas Aquinas on the just war, but they no longer share the facile assumptions of the 1960s that nearly all institutions in Latin America were "structures of sin" (Medellín) that required revolutionary transformation. (Cuba was an exception since it had had its revolution.)

2. There is a more nuanced attitude toward Marxism. At the outset liberation theologians argued that theology should learn from social science. The dominant social analysis in the Latin American universities in the late 1960s was Marxist—although dependency analysis (on which Gutierrez and others also relied heavily) was also influential. From the beginning, the liberation theologians rejected the atheism and determinism of Marx. However, they were concerned with liberation from oppression and domination, and Marxism gave them a ready explanation of the source of oppression—capitalist exploitation and imperialism on the part of the capitalist powers, especially the United States. Anticapitalism remains as an element in nearly all liberationist writings, but more recently liberation theologians have recognized that there are other sources of oppression—sexual, political, racial, ethnic, and ecological. Still for most liberationists, capital-

ism remains the principal variety of sinful structure, although they are willing to admit that the historical examples of "real socialism" in the Marxist-Leninist governments of Eastern Europe and the Soviet Union cannot be viewed as genuine instances of liberation.

The liberation theologians accept Marx's critique of the ideological character of many contemporary ideas and institutions, and Leonardo Boff has used it to demythologize structures of authority in the church. Class struggle analysis is drawn on, but it is a struggle between rich and poor rather than bourgeoisie and proletariat. However, private ownership of the means of production is now less suspect. Recent statements by Gustavo Gutierrez, quoted in the last chapter, accept it as one of several coexisting economic arrangements. Hugo Assmann describes the initial capitalism-socialism dichotomous way of thinking as "an original sin of liberation theology that must be overcome." A recent work by a Brazilian liberation theologian, J. B. Libanio S.J., argues that "in place of socialism, liberation theology now speaks of an alternative to capitalism."[1] And, despite the accusation that the leaders or advisers of the Christian Base Communities use the concept of *conscientização* to indoctrinate and mobilize the poor, except for some statements in the writings of Juan Luis Segundo and Franz Hinkelammert, there is no evidence of a theological "vanguardism" of the Leninist variety on the part of the liberation theologians.

Most liberation theologians, however, continue to identify themselves as socialists. What that means, however, is not developed in their writings. There is no attempt to draw on current discussions as to the contemporary meaning of socialism. (See, for example, Norberto Bobbio, *Which Socialism? Marxism, Socialism, and Democracy,* Oxford: Polity Press, 1987; and Adam Przeworski, *Capitalism and Social Democracy,* New York: Cambridge University Press, 1985). It remains a utopian ideal of a cooperative equalitarian, non-exploitative social order—with the details to be filled in later. (The lack of a blueprint in Marx for the socialist society that was to follow the overthrow of capitalism enabled Joseph Stalin to create—in the name of socialism—one of the bloodiest tyrannies in world history.)

3. While liberation theologians still blame most of Latin America's ills on "dependent capitalism," some of them—Gutierrez, for example—are aware that the theory of dependence that also first emerged twenty years ago and was adopted by most liberation theologians has come in for considerable criticism since that time. The success, at least for a decade or so, of the OPEC cartel demonstrated

that *dependencia* does not always go in a single direction. And the debt crisis in which both debtors and lenders are painfully aware of their interdependence and mutual interest in maintaining the international economic system also raised questions about the one-way character of the original theory—even if more of the adverse consequences have been borne by the Third World debtors. Meanwhile, as Cuba's economic and military dependence on the Soviet Union became ever larger, with the total Soviet subsidy now estimated at $4 billion a year, it was difficult to describe *dependencia* as an exclusively capitalist phenomenon. On the other hand, the economic success of the capitalist economies on the rim of Asia, as well as that of Brazil before the high cost of imported oil took its toll, called into question the claim of the original dependence theorists that the consequences of dependent development are always negative. Conversely, the solution of the *dependentistas*—a socialist break with the capitalist world—looked less attractive when the models of socialism either seemed to be bankrupt, or were resorting to market incentives and private enterprise, even inviting multinational investment. Gustavo Gutierrez, in "Theology and the Social Sciences" (see Appendix II), argued that theology should be critical of all social theories, but the original force of the social criticism of liberation theology was considerably weakened when its principal instruments of "social analysis"—dependency and Marxism—were no longer considered adequate explanations of Latin American poverty and underdevelopment.

4. Liberation theology began as a revolt against "developmentalism," the optimistic view associated with the Alliance for Progress that economic development would solve, or at least considerably ameliorate, Latin America's social, economic, and political problems. Part of that criticism was also aimed at "bourgeois democracy" and at the Social Christian or Christian Democratic Parties, which were seen as, at worst, defenders of unjust social structures, or at best, incapable of achieving satisfactory solutions. Now, after two decades in which the fragile structures of democratic government were destroyed by brutally repressive military governments in most of Latin America, which in turn have yielded power to elected governments, the liberation theologians have learned from bitter experience ("praxis"?) the value of Assmann's "minimal consensus" or the Third World theologians' "space" for the popular majorities. The reformists—in particular, the Christian Democrats—are still criti-

cized, especially in Central America, where they are seen as "legiti-mizing a new system of domination,"[2] but the central importance of political democracy is now appreciated in ways that were not evident twenty years ago. Except in São Paulo, where in November 1988 it elected a woman mayor with strong ties to the Base Communities, the Workers Party (PT) in Brazil has not been able to create a nation-wide mass basis out of the Base Communities structures but it has be-come an important element in the Brazilian party spectrum. The church and Base Community support have kept agrarian reform as a central issue in Brazilian politics. In Chile, the liberation groups have recognized the need for cooperation with the center and the right against the Pinochet dictatorship even if it means the return of 1960s-style reformism of the Christian Democrats (which the polls now show was the most popular government in recent Chilean history). If praxis means more than a refusal to set out conditions of action in advance, it means that one can learn from experience. Such a learn-ing process seems to have begun, leading to a more positive attitude to the value of democratic participation, balance, and accommoda-tion—however remote such a process is from the revolutionary trans-formation desired by the liberationists.

5. At no point did the liberation theologians reject the hierarchical structure of the church. However, at the outset their criticism of the involvement of the church in socioeconomic structures of oppression, and their advocacy of a "popular church"—based on the poor—seemed to challenge the Catholic tradition. Several liberation theo-logians had problems with the Vatican that we have described in earlier chapters. The result of those difficulties, however, was to re-affirm the adherence of the liberation writers to a belief in a highly decentralized but still hierarchical church. They obeyed Rome; ac-cepted, at least verbally, many of the Vatican's criticisms and cen-sures; and reaffirmed their belief in traditional church dogmas such as the Eucharist, the divinity of Christ, the Trinity, and veneration of the Virgin Mary. While they challenged the position of women in the church, there was no public questioning of the Church's position on birth control, abortion, even divorce—of the type that has been voiced frequently in Europe and the United States. It is true that some of the early criticisms by Gutierrez of the excessive dualism of Catholic moral theology, or by Juan Luis Segundo of the church's attempt to develop deductive ethics may sound dangerously close to a "situation ethics" that refuses to develop standards of moral or

political evaluation for fear that they will be too static or status quo oriented. On this issue, however, Clodovis Boff, for example, is clear. Praxis requires ethical mediation that will

> enrich it with its specific determinations, especially in the form of natural law. . . . We may not embrace the ideology of orthopraxis or praxiology, dispensing ourselves from a thorough reflection on the ethical content of a given practice. . . . Faith measures, criticizes, stimulates, and orients social transformation, which in turn, expresses, realizes, and verifies the truth of faith and its values.[3]

The moral teaching authority of the church (the *magisterium*) is not in question, only its application and interpretation where it has been removed from actual experience and distorted by power interests.

6. The final shift is more one of emphasis than of content—the greater emphasis on the spiritual sources and implications of the concept of liberation. At the outset there was indeed the tendency toward political reductionism noted by later critics. While Gutierrez in particular spoke of the necessity of a spirituality of liberation, and Assmann cited the differences from Marxism that resulted from his Christian belief, the dominant thrust of the sources, arguments, and implications of the period from 1968 to 1975 was political. The early books on liberation theology often had few biblical references and much Marxist or *dependentista* social science. This is much less true today; recent works by Gutierrez and others stress the rootedness of liberation theology in the Bible and in the experience of the poor. St. Bernard, Job, Mary's Magnificat, and Matthew's account of the last judgment (ch. 25) are the sources of reflection, rather than the European Marxists and theologians of the early works. This can be viewed as simply a defensive reaction against the attacks of recent years, but these are writings by priests and laypersons with theological training and interests, and it should not be surprising that they argue from religious sources—although those sources are less likely to be theological in the traditional sense than biblical and experiential.

Has liberation theology changed to the extent that it has been "coopted" by the status quo? What remains after twenty years, and how should it be evaluated? If the evidence set out in this book is correct, liberation theology still maintains much of its original radical thrust. It still sees the world as more characterized by conflict than compromise, inequality rather than equality, oppression rather than liberation. It maintains what was called at the beginning of this book its structural anticapitalism, its belief in the need to replace capitalist structures with those of a socialist inspiration. It also still retains its grass-roots populism—its belief in the special religious character of the poor both as the object of God's particular love and the source of religious insights. Finally, it is still as suspicious of the liberal tradition in politics and philosophy, and of the social doctrine of the church insofar as this is seen as a disguised form of liberalism.

Since this is a concluding chapter, I should state clearly where I stand on these issues. I endorse the effort to develop a radical socio-economic critique of the status quo from the Catholic and biblical tradition but I have problems with aspects of each of these views. Specifically, I believe that the liberation theologians are wrong in holding (a) that the primary source of oppression is capitalism and of liberation is socialism, (b) that the poor have a superior insight into religious truth, and (c) that liberalism is to be rejected by biblically oriented Christians.

The Cause and Cure of Poverty in Latin America

The identification of capitalism as the primary obstacle to liberation can be explained in terms of the currents dominant in Latin American thought in the 1960s—particularly among students, intellectuals, and certain sectors of the church. Gustavo Gutierrez has been quoted earlier as saying that he made three discoveries after his return from his European studies—that it was necessary to fight against poverty, that the poor were an identifiable class, and that "poverty was not accidental . . . not just a matter of chance, but the result of a structure."[4]

In the 1960s the search for the structural causes of underdevelopment was a common theme in Latin American social science. At the Medellín Conference, that search was reflected in its passages about "structures of sin." When theologians suddenly became aware that poverty was not inevitable but had causes, they were likely to find in the social sciences in Latin America a blend of Marxist-influenced sociology and economics in the Latin American universities and the structuralist economics of the United Nations Economic Commission for Latin America (CEPAL) in Santiago. The dominant Marxist currents in Latin American sociology rejected the status quo orientation that they saw in contemporary American and European functionalist and systemic approaches to sociology. They identified domestic exploitation (the low level of wages, especially in the countryside, and the concentration of income in the upper classes) as the product of domestic and international capitalism. The CEPAL economists blamed the lack of progress in Latin America on its dependence on the developed world, especially the United States, citing the increasing dominance of multinational corporations, Latin America's military links with the United States through the Rio Treaty, and the cultural orientation of Latin American elites to Europe and North America. Some argued that an improvement in bargaining strength through economic integration, and nationalization of mineral and other resources was the solution, but for most dependence theorists the remedy was to break the links with the capitalist world through a socialist revolution of the Cuban variety. This is what the liberation theologians learned when they consulted Latin American social scientists. The cause of Latin American poverty is dependent capitalism, and the solution is a socialist revolution. Were they right?

The history of the last twenty years and the debates described in this book provide at least a partial answer. There have been many examples of sinful structures in that period—brutal military regimes that slaughtered thousands of innocent people in Argentina, Chile, Guatemala, Nicaragua, and El Salvador, for example. Some of those regimes were supported by domestic and international capitalists, but it is a vast oversimplification to explain the military interventions in those countries as simply the product of dependent capitalism. More often the military were defending their own corporate existence against inflation, chaos, and—yes—a threat from the left. But during the last twenty years, there have been enough examples of noncapitalist ruling elites, whether domestic or international, defending themselves by repression in Poland, Afghanistan, Burma, Ethiopia, China, and Cuba to raise doubts that the principal obstacle to liberation is always capitalism. In addition, the emergence of other liberation movements involving women, racial minorities, and ethnics, as well as those concerned with sexual and psychological liberation, indicated that economics was not the only source of oppression and alienation.

The liberation theologians never did spell out in detail the mechanisms through which capitalism *causes* poverty. They did not resort directly to Marx's explanation—namely, the alienation by the capitalist of surplus value—the amount of the labor value added by workers beyond what was necessary to keep them and their families alive. More often the mere *existence* of large-scale poverty in Latin America was taken to prove that the system is unjust. There *must* be something wrong with a system that allows the majority of the people to live in squalor and poverty while a small minority enjoys all the luxuries of the modern world. As a recent liberation theologian in the Orbis series argues, because economic inequality exists in a world in which there is hunger and poverty, "The logic of capitalism clearly collides with the biblical logic of the majorities. . . . The values, assumptions, and workings of the capitalist system are so hostile to biblical values that capitalism must be judged a fatally flawed system."[5]

There is no doubt that tension exists between the pursuit of profit as an operational goal in capitalism, and the pursuit of righteousness in the eyes of God, as the aim of the Christian message. However, if the market is operating competitively (often a big "if" in Latin America), this does not mean that profit is immoral. As economists have told us, it is a measure of efficiency, and an incentive to make the economic system work. This does not mean that the pursuit of profit is to become the world view of the rational economic actor, but that in this particular area—the market—a game is played according to certain rules that will benefit the whole society. When the invisible hand does not operate to harmonize individual and social ends, government can intervene to correct market failures—monopoly, pollution, lack of bargaining power of labor, false advertising, and so on. Similarly when the adjustment of the system to innovation produces social imbalances, government can and should act to ease the transition ("the safety net," job retraining, tax incentives for decentralization, and so forth). Development often increases inequality in relative—although usually not in absolute—terms, as many income distribution studies have shown, but this is usually followed later by a decline in inequality and the growth of a middle class as urbanization, industrialization, and often democratization proceeds.

We need not engage in biblical exegesis on the relation of Christianity and capitalism. Even capitalists can quote the Bible to their own advantage, and the Parable of the Talents in Luke 19 has been interpreted to endorse investment and profit.[6] There are some economic activities that are unethical and/or illegal, but if those constraints are observed, the pursuit of profit is not in and of itself unchristian—despite medieval Christian views on the sin of usury, which were based primarily on a faulty analysis by Aristotle of the nature of investment. Where the market or its failure produces results that offend the moral sense of the community, democratic procedures can produce a law to forbid such conduct or to support a more equitable distribution of profit. But it is not the workings of capitalism that are the *cause* of poverty: *Properly regulated,* they can help to cure it.

Instead of directing their wrath at capitalism, the liberation theologians should—and now are beginning to—direct more attention to promoting a genuine participatory democracy that will work to restrain the excesses of economic power, whether capitalist or socialist. They should work to expose the behind-the-scenes manipulation and corruption that characterize both capitalist and socialist governments, and to assure that the voice of the poor is heard—in the press, in the media, and in the halls of government—rather than simply writing off all existing capitalist systems as structures of sin.

In the market economies of Europe, the United States, Japan, and the rim of Asia, economic growth has enabled the government and private groups and individuals to provide access to health, education, culture, and employment that were unknown in earlier periods. And there is ample evidence today that it is not imperialist exploitation that was responsible for most of that improvement but technology, organization, and expanded markets.[7]

It is true that some, mainly Marxist socialist states have launched a frontal attack on poverty by providing jobs, education, health care, and social security to broader sectors of the population than all but the most advanced capitalist states. However, it seems that this has been done at the cost of both economic efficiency and political liberty, and that when as in recent years they attempt to provide more economic incentives, this may threaten both political control and economic equality. Perhaps the changes in China and the Soviet Union may ultimately lead to a mixed regime that combines social justice, economic efficiency, and political democracy, but so far, no socialist system has been able to achieve that combination.

The problem is not capitalism. It is what Charles Lindblum called, in his book of the same name, politics and markets (New Haven: Yale University Press, 1978)—how to combine the efficiency of the market system with the equity of the welfare state. It is not obvious that utopian references to socialism provide an answer. In this book, only José Comblin has made a serious effort to spell out the details of a humanistic democratic socialism with a decentralized economic system based on cooperatives and a tax and investment policy that favors the poor. For the others it is enough to know that capitalism is the root of all evil, and to endorse a vague utopian socialism that will abolish it.

Alec Nove, an English economist and specialist on Eastern Europe, has written on *The Economics of a Feasible Socialism* (London: Allen and Unwin, 1983). For Nove a genuinely noncapitalist but democratic system would involve opting out of the capitalist-dominated international economic system in a way similar to that pursued by Burma over the last twenty-five years. A price would be paid (and has been paid in the Burmese case) in lack of access to markets, technology, and capital, but this would avoid large concentrations of income and property, and permit democratic decision-making on major economic policies, as well as an orientation of government policy toward the needs of the poor. (Neither has happened in Burma.) Nove warns, however, that the experience of many Third World experiments with government efforts in this direction through agrarian reform, price controls, subsidies for basic foods and necessities, and wage increases for the lowest income groups has led to inflation, black markets, and steep declines in agricultural and industrial production. If the socialism that the liberation theologians espouse leads to a collapse in the economy, are they in fact exercising "the preferential option for the poor"?

Why is there no discussion by liberation theologians of the mixed economy and the welfare state as alternatives to both "unbridled" capitalism and collectivist socialism? Perhaps this is so because the welfare-state oriented Christian Democratic parties and the Catholic social doctrine against which the liberation theologians were reacting in the late 1960s used a type of "third position" terminology that the liberation theologians saw as a "naive reformism" and an ideological justification for capitalism. Yet without engaging in a Reaganite apology for "the magic of the market," it does seem that the experience of the last twenty years in many Latin American countries indicates that in order to redistribute, it is necessary first to produce a redistributable surplus, that state enterprises and bureaucracies are notoriously unproductive and economically inefficient in achieving that goal,[8] and even that worker cooperatives need very special conditions to succeed economically.[9] Is it necessary, however, to give special privileges to private investors in order to coax them into providing the capital for a healthy economy, as Lindblum has maintained? Or could a functioning and productive economy be based on social recognition and public esteem rather than private greed, as Joseph Carens has argued in *Equality, Moral Incentives, and the Market* (Chicago: University of Chicago Press, 1981)? How far can the public regulation and democratic participation in economic decision-making advocated by democratic socialists like Michael Harrington (*Socialism, Past and Future,* New York: Arcade, 1989) be extended without undermining the incentives and structures necessary for technological innovation, and the "bottom-line" mentality that produces economic efficiency?

These questions are raised only to demonstrate that there is no clear consensus among social scientists on the best way to implement the preferential option for the poor (and this is without getting into specifics such as the negative income tax, food stamps, employment training, and so on that are the central themes in discussions of anti-poverty programs in this country). Lacking such a clear consensus one may ask, then, why the liberation theologians continue to argue—or more accurately, to assume—that "social analysis" demonstrates that capitalism is *the* cause of Latin American poverty, and that socialism is *the* cure.

The Religious Role of the Poor

One of the great innovations of liberation theology was invented before it was ever heard of—the Ecclesial Base Community. As a result of the ideological response of the Brazilian left to the concentration of elite power, and a practical response of the Brazilian church and later those of other Latin American churches to the lack of clergy, there emerged a structure that was new for Roman Catholicism—small Bible-study groups that attempted to relate the Word to their everyday experience. Around those structures grew a mystique, a number of mass movements, and a large literature, much of it by liberation theologians. The theologians saw the Base Communities as the basis of a new church ("ecclesiogenesis") that would right the imbalance of authority in Roman Catholicism, and even as the basis for the political and social transformation of Latin American societies. The link between decentralization of the church and political transformation was that the Base Communities were supposed to be composed of the poor and the oppressed, and they were to be agents of their own spiritual *and political* liberation. By the end of this process, "the preferential option for the poor" had been interpreted in terms of a quasi-class alignment, with the poor against the rich. This led the Vatican to substitute the phrase "preferential love or love of preference for the poor." The more sophisticated liberation theologians such as Gustavo Gutierrez also broadened the concept of the poor to include all the oppressed and excluded, as well as those who identify with them, but the conflictual model adopted at the outset still created problems. In the case of the Base Communities, the issue was whether they would be limited to the poor and their supporters, or whether members of the middle or upper classes would be allowed to form Base Communities and to interpret *their* experience in the light of the Bible. If Christianity was open to all and called all to conversion, why the differential in favor of one group?

One critic of liberation theology accused it of going even further in its adulation of the poor. James Burtchaell ("How Authentically Christian Is Liberation Theology?" *The Review of Politics* (50), 2, Spring 1988, 264–81) quotes passages from Gustavo Gutierrez's *The Power of the Poor in History* (Maryknoll, NY: Orbis Books, 1983) asserting that "God loves the poor with a special love because they are poor and not necessarily because they are good" (p. 116, see also p. 140) to argue that the liberation theologians believe that the Gospel does not call the poor to conversion because "their miseries have exempted them from the struggle between sin and grace" (p. 271). This may be something of an overstatement, but it is true that liberation theologians have exaggerated the special status of the poor, both as the preferred source of religious insight and the agents of liberation.

The Bible is full of critical statements about the rich, and promises of liberation for the poor. We need only think of the initial statement of Christ's purpose in Luke 4:18, preaching the good news to the poor; Mary's praise of God in her hymn, the Magnificat (Luke 1:53), "He has filled the hungry with good things, the rich he has sent away empty"; the consignment of the rich man to hell while Lazarus is in Abraham's bosom (Luke 17:22ff.); and the comparison of the camel and the eye of a needle with the chances of the rich gaining heaven (Luke 18:25). But having a special concern for the poor and a recognition of God's love for them and of the value of their acting in community to apply the Bible to their own lives is different from making them a privileged source of religious truth, and consigning the nonpoor to the status of class enemies who must be overcome. Christ's message was to rich and poor alike; both are the objects of his love and both need to be converted. Likewise in the church, there is a role for the religious insights of the poor, but there is also a role for the community as a whole, and in the case of Roman Catholicism, for the hierarchy as keepers and interpreters of the tradition.

There is also a place for private property—not as the object of individual greed and selfishness but as the most efficient and effective way to provide the economic growth that makes it possible to act against poverty, through the creation of new jobs, technological innovation, and tax revenues to finance welfare programs, education, health, and care for the elderly, the sick, and the disabled. The middle class, the wealthy, and the innovative entrepreneur have a role other than that of class enemies if we are to exercise the preferential option for the poor. To degrade their religious status and indeed threaten their very existence is not an effective way to carry out that option—as the experience of Chile under Allende between 1970 and 1973 demonstrated.

Allende terrified the relatively large middle class in Chile when he said, contrasting his view of his office with that of his Christian Democratic predecessor, "I am not president of all Chileans." Seeking to expand his base among the poor by class appeals he succeeded in creating much more intense middle- and upper-class opposition against him than lower-class support, polarizing the country to the point that the military felt that it had majority support—the March 1973 election had resulted in a 56 percent to 43 percent vote against Allende—for the coup in September 1973 that ended democracy in Chile.[10]

Liberation Theology and Liberalism

Liberation theology began as a reaction against reformist liberalism and modernization, which were seen as inadequate responses to the problem of poverty in Latin America. Twenty years later, however, that response looks like an overreaction. There is a difference between criticism of the direction of programs and policies, and totalistic rejection—and the latter was the explicit initial thrust of liberation theology. In many other areas, liberation theology has modified its position. Now it is time for it to rethink its opposition to liberalism, especially as expressed in the institutions of constitutional democracy. In the past, liberation theology has described liberal democracy with such terms as *fraudulent* and *a lie,* arguing that constitutions, political parties, and elected governments were responsive to the powerful and the wealthy rather than the poor. Earlier, the very word *liberalism* in the Catholic tradition had been identified with a rampant free enterprise system, rather than with political freedom and individual rights. By the 1960s, however, in such documents as *Pacem in Terris* (1963) of Pope John XXIII and *Gaudium et Spes* (1965), the Declaration of the Second Vatican Council on the Church in the Modern World, support for democracy and human rights were incorporated into the mainstream of Catholic teaching without the word *liberalism* being used to describe what was taking place. Yet for the Anglo-Saxon world, and increasingly in Western Europe, modern liberalism involves a commitment to human rights, the rule of law, and equality of opportunity, as well as a government role in responding to basic needs of housing, employment, health, and "a safety net" against sudden catastrophes.

This is an argument, therefore, for more awareness on the part of the liberation theologians of the nature of contemporary liberal thought—including its concern for equality and for the disadvantaged. It is also a plea for the incorporation within liberationist thinking of a more explicit concern for legal guarantees and human rights as they are articulated in the liberal tradition.

To show how ignorant contemporary writers on liberation theology are of current liberal theory one need only look at *Liberation Theology,* an introductory survey by Philip Berryman (New York: Pantheon, 1987). Chapter 7, subtitled "A Critical Vision of Human Rights," describes "the Western liberal definition of human rights with its individualistic thrust," as "a trap" and asserts that liberation theologians believe that "one should not speak simply of 'human rights' in general but of 'the rights of the majorities' or the 'rights of the poor'" since this is "closer to the Bible's image of a God who sides with the poor against their oppressors." Moreover, as we have seen earlier in this book, "some rights are prior to others" especially "the right to life, and consequently the right to the means of life that is employment and land." Berryman summarizes these theologians' views as rejecting "the Western notion of human rights . . . which could easily become an ideology masking the daily suffering and death of the poor majority" and arguing for "a new language about human rights" that would "express the subsistence rights of the poor majority of humankind, including their collective rights as peoples" (pp. 116–18).

There are serious problems with this formulation. In the first place, contemporary liberalism is not nearly as individualistic as the liberation theologians believe. In practice, it has led to the expansion of the welfare state in Britain and America in ways that, however controversial their results, have been aimed at helping the poor and marginalized. Many contemporary liberals support government welfare programs financed by progressive taxes, arguing that basic human needs must be satisfied as a condition for the effective exercise of freedom. In the case of the best-known contemporary liberal theorist, John Rawls (*A Theory of Justice,* Cambridge, MA: Harvard University Press, 1971), a central feature of his theory is the "difference principle," which evaluates political and economic systems in terms of their effects on the "least-advantaged." (Note, however, that Rawls' difference principle defers to "the principle of equal liberty" as a priority, while the liberationists do not do so.) Rawls's theory can lead to quite broad-ranging public policies that amount to a "preferential option for the poor," but it is an indication of the ignorance of contemporary liberal thought on the part of liberation theologians (and, one might add, of the Vatican as well) that the liberalism that appears in their writings equates it with the theories of Adam Smith and Herbert Spencer.

There is a second problem with the liberationist critique of liberal rights theories. Suspicious of "bourgeois" legalism and "individualistic" rights, the liberationists may allow the fabric of the rule of law and constitutional guarantees to be destroyed in the name of the "logic of the majority" by a populist or Marxist-Leninist *caudillo* or elite, leaving the individual dissenter or the opposition party without protection or recourse. To be effective, democracy must include the right of the minority to express effective dissent against those who claim to speak for the people or for the poor and the oppressed. When that right is removed, even by a populist regime (such as that of Perón in Argentina), the ultimate recourse is to force—and, as

Hobbes once said, "when no other cards are agreed upon, clubs are trumps." And it is not usually the poor who have the necessary instruments of coercion to win such a contest.

It is true that national uprisings against unpopular and repressive regimes in Cuba and Nicaragua brought leftist leaders to power with control over the instruments of coercion. However, in most other cases—the urban guerrillas in Brazil of the late 1960s, the Movement of the Revolutionary Left (MIR) in Chile, the Tuparamos in Uruguay, and the Montoneros in Argentina—the result of revolutionary guerrilla activity was to polarize society and to bring the military and the technocrats to power with policies that were far more destructive to the welfare of the poor than those of the "bourgeois" democracies that preceded them.

Recognizing the counterproductive character of much of the revolutionary fervor of the late 1960s, Gustavo Gutierrez now argues that liberation theology accepts the traditional "just war" doctrine of St. Thomas governing the permissibility of the use of violence. Yet he cannot disguise his admiration, even enthusiasm, for the Christian guerrillas in Somoza's Nicaragua—as well as for the nonviolent approach of Archbishop Romero in El Salvador (*We Drink From Our Own Wells*, Maryknoll, NY: Orbis Books, 1984, chs. 9–10).

The basic issue is the relation of liberal democracy to property rights. However liberalism from the outset (for example, Locke's *Second Treatise of Civil Government*) recognized the right of the majority to limit private property by taxation for common purposes and legal procedures such as eminent domain. (In section 47 of the *First Treatise* Locke went even further, arguing that there was an enforceable right of the starving person to the surplus property of those with more resources. He derived that right from the divine command that man preserve himself, a Lockean—and medieval scholastic—version of the right to "the means of life" discussed by Berryman.)

Liberation theology and Catholic social thought in general give more explicit attention to the "social function of property" than do liberals. However, contemporary liberal thinkers such as Rawls, welfare state liberals of the late nineteenth century such as T. H. Green, and even the classical expressions of political liberalism such as the writings of John Locke and John Stuart Mill do not erect private property into the absolute right that appears in the liberationist critique of liberalism. There are differences of emphasis in the value placed on individual economic and political freedom, and there is a difference of degree in their attitude toward social conflict and domination,[11] and while these differences probably distinguish liberalism and radicalism from one another more generally, it is simply not true that liberalism and laissez-faire free enterprise are synonymous, as the liberationists seem to think. Political liberals believe in equality, majority rule and minority rights, restraints on power, and due process; liberation theologians believe in the logic of the majorities and an end to domination by the rich and powerful. What I am suggesting is that constitutionalism and due process are also a form of liberation—"those wise restraints that make men free"—and that liberation theology should recognize this.

Many liberals accept aspects of the Marxist critique of capitalism. It is difficult, since Marx wrote, not to be aware of the importance of class differences, particularly in less developed countries. Marx has also made us aware of the reality of economic power behind the facade of liberal democracy, and the ideological justifications for existing socioeconomic arrangements. Modern democracies have also recognized the need for trade unions and legislation to counterbalance the stronger bargaining position of employers in arriving at the wage contract. But if this is what the liberation theologians mean by using Marxist tools of analysis, it is a use that is employed by most intelligent social critics. What is not accepted and what has created problems for the liberation theologians is Marxism's reduction of all social ills to the capitalist nature of the underlying mode of production, its emphasis on structural conflict to the point that it seems that only violence will resolve it, its utopianism about the possibility of transforming human nature through changes in socioeconomic structures, and, for religious believers, its denial of God. For purposes of the central thesis of this book, a further criticism would be Marx's rejection of the importance of representative democracy and constitutional guarantees of rights.[12]

This is not to argue that the liberation theologians should become liberals. They will and should continue to criticize structures that dominate, exploit, or oppress the poor. It is only to insist that the structural critique should incorporate a recognition of the value of democracy, individual and social rights, and the rule of law. It is also to suggest that there are many kinds of radicalism—not only the Marxist variety. There are democratic socialists, there are anarchists, there are pacifists, and there are grass-roots populists—and there is a radicalized form of liberalism that insists that fundamental structural changes are necessary if human beings are to be free.

This book has argued for a movement away from Marxist reductionism to communitarian participatory radicalism in the development of liberation theology over the last twenty years. The next step, I would suggest, is a dialogue with liberalism (and its somewhat more "communitarian" religious counterpart, Christian Democracy) to identify areas of common agreement, including democracy and human rights, and areas where the more prophetic criticism of the liberationists still differs from the liberals. That dialogue would recognize, as the early liberation theologians did not, the need for pluralism in the derivation of proximate political and economic solutions from a common faith (a return of the "two planes"?).

The dialogue could also include representatives of the recent wave of "communitarian" critics of Anglo-American liberalism, some of whose views resemble those of the liberationists. Michael Sandel, Alasdair MacIntyre, Michael Walzer, and Roberto Unger criticize classical and contemporary liberals for their absence of a shared conception of the good, their unrealistic view of the person, and their effort to derive ideas of community from an artificial contract that bears no relationship to actual experience. The communitarians do not always share the liberation theologians' commitment to the poor, but they stress the social and community basis of political life in ways that resemble the arguments of the liberation writers—although with a somewhat greater emphasis on shared values and traditions. (The liberation theologians are more likely to stress the shared values and traditions of the poor and the oppressed.) As did the liberation theologians, however, the communitarians set up an egoistic and individualistic caricature of liberalism, and fail to recognize the moral elements in liberal theory, from Locke's natural law through Mill's revisionist utilitarianism to Rawls' reflective equilibrium.[13]

As do the communitarians, the liberationists force the liberals to rethink their easy assumptions about formal democracy, the rule of law, and property rights—and to look more deeply at the actual operation of liberal democracy to see if it is in fact promoting liberty and equality effectively. They also may persuade the liberals to accept the political and human fact that most people, even in the modern world, base their politics on religious or quasi-religious assumptions. In the case of Latin America, for a sector of those influenced by the Catholic tradition, those assumptions lead to conclusions that make them suspicious of the individualism, relativism, and hedonism of those who interpret liberalism as an endorsement of selfishness and the pursuit of profit in disregard of moral constraints. If this misinterprets the views of the welfare state liberals, it still applies to a significant sector (for instance, the "yuppies") of those influenced by modern capitalism. And at a time when American liberals have lost the optimistic outlook of the 1960s' war on poverty, the liberation theologians remind them that the issue is still an important one, both in the United States and Latin America.

Conclusions and Questions

By the standard that the theologians themselves set—the preferential option for the poor—liberation theology has some major accomplishments but some serious failings. Its accomplishments include committing the Latin American church to the defense of the poor and oppressed, reasserting the biblical critique of the wealthy, promoting reflection on the Bible at the local level, and giving a sense of dignity, self-respect, and efficaciousness to thousands of the poor and marginalized in Latin America. It has trained some of the leaders of the new democracy in Brazil, encouraged grass-roots community action in many Latin American countries, and continually pressed for policies that support the struggles of the poor. On the negative side, in its early stages, it also promoted a mindless revolutionism and continues to support—although critically in most cases—Castro, the Sandinistas, and the Marxist-dominated opposition in El Salvador. It is ignorant of contemporary liberal thought and has a close-minded attitude about the market system and the possibilities of reform of Latin American capitalism. The same close-mindedness was also evident at an earlier point in its attitude to "bourgeois" democracy, but here there are signs of a change, which is related to a shift in their thinking from a view of the poor as the social base for the overthrow of capitalism to a concern with their empowerment and participation to make democracy effective. But except in Brazil and perhaps in Central America, the Base Communities are small and not politically active. The specter of a continent-wide revolutionary movement fuelled by an alliance of Marxists and liberation theologians, as cited by Latin American and American conservatives, is no longer persuasive, but neither is the likelihood of a continent-wide grass-roots democracy movement based on the Basic Ecclesial Communities.

Is liberation theology reformist or revolutionary? In politics it is undecided between grass-roots communitarian democracy and the revolutionary transformation of society to create "the new man." In economics it is still committed to replacing capitalism with an alternative system, usually described as socialism, although it is less sanguine about this possibility. In the institutional church, it represents reform and a reorientation toward the Base Communities, rather than replacement of the hierarchy by the popular church. In theology the mainstream of the Catholic church has accepted central elements of its message—the Christian Base Communities, the preferential option (which is to be "nonexclusive" or reformulated as "preferential love") for the poor, and the application of the Bible to daily experience. Gutierrez's most recent writings are, rather than a radically new theology, more a series of meditations or sermons on the meaning of God as revealed in the Bible in relation to human suffering and oppression.

Liberation theology may have lost some of its early revolutionary fervor and its emphasis may have shifted from the class struggle to solidarity with the poor and oppressed, but it still can exercise a radical "prophetic" role in reminding complacent elites of the religious obligation of social solidarity, and in combatting oppression and promoting the empowerment of the poor. In the past, it has been mainly Protestant Christianity that has provided a radical critique of social and economic structures. Now Roman Catholicism has broadened the range of political perspectives that can be developed out of its tradition, to include a biblically based radicalism.[14]

Liberation theology has shown itself responsive to dialogue and to experience. In the spirit of that dialogue, and keeping in mind the experience of the last two decades, we may conclude by suggesting a number of questions that might be topics for a discussion between a social scientist committed both to the values of Christianity and to modern reformist liberalism, and a liberation theologian concerned to learn from social science how best to exercise the preferential option for the poor and oppressed:

1. Does theological reflection on the experience of the poor and oppressed always lead to the conclusion that capitalism must be re-

placed by a socialist system? If not, are there alternatives combining the efficiency of the market with the equity of the "preferential love for the poor"? If socialism is the alternative, what would an ideal socialist state look like?

2. What is the relation of private property and liberation? Is private property always to be viewed as an obstacle to liberation, or are there important ways—for instance, the small family farm or innovative new business—in which it can contribute to free people from oppression, whether by private interests or public authorities?

3. How can human rights—especially, but not only, the rights of the poor—be best promoted in the modern state? What is the place of courts, private groups, or the media in guaranteeing those rights? Does the dialectical approach that many liberation theologians employ make it conceptually difficult to develop a theory of rights? Does the preference for the poor imply a kind of "affirmative action" that may undermine the ideal of equal treatment under law?

4. What is liberation theology's attitude toward the redemocratization of Latin America? Is it to be rejected as "fraudulent," as was the case in the early 1970s? Can the fragile new democracies of Latin America promote participation and greater opportunity for the poor and oppressed, or is total socialist transformation—all or nothing—the only possibility? If so, what lessons in revolutionary *praxis,* in terms of its impact on the well-being of the poor, are to be drawn from the failure of the revolutionism of Latin America in the 1960s?

5. What is the "prophetic" role of the theologian? Is it only to remind the people of their moral duties to others, especially to the poor and oppressed? Or are there more specific criticisms, denunciations, and proposals that theologians can offer? Does the Bible in fact offer a blueprint for the good society? Are those liberation theologians who believe that it does so running the same risk of identifying a particular ideology with God's purposes in history that was run by the right-wing Catholic integralists and reformist Christian Democrats whom they denounce?

6. Finally, if the cure for the weaknesses and failures of democracy is more democracy, should not the liberation theologians devote their primary energies to developing a spirituality of socially concerned democracy, whether capitalist or socialist in its economic

form, rather than to denouncing dependency, imperialism, and capitalist exploitation? If those theories are inadequate explanations of poverty and underdevelopment ("the rich are not rich because the poor are poor"), should not the very considerable abilities of the liberation theologians be devoted now to promoting democratic participation, protecting human rights, and satisfying basic needs rather than to the sterile revolutionism that characterized their earlier writings?

It took the official Roman Catholic church a century and a half to recognize that democracy and freedom were central elements in the Christian message. It has taken only two decades for it to relate that message to human liberation. The secular left earlier defined liberation either as the overthrow of capitalism and the abolition of private ownership of the means of production (Marx), or as the extension of democracy and equality to all human beings, regardless of sex, race, or social class (Rousseau). Liberation theology will have to choose which it is to represent—democracy or revolution.

Appendix I

Notes for a Theology of Liberation (1970)*

GUSTAVO GUTIERREZ M., *Lima, Peru*

To get at the theological meaning of liberation, we first have to define our terms. That will make up the first part of this article. It will permit us to emphasize that in these pages we are particularly sensitive to the critical function of theory regarding the Church's presence and activity in the world. The principal fact about that presence today, especially in underdeveloped countries, is the participation by Christians in the struggle to construct a just and fraternal society in which men can live in dignity and be masters of their own destinies. We think that the word "development" does not well express those profound aspirations. "Liberation" seems more exact and richer in overtones; besides, it opens up a more fertile field for theological reflection.

The situation of Latin America, the only continent of underdeveloped and oppressed peoples who are in a majority Christians, is particularly interesting for us. An effort to describe and interpret the Church's ways of being present there will enable us to pose the fundamental question upon which we can then turn our theological reflection. That will make up the second part of this article.

This will permit us to see that asking the theological meaning of liberation is really asking the meaning of Christianity itself and the Church's mission. There used to be a time when the Church answered problems by calmly appealing to its doctrinal and vital reserves. Today,

* *Theological Studies* (31) 2, June 1970. Used by permission.

however, the gravity and scope of the process we call liberation is such that Christian belief and the Church itself are called radically in question. They are asked what right they have to address the mighty human task now before us. A few paragraphs will allow us to outline that problem, or rather to state, without attempting to answer them, the new questions.

Definitions

To approach this question properly, we should explain precisely what we mean by "theology" and by "liberation."

Theology

Theological reflection is inherent in the life of faith and the life of the Church. However, the focus of theological study has varied down through the history of the Church. That evolution has been accelerated in recent years.

Through the Church's history, theology has carried out various functions. Two stand out in particular. In the first centuries, what we today call theology was closely allied to the spiritual life. Primarily it dealt with a meditation on the Bible, geared toward spiritual progress. From the twelfth century on, theology began to be a science. The Aristotelian categories made it possible to speak of theology as a "subordinate science." This notion of science is ambiguous and does not satisfy the modern mind. But the essential in the work of St. Thomas is that theology is the fruit of the meeting between faith and reason. Perhaps we do better, then, to speak of a rational knowledge. In résumé, theology is necessarily spiritual and rational knowledge. These two elements are permanent and indispensable functions of all theological reflection.

Another function of theology has slowly developed and been accepted in recent years: theology as a critical reflection on the Church's pastoral action.

The renewed stress on charity as the center of the Christian life has brought us to see faith more biblically, as a commitment to God and neighbor. In this perspective the understanding of faith is likewise seen to be the understanding of a commitment, an attitude, a posture toward life, in the light of the revealed Word.

At the same time, the very life of the Church has become a *locus theologicus*. This was clear in the so-called "new theology," and has frequently been emphasized since then. God's word, which assembles us, is incarnated in the community of faith totally devoted to the service of all men.

Something similar happened with what has been called since Pope John and Vatican II a theology of the signs of the times. Let us not forget that the signs of the times are not only a call to intellectual analysis. They are, above all, a demand for action, for commitment, for service of others. "Scrutinizing" the signs of the times takes in both elements (*Gaudium et spes,* no. 44).

All these factors have brought us to rediscover and make explicit theology's function as a critical reflection on the Church's presence and activity in the world, in the light of revelation. By its preaching of the gospel message, by its sacraments, by the charity of its members, the Church announces and accepts the gift of the kingdom of God into the heart of human history. The Church is effective charity, it is action, it is commitment to the service of men.

Theology is reflection, a critical attitude. First comes the commitment to charity, to service. Theology comes "later." It is second. The Church's pastoral action is not arrived at as a conclusion from theological premises. Theology does not lead to pastoral activity, but is rather a reflection on it. Theology should find the Spirit present in it, inspiring the actions of the Christian community. The life of the Church will be for it a *locus theologicus*.

Reflecting on the Church's presence and activity in the world means being open to the world, listening to the questions asked in it, being attentive to the successive stages of its historical growth.[1] This task is indispensable. Reflection in the light of faith should always accompany the Church's pastoral efforts. Theology, by relativizing all its undertakings, keeps the Church from settling down into what is only provisory. Theology, by harking back to the sources of revelation, will guide action, setting it into a broader context, thus contributing to keep it from falling into activism and immediatism.

As reflection on the Church's activity, theology is a progressive and, in a certain sense, variable understanding. If the commitment of the Christian community takes on different forms down through history, the understanding that accompanies that commitment will constantly take a fresh look at it—and may then take suprising initiatives.

Theology, therefore, as a critical reflection on the Church's presence and action in the world, in the light of faith, not only complements the other two functions of theology (wisdom and rational knowledge) but even presupposes them.

Development or Liberation?

Today's world is going through a profound sociocultural transformation. Modern man has also become fully aware of the economic basis for that transformation. In the poor countries, where the immense majority of the world's population lives, the struggle for social change is being made with great urgency and is starting to become violent.

The term "development" does not seem to express well the yearning of contemporary men for more human living conditions. A basic problem is: the notion of development is not univocal; a considerable number of definitions are given. Instead of looking at them one by one, let us see the perspectives they start from.

First, development can be taken in a purely economic sense, as synonymous with *economic growth.* In that case, a country's develment will be measured, e.g., by comparing its GNP or its per capita income with those of some country assumed to have achieved a high level of development. This yardstick can be improved on and made more sophisticated, but the basic presumption will be that development is primarily an increase of wealth. Those who speak this way, explicitly at least, are few today.[2] Such a yardstick is used rather to contrast with other, more integral norms. One may still ask, however, if all the norms do not retain something of the capitalist concept of development.

The inadequacies of the purely economic yardstick have popularized another, more important and frequent today, which looks on development as a *global social process,* with economic, social, political, and cultural aspects. This strategy of development, keeping in view all these aspects, permits a people to make global progress and also avoid certain dangerous pitfalls.

Seeing development as a global social process involves, of necessity, ethical values, and that implies ultimately a concept of what man is. A detailed explicitation [sic] of such a *humanist perspective* in development takes time and extends, without contradicting it, the point of view just presented. Fr. L. J. Lebret strove constantly in that direction. For him, developmental economics is "the discipline covering the passage from a less human to a more human phase." The same notion is contained in that other definition of development: "having more in order to be more."[3] This humanistic view places the notion of development in a broader context: a historical vision, in which humanity takes charge of its own destiny. But that involves a change of perspective, which we prefer to call "liberation." That is what we shall try to explain in the following paragraphs.

In recent decades the term "development" has been used to express the aspirations of the poor nations. Of late, however, the term has seemed weak. In fact, today the term conveys a pejorative connotation, especially in Latin America.

There has been much discussion recently of development, of aid to the poor countries; there has even been an effort to weave a mystique around those words. Attempts to produce development in the 1950's aroused hopes. But because they did not hit the roots of the evil, they failed, and have led to deception, confusion, and frustration.

One of the most important causes of this situation is the fact that development, in its strictly economic, modernizing sense, was advanced by international agencies backed by the groups that control the world economy. The changes proposed avoided sedulously, therefore, attacking the powerful international economic interests and those of their natural allies: the national oligarchies. What is more, in many cases the alleged changes were only new and concealed ways to increase the power of the mighty economic groups.

Here is where conflict enters the picture. Development should attack the causes of our plight, and among the central ones is the economic, social, political, and cultural dependence of some peoples on others. The word "liberation," therefore, is more accurate and conveys better the human side of the problem.

Once we call the poor countries oppressed and dominated, the word "liberation" is appropriate. But there is also another, much more global and profound view of humanity's historical advance. Man begins to see himself as a creative subject; he seizes more and more the reins of his own destiny, directing it toward a society where he will be free of every kind of slavery.[4] Looking on history as the process of *man's emancipation* places the question of development in a broader context, a deeper and even a more radical one. This approach expresses better the aspiration of the poor peoples, who consider themselves primarily as oppressed. Thus the term "development" seems rather antiseptic, inaccurately applying to a tragic, tense reality. What is at stake, then, is a dynamic and historical concept of man as looking toward his future, doing things today to shape his tomorrow.[5]

This topic and this language are beginning to appear in certain actions of the magisterium. One isolated text of *The Development of Peoples,* e.g., speaks of "building a world where every man, regardless of race, religion, or nationality, can live a fully human life, free of the servitude that comes from other men and from the incompletely mastered world about him." The notion is more forcibly expressed in the *Message of Fifteen Bishops of the Third World,* published in reply to *The Development of Peoples.* The topic of liberation comes up frequently, almost as the leitmotif of the document, in another text of greater importance because of its doctrinal authority: in the Medellín *Guidelines.*

Liberation, therefore, seems to express better both the hopes of oppressed peoples and the fulness of a view in which man is seen not as a passive element, but as an agent of history. More profoundly, to see history as a process of man's liberation places the issue of desired social changes in a dynamic context. It also permits us to understand better the age we live in. Finally, the term "development" clouds up somewhat the theological issues latent in the process. To speak of liberation, on the other hand, is to hint at the biblical sources that illuminate man's presence and actions in history: the liberation from sin by Christ our Redeemer and bringing of new life.

In résumé, then, there are three levels of meaning to the term "liberation": the political liberation of oppressed peoples and social classes; man's liberation in the course of history; and liberation from sin as condition of a life of communion of all men with the Lord.

The Option Facing the Latin American Church

We have seen that one of theology's functions is to be a critical reflection on the Church's pastoral activity. The flow of history reveals unsuspected aspects of revelation, and the role of Christians in that history constitutes, we have said, a real *locus theologicus.* In this regard it may help to recall, on broad lines, the option or choice that important sectors of the Church are making in the only continent with a majority of its people Christian. Crucial and difficult problems connected with liberation face the Latin American Church.

The Process of Liberation in Latin America

After many years of genuine ignorance of what was going on, and after a brief moment of induced and artificial optimism, Latin America is now acquiring at least a partial, but more global and structural understanding of its situation. The most important change in the understanding of Latin America's reality lies in the fact that it is not a mere description, prescinding from the deep causes; rather, it gives particular attention to those causes and examines them in a historical perspective.

The decade of the 1950s was marked in Latin America by a great optimism in the possibilities of achieving economic development. The hope was based on a favorable historical moment and was theoretically expressed in a number of masterly economic studies. The developmental models popular in those years were the ones proposed by international agencies.[6]

For them, however, to develop meant imitating the processes followed by the more developed societies. The ideal imitated was the "modern society" or the "industrialized society." This approach was supposed to solve all the problems the underdeveloped countries were experiencing because they were "traditional societies." Thus underdeveloped countries were thought of as in some "prior stage" to that of the developed ones and as having to go through, more or less, the same historical experience they did in their progress to becoming modern societies. The result was some timid and, as later seen, misdirected efforts at change, which merely consolidated the existing economic system.[7]

In the 1960s a new attitude emerged. The developmental model has not produced the promised fruits. A pessimistic diagnostic has now replaced the former optimistic one.[8] Today we see clearly that the proposed model was an improper one. It was an abstract model, an ahistorical one, which kept us from seeing the complexity of the problem and the inevitably contradictory aspects of the proposed solution. The process of underdevelopment should be studied in historical perspective, i.e., contrasting it with the development of the great capitalist countries in whose sphere Latin America is situated.

Underdevelopment, as a global social fact, can be seen as the historical subproduct of the development of other countries.[9] The dynamics of capitalistic economics lead simultaneously to the creation of greater wealth for fewer, and of greater poverty for more. Our national oligarchies, teamed up in complicity with these centers of power, perpetuate, for their own benefit and through various subterfuges, a situation of domination within each country.[10] And the inequality between developed and underdeveloped countries is worse if we turn to the cultural point of view. The poor, dominated countries keep getting farther and farther behind. If things go on this way, we will soon be able to speak of two human groups, two kinds of men.[11]

All these studies lead us to conclude that Latin America cannot develop within the capitalistic system.

Labeling Latin America an oppressed and dominated continent brings us naturally to speak of liberation and to start acting accordingly. Indeed, this is a word that reveals a new conviction of Latin Americans.

The failure of the efforts at reform has accentuated this attitude. Today the most "conscientized" groups agree that there will be a true development for Latin America only through liberation from the domination by capitalist countries. That implies, of course, a showdown with their natural allies: our national oligarchies. Latin America will never get out of its plight except by a profound transformation, a social revolution that will radically change the conditions it lives in at present. Today, a more or less Marxist inspiration prevails among those groups and individuals who are raising the banner of the continent's liberation. And for many in our continent, this liberation will have to pass, sooner or later, through paths of violence. Indeed, we recognize that the armed struggle began some years ago. It is hard to weigh its possibilities in terms of political effectiveness. The reverses it has suffered have obliged it to rethink its program, but it would be naive to think that the armed struggle is over.

We must remember, however, that in this process of liberation there is, explicitly or implicitly, an added thrust. Achieving the liberation of the continent means more than just overcoming economic, social, and political dependence. It also means seeing that humanity is marching toward a society in which man will be free of every servitude and master of his own destiny.[12]

The Church in the Liberation Process

The Latin American Church has lived, and still does, largely in a ghetto state. Thus the Church has had to seek support from the established powers and the economically powerful groups, in order to carry out its task and, at times, face its enemies. But for some time now, we have been witnessing a mighty effort to end that ghetto situation and shake off the ambiguous protection offered by the upholders of the unjust order our continent lives in.

The pastoral goal of setting up a "new Christianity" has brought about a political commitment by many Christians to create a more just society. The lay apostolic movements, in particular those of youth, have given their best leaders in years gone by to the political parties of Social Christian inspiration. Today, however, the apostolic youth movements have gone more radical in their political stance. In most Latin American countries the militants no longer gravitate toward the Social Christian parties, or if they do, they become their more radical wing. The increasingly more revolutionary political postures of Christian groups frequently lead the lay apostolic movements into conflict with the hierarchy, open the question of where they fit into the Church, and cause serious conscience problems for them. In many cases the laymen's interest in social revolution is gradually displacing their interest in the kingdom.

Clearer notions about the continent's tragic plight, sharp breaks provoked by the political polarization, the trend toward more active participation in the Church's life as urged by the Council and Medellín—all of these have made the clergy (including religious) one of the most dynamic and restless segments of the Latin American Church. In many countries groups of priests have organized to channel and accentuate the growing restlessness. They call for radical changes in the Church's presence and activity. These activities, and other factors, have in a number of cases led to frictions with local bishops and nuncios. It seems probable that, unless radical changes take place, these conflicts will multiply and get even worse in coming years. Many priests, as well, feel bound in conscience to engage actively in the field of politics. And it happens frequently today in Latin America that priests are labeled "subversives." Many of them are watched or sought by the police. Others are in jail, are exiled, or are even assassinated by anticommunist terrorists.

These new and serious problems facing the Latin American Church cause conflicts, and many bishops are ill prepared to cope with them. Yet there is a gradual awakening to the social overtones of the Church's presence and a rediscovery of their prophetic role. Bishops in the more impoverished and exploited areas have most vehemently denounced the injustices they witness. But as soon as they point out the profound causes behind these evils, they collide with the great economic and political blocs of their countries. Inevitably they are accused of intruding into matters that do not pertain to them and called Marxists. Often it is Catholic conservatives who most readily make those charges.

These activities have led to manifestoes expressing them and developing theologico-pastoral bases for them. In the past two years we have seen a flurry of public statements: from lay movements, groups of priests and bishops, and entire episcopates. A constant refrain in these statements is the admission of the Church's solidarity with Latin America's plight. The Church refuses to disregard that plight, seeking instead to accept its responsibility to correct the injustices.[13] The poverty, injustice, and exploitation of man by fellow man in Latin America is often called "institutionalized violence." Theologically, that phenomenon is called a "situation of sin."[14] The reality so described is more and more obviously the result of a *situation of dependence,* i.e., the centers where decisions are made are located outside our continent—a fact that keeps our countries in a condition of neocolonialism.[15]

In all these statements, from a variety of sources inside the Latin American Church, the term "development" is gradually being displaced by the term "liberation."[16] The word and the idea behind it express the desire to get rid of the condition of dependence, but even more than that they underline the desire of the oppressed peoples to seize the reins of their own destiny and shake free from the present servitude, as a symbol of the freedom from sin provided by Christ.[17] This liberation will only be achieved by a thorough change of structures. The term "social revolution" is heard more and more—and ever more openly. . . .[18]

In the Latin American world, where the Christian community should live and rejoice, its eschatological hope is that of social revolution, where violence is present in different ways. Its mission is before it. The choices which (with the limits already indicated) the Church is making are confronting her more and more with the dilemma which she presently is living on the continent: reform or revolution. Faced with this polarization, can the ecclesiastical authority stay on the level of generalized declarations? But can it go further without leaving that which is normally considered as its specific mission?

For the Latin American Church to be *in* the world without being *of* the world means concretely and more clearly to be in the system but not of the system. It is evident, in effect, that only a break with the unjust present order and a frank commitment to a new society will make believable to the men of Latin America the message of love of which the Christian community is carrier. This demand should lead to a profound revision of the way it preaches the Word. . . .

The Faith and the New Man

What ultimately brings Christians to participate in liberating oppressed peoples is the conviction that the gospel message is radically incompatible with an unjust, alienated society. They see clearly that they cannot be authentic Christians unless they act. But what they are to do to achieve this just world calls for great effort and imagination.

Theology, as a critical reflection in the light of faith on the presence of Christians in this world, ought to help us find our answer. It ought to verify the faith, hope, and charity contained in our zeal. But it ought also correct possible deviations and omissions in our Christian living that the demands of political action, however nobly inspired, may make us fall into.[19] This too is a task for critical reflection.

In addition to the struggle against misery, injustice, and exploitation, what we seek is the *creation of a new man*. This aspiration questions and challenges our Christian faith. What that faith can say about itself enables us to see its relation with the yearning of men who fight to emancipate other men and themselves. . . .

We do not seem to have drawn all the conclusions latent in the rediscovery of the truth of universal salvation. This is a bigger question than merely asking if one can be saved outside the visible Church. To talk of the presence of grace, accepted or rejected, in all men implies also forming a Christian judgment on the very roots of human actions. It makes it impossible to talk about a profane world; for human existence is ultimately nothing but a yes or a no to the Lord.

There are not, then, two histories, one profane and one sacred, juxtaposed or interrelated, but a single human progress, irreversibly exalted by Christ, the Lord of history. His redemptive work embraces every dimension of human existence. Two great biblical themes illustrate this view: the relation between creation and salvation, and the eschatological promises.

In the Bible, *creation* is presented not as a stage previous to the work of salvation, but as the first salvific action: "God chose us before the creation of the world" (Eph 1:3). It is part of the process of salvation, of God's self-communication. The religious experience of Israel is essentially history, but that history is merely a prolongation of the creative act. Hence the Psalms sing of God simultaneously as Creator and Saviour (cf. Ps 135, 136, 74, 93, 95). God, who made a cosmos out of a chaos, is the same who acts in salvation history. The work of Christ is seen as a re-creation and narrated for us in a context of creation (Jn 1). Creation and salvation thus have a Christological meaning: in Him everything was created and saved (cf. Col 1:15–20).

So when we say that man realizes himself by continuing the act of creation through work, we are saying that he thereby places himself in the interior of salvation history. Mastering the earth, as Genesis bids him do, is a work of salvation meant to produce its plenitude. To work, to transform this world, is to save. The Bible reveals the profound meaning of that effort. Building the temporal city is not a mere step in "humanizing," in "pre-evangelizing," as theologians used to say a few years back. Rather, it means participating fully in the salvific process that affects the whole man.

A second great biblical theme brings us to similar conclusions. This is the theme of *eschatological promises,* i.e., the events that herald and accompany the eschatological era. This is not a once-mentioned theme; rather, like the first one, it occurs repeatedly all through the Bible. It is vividly present in the history of Israel and hence deserves a place in the present progress of the people of God.

The prophets spoke of a kingdom of peace. But peace supposes the establishment of justice (Is 32:17), defense of the rights of the poor, punishment of the oppressor, a life without fear of being enslaved. A poorly understood spirituality has often led us to forget the human message, the power to change unjust social structures, that the eschatological promises contain—which does not mean, of course, that they contain nothing but social implications. The end of misery and exploitation will indicate that the kingdom has come; it will be here, according to Isaiah, when nobody "builds so that another may dwell, or plants so that another may eat," and when each one "enjoys the work of his hands" (65:22). To fight for a just world where there will be no oppression or slavery or forced work will be a sign of the coming of the kingdom. Kingdom and social injustice are incompatible. In Christ "all God's promises have their fulfilment" (2 Cor 1:20; cf. also Is 29:18–19; Mt 11:5; Lv 25:10; Lk 4:16–21).

The lesson to be drawn from these two biblical themes is clear: *salvation embraces the whole man.* The struggle for a just society fits fully and rightfully into salvation history. That conclusion is emphasized in *The Development of Peoples* (21), where it is said that "integral development" (viz., salvation) of man extends, without discontinuity, from the possession of what he needs to communion with the Lord, the fulness of the salvific work.

Christ thus appears as the Saviour who, by liberating us from sin, liberates us from the very root of social injustice. The entire dynamism of human history, the struggle against all that depersonalizes man—social inequalities, misery, exploitation—have their origin, are sublimated, and reach their plenitude in the salvific work of Christ. . . .

Political theology seeks to focus on the social dimensions of the biblical message. The Bible tells us not only of a *vocation* to communion with God but of a *convocation.* That fact ought to have an impact on the political behavior of Christians.

This conclusion is particularly appropriate in Latin America, where the Christian community is accepting more and more delicate and even radical political involvements. But some questions arise. Will political theology stop at analyzing the meaning of those involvements? Or will it go further and inspire a new political doctrine for the Church? In the latter case, how can we avoid a return to the familiar old problem of Christendom? Shall theology become a new "ideology"? The challenge will be to find a way between a Christian politics and an abstention. Very likely no solution can be found by hit-and-miss methods. Yet it is hard to work out in advance (as we used to believe we could) the precise norms that should govern the Church's conduct, which will probably have to be decided by the needs of the moment, with the lights the Church has at its disposition, and with a mighty effort to be true to the gospel. There are certain chapters of theology that can only be written afterwards.

In any event, if we can recapture a historical vision focusing on the future and animated by hope that Christ will bring about the fulness we wait for, we shall see in a fresh light the *new man* we are trying to create by our activity in the present. If we hope in Christ, we will believe in the historical adventure—which opens a vast field of possibilities to the Christian's action. . . .

In Latin America the Church must realize that it exists in a continent undergoing revolution, where violence is present in different ways. The "world" in which the Christian community is called on to live and celebrate its eschatological hope is one in social revolution. Its mission must be achieved keeping that in account. The Church has no alternative. Only a total break with the unjust order to which it is bound in a thousand conscious or unconscious ways, and a forthright commitment to a new society, will make men in Latin America believe the message of love it bears. The Church's critico-political function becomes doubly important in Latin America, where the ecclesial institution carries so much prestige. In consideration, then, of the Church's mission, concrete circumstances should affect not only pastoral attitudes but theological thought itself.

Poverty—in Solidarity and in Protest

For several years we have been hearing a growing call in the Church for an authentic witness of poverty. It is important, however, to grasp very precisely the point of this witness and to avoid sentimentalism (there has been trivial talk of the "eminent dignity of the poor in the Church"), as well as the fanciful project of making poverty into an ideal (which would be ironic indeed for those who undergo real misery).

In the Bible poverty, as deprivation of the basic needs for living, is considered an evil, something that degrades man and offends God; the words it uses in referring to the poor show this (cf. Is 10:2; Amos 2:6–7; 5:1–6; 2:1). On the other hand, spiritual poverty is not merely an interior indifference to the goods of this world, but an attitude of openness to God, of spiritual simplicity (Wis 2:3; Is 66:2; Ps 25, 34, 37, 149; Prv 22:4; 15:33; 18:2; Mt 5:3).

Christian poverty makes no sense, then, except as a promise to be one with those suffering misery, in order to point out the evil that it represents. No one should "idealize" poverty, but rather hold it aloft as an evil, cry out against it, and strive to eliminate it. Through such a spirit of solidarity we can alert the poor to the injustice of their situation. When Christ assumed the condition of poverty, He did so not to idealize it, but to show love and solidarity with men and to redeem them from sin. Christian poverty, an expression of love, makes us one with those who are poor and protests against their poverty.

Yet we must watch the use of that word. The term "poor" can seem vague and churchy, sentimental, even antiseptic. The "poor" man today is the one who is oppressed, who is kept marginal to society, the proletarian or subproletarian struggling to get his most elemental rights. The solidarity and protest we are talking about have a real political overtone in today's world.

Making oneself one with the poor today can entail personal risk, even of one's life. That is what many Christians—and non-Christians—who are dedicated to the revolutionary cause are finding out. Thus new forms of living poverty, different from the usual "giving up the goods of this world," are being found.

Only by repudiating poverty and making itself poor in protest against it can the Church preach "spiritual poverty," i.e., an openness of man and the history he lives in to the future promised by God. Only in that way can it fulfill honestly, and with a good chance of being heard, the critico-social function that political theology assigns. For the Church of today, this is the test of the authenticity of its mission. . . .

Appendix II

Theology and the Social Sciences
*(1984)**

Gustavo Gutierrez

Social Analysis and Critical Response

As I have pointed out a number of times in my books, scientific application of the social sciences is undeniably in its early stages and still
marked by uncertainties. Nonetheless, these sciences do help us understand better the social realities of our present situation. We need
discernment, then, in dealing with the social sciences, not only because of their inchoative character, which I just mentioned, but also
because to say that these disciples are scientific does not mean that
their findings are apodictic and beyond discussion. In fact, the contrary is true. What is really "scientific" does not seek to evade critical
examination but rather submits to it. Science advances by means of
hypotheses that give various explanations of one and the same reality.
Consequently, to say that something is scientific is to say that it is
subject to ongoing discussion and criticism. This statement holds in a
special way for the ever-new and changing field of social realities. . . .

The same critical approach (which expresses an authentic rationality and personal freedom) must be taken to movements of liberation.
Like every human process, these are ambivalent. We must therefore
be clear in our minds regarding them, not out of any aversion to history but, on the contrary, out of loyalty to the values they embody
and solidarity with the individuals committed to them.

* From Gustavo Gutierrez, *The Truth Shall Make You Free: Confrontations*,
trans. Matthew McConnell, © 1990 by Orbis Books, Maryknoll, NY 10545,
by permission. First published in *Páginas* 63–64 (September 1984).

The longing for liberation is undoubtedly one of the "signs of the times" in our age. "For many persons in various ways this aspiration—in Vietnam or Brazil, New York or Prague—has become a norm for their behavior and a sufficient reason to lead lives of dedication" (*A Theology of Liberation*, p. 21). In all these places, men and women will have to be faithful to a quest for freedom that no political system guarantees. This, even though the quest may cost them their lives—in capitalist societies, but also in the world of what today is called "real socialism." It was for this reason that I rejected, thirteen years ago, the attitude of "those who sought refuge in easy solutions or in the excommunication of those who did not accept their pat answers, schematizations, and uncritical attitudes toward the historical expressions of socialism" (*A Theology of Liberation*, p. 56).

Recent historical events have validated that rejection and have dispelled illusions regarding concrete historical systems that claim to eliminate all evils. As a result, we have launched out upon new and more realistic quests; quests, too, that are more respectful of all dimensions of the human.

Social Sciences and Marxism

Elements of Marxist analysis play a part in the contemporary social sciences that serve as a tool for studying social reality. This is true of the social sciences generally, even where they differ from or are opposed to Marx (as in the case, for example, of Max Weber). But the presence of these elements does not at all justify an identification of the social sciences with Marxist analysis, especially if one takes into account what Father Arrupe, in a well-known letter on the subject, called "the exclusive character" of Marxist analysis ("Letter on Marxist Analysis," December 1980, no. 6).

The Theory of Dependency

The very fact that liberation theology has regarded the theory of dependency as important for an analysis of Latin American social situations is enough to prevent the kind of identification just mentioned. For this theory had its origin in a development of the social sciences proper to Latin America, and is held by prominent theoreticians, who do not regard themselves as Marxists. Nor may we overlook the fact that representatives of Marxism have severely criticized the theory.

We are dealing here with a very important point of theory. Marx said: "The industrially more developed countries only present the less developed with an image of their own future" (*Capital,* I, p. 17). This outlook, however, the theory of dependency rejects. A Latin American social scientist writes that "to begin with, this theory challenged the supposedly 'linear' pattern of the evolution of human society and branded as 'Eurocentric' Marx's observations on the subject." Elsewhere, speaking of the views of Fernando Henrique Cardoso, the most important representative of the theory, the same writer says: Cardoso maintains a "theoretical posture that is worlds removed from that of Marx." (Agustín Cueva, "El Uso del Concepto de Modos de Producción en América Latina," *Modos de Producción en América Latina* [Lima, 1976], pp. 24, 26.)

The nature of this article does not permit me to dwell on this point or to offer further evidence or go into the matter in greater depth. My intention in harking back to the theory of dependency—which was very much to the fore in early writings on liberation theology[1]—is simply to make the point that neither the social sciences generally nor the Latin American contribution to them can be reduced to the Marxist version. I am not denying the contributions Marxism has made to our understanding of economic and social matters; I do, however, want the necessary distinctions to be clearly grasped.

Furthermore, the use (a critical use, as we have seen) of the theory of dependency does not mean a permanent commitment to it. In the context of theological work, this theory is simply a means of better understanding social reality.

Ideological Aspects and Marxist Analysis

In the contemporary intellectual world, including the world of theology, references are often made to Marx and various Marxists, and their contributions in the field of social and economic analysis are often taken into account. But these facts do not, by themselves, mean an acceptance of Marxism, especially insofar as Marxism embodies an all-embracing view of life and thus excludes the Christian faith and its requirements. The matter is a complex one and would require a close study of texts, a presentation of divergent interpretations in this area, and the resultant distinctions and critical observations. Without getting into details I shall state my views on some questions.

Let me begin by clarifying a first point. There is no question at all of a possible acceptance of an atheistic ideology. Were we to accept this possibility, we would already be separated from the Christian faith and no longer dealing with a properly theological issue. Nor is there any question of agreement with a totalitarian version of history that denies the freedom of the human person. These two options—an atheistic ideology and a totalitarian vision—are to be discarded and rejected, not only by our faith but by any truly humanistic outlook and even by a sound social analysis.

The question of how closely connected the ideological aspects of Marxism are with Marxist social analysis is a question much discussed in the social sciences. The same is true even within Marxism itself: for some Marxists (in a line represented by Engels and Soviet Marxism, to give two examples) Marxism is an indivisible whole; for others (Gramsci, J. C. Mariátegui, and many more) Marxist analysis or the scientific aspects of Marxism are not inseparably linked to "metaphysical materialism."

I must make it clear, however, that in the context of my own theological writings, this question is a secondary one. In fact, given the situation in which Latin America was living, it seemed to me more urgently necessary to turn to more clearly theological questions (in this I differed from European writings on similar subjects). That is why I wrote, in a note in *A Theology of Liberation:* "We hope to present soon a study of certain questions concerning the ambiguities in the use of the term *materialism* and the various conceptions of Marxism as a total conception of life or a science of history. We hope therefore to situate the vision of human nature and atheistic ideology in Marxism" (p. 201, note 41). In the promised study (the promise has only partially been fulfilled in courses and lectures), my intention was to deal in greater detail with the ideological and philosophical aspects of Marxism, as well as with the connection between these aspects and the more scientific levels of analysis. But my concern was equally to show that the contributions of Marxist analysis needed to be critically situated within the framework of the social sciences. Otherwise, the importance of these contributions is likely to be exaggerated both by their defenders and by their opponents.

Others have made a similar study and drawn similar boundaries. I wish to take part in the effort, and I hope for the opportunity to go into the matter more fully. But I must call attention to the fact that in a Christian perspective, importance does not attach exclusively to the theoretical side of the question. There are also pastoral concerns that are urgently important for all and especially for the church's magisterium. The church has therefore issued several recent pronouncements on the subject and taken account therein of the new problematic and the set of theoretical and practical questions it raises. Thus the Encyclical *Pacem in Terris* of John XXIII made some fruitful distinctions. The Letter *Octogesima Adveniens* of Paul VI touched on the subject in an open and authoritative way, pointing out the values and dangers of Marxism in this area (see esp. no. 34); it also pointed out the connections between analysis and ideology in Marxism and described the conditions required of a work that would go more deeply into the subject. The Puebla Conference returned to the question (see no. 92 and especially nos. 543–45); it also drew attention to the way in which these problems arise in the Latin American context.

The letter of Father Arrupe to which I referred earlier drew its inspiration from these documents of the magisterium. In that letter we find distinctions, appraisals, warnings, and rejections with which I am in full agreement and which must be taken into account both in pastoral practice and in any theoretical discussion of the subject. . . .

Theology and Social Analysis

My purpose in my theological writings was stated in the opening words of *A Theology of Liberation*: "This book is an attempt at reflection, based on the gospel and the experiences of men and women committed to the process of liberation in the exploited and oppressed land of Latin America" (p. xiii)—in the light, therefore, of the gospel, and in a world of poverty and hope.

At no time, either explicitly or implicitly, have I suggested a dialogue with Marxism with a view to a possible "synthesis" or to accepting one aspect while leaving others aside. Such undertakings were indeed frequent during those years in Europe (see the movement created by the Salzburg conversations in the 1960s) and were beginning to be frequent in Latin American circles. Such was not my own intention, for my pastoral practice imposed pressing needs of a quite different kind.

As I have reminded the reader, once the situation of poverty and marginalization comes to play a part in theological reflection, an analysis of that situation from the sociological viewpoint becomes important, and thinkers are forced to look for help from the relevant disciplines. This means that if there is a meeting, it is between theology and the social sciences, and not between theology and Marxist analysis, except to the extent that elements of the latter are to be found in the contemporary social sciences, especially as these are practiced in the Latin American world.[2]

Use of the social disciplines for a better understanding of the social situation implies great respect for the so-called human sciences and their proper spheres, and for the legitimate autonomy of the political order. The description that these sciences give of a situation, their analysis of its causes, the trends and searches for solutions that they propose—all these are important to us in theology to the extent that they involve human problems and challenges to evangelization. It is not possible, however, to deduce political programs or actions from the gospel or from reflection on the gospel. It is not possible, nor should we attempt it; the political sphere is something entirely different.

I said as much, and with all desirable clarity, on the very first page of *A Theology of Liberation:*

> My purpose is not to elaborate an ideology to justify postures already taken, or to undertake a feverish search for security in the face of the radical challenges that confront the faith, or to fashion a theology from which political action is "deduced." It is rather to let ourselves be judged by the word of the Lord, to think through our faith, to strengthen our love, and to give reason for our hope from within a commitment that seeks to become more radical, total, and efficacious. It is to reconsider the great themes of Christian life within this radically changed perspective and with regard to the new questions posed by this commitment. This is the goal of the so-called *theology of liberation.* [p. xiii]

In this area an insistent demand is made, motivated by the desire to do something concrete and active, but it can also distort the perspective and limits of theological reflection. In the dialogues sponsored by CELAM over ten years ago, this point was discussed; the result was clarifications that are worth recalling here. One of the participants asked what strategic lines were to be followed that would bring the theology of liberation to bear on the great social problems of Latin America. This gave me an opportunity to reply that there are three things that may be asked of theology: "Liberation theology must be required to supply a concrete language. But we must not ask of theology what it cannot and ought not give."

It is not the function of liberation theology "to offer strategic solutions or specifically political alternatives. . . . In my opinion, the 'theology of revolution' set out on that path, but it seems to me that it was not a theologically sound course to follow; in addition, it ended up 'baptizing' revolution—that is, it did not acknowledge the autonomy proper to the political sphere." It is, however, right "to ask theology to play a part in the proclamation of the word," for this is in keeping with the nature of reflection that "positions itself in the light of faith and not in the light of sociology (I understand the temptations of sociologists; theologians, however, operate in the light of the faith as lived in the Christian community)."

Theology may also be asked to help us avoid losing a comprehensive vision of a given historical process and reducing it instead to its political dimension:

> Theology must be aware that the problem is not solved solely by economic, social, and political structures. Theologians must, on the contrary, be aware of deeper changes that can take place in the human person, of the search for a different kind of human being, of liberation in the many dimensions of the human and not just in the economic and political dimension, although, of course, all these aspects are closely connected.

Most importantly:

> theology must be asked to show the presence of the human relationship to God and the rupturing of that relationship at the very core of the historical, political, and economic situation; this is something that no social analysis can ever bring to light. A sociologist will never come to see that sin—the breaking of the relationship with God and therefore with others as well—is at the very heart of any unjust situation. If a theology does not tell us this when it takes a social situation into account, then, in my opinion, theology is not reading the situation in the light of faith. Faith will not provide strategies, but it will indeed tell us, as Medellín says, that sin is at the heart of every breaking of brotherhood and sisterhood among human beings; it will therefore call for a particular behavior and an option. [all these passages are from *Diálogos en el CELAM,* pp. 229–30]

In my view, the requirements and tasks I have outlined here are fundamental for theology. They are part of its proper sphere; what is unacceptable is to turn theological reflection into a premise in the service of a specific political choice. This statement does not suggest a lack of interest in the serious questions raised by the struggle for social justice; it signifies only that we must be clear regarding the scope and limits of every contribution to so vast and complex a subject.

The presence of the social sciences in theology at the point when it is important to have a deeper understanding of the concrete world of human beings does not imply an undue submission of theological reflection to something outside it. Theology must take into account the contribution of the social sciences, but in its work it must always appeal to its own sources. This point is fundamental, for whatever the context in which theological reflection takes place, "theology must now take a new route, and in order to do so it will have to appeal to its own fonts" (*The Power of the Poor in History,* p. 60).

Furthermore, the absolutely indispensable use of some form of rational discourse in theological work does not mean an uncritical acceptance of that form or an identification with it: "Theology is not to be identified with a method of analyzing society or with a form of philosophical reflection on the person. . . . It never makes use of a rational tool without in some way modifying it. This is in the very nature of theology, and the entire history of theology is there to prove it" (*Diálogos,* pp. 88–89). . . .

Conflict in History

A Question of Fact

To speak of conflict as a social fact is not to assert it apodictically as something beyond discussion, but only to locate it at the level of social analysis. I cannot, for pastoral or theological reasons, simply deny social facts; that would be to mock those Christians who must confront these facts every day. For this reason I made the following statement over ten years ago, during a discussion of the subject and at a bishop's request:

> The problem facing theology is not to determine whether or not social classes are in opposition. That is in principle a matter for the sciences, and theology must pay careful attention to them if it wishes to be *au courant* with the effort being made to understand the social dimensions of the human person. The question, therefore, that theology must answer is this: If there is a struggle (as one, but not the only form of historical conflict), how are we to respond to it as Christians? A theo-

logical question is always one that is prompted by the content of faith—
that is, by love. The specifically Christian question is both theological
and pastoral: How are Christians to live their faith, their hope, and
their love amid a conflict that takes the form of class struggle? Suppose
that analysis were to tell us one day: "The class struggle is not as important as you used to think." We as theologians would continue to say
that love is the important thing, even amid conflict as described for us
by social analysis. If I want to be faithful to the gospel, I cannot disregard reality, however harsh and conflictual it may be. And the reality
of Latin America is indeed harsh and conflictual. [*Diálogos,* pp. 89–90]

The conditional sentence ("Suppose that analysis . . .") in that
paragraph is important for situating the problem, for it leaves the door
open, in an undogmatic way, to other possibilities.[3]

I spoke earlier in these pages of the critical stance to be maintained
toward social analysis, but also of a proper acknowledgment of its
contribution.

When I speak of conflict in history I always mention different aspects of it. That is why I continually refer to races discriminated
against, despised cultures, exploited classes, and the condition of
women, especially in those sectors of society where women are
"doubly oppressed and marginalized" (Puebla, no. 1134, note). In
this way, I take into account the noneconomic factors present in situations of conflict between social groups. The point of these constant
references is to prevent any reduction of historical conflict to the fact
of class struggle. I said earlier that in *A Theology of Liberation* (pp.
272–97 of the first edition), I was discussing the class struggle aspect
of the general problem because it is the one that poses the most acute
problems for the universality of Christian love. If it is possible to
clear that obstacle, then we have an answer to the questions raised
by other, perhaps less thorny, kinds of conflict. For it is evident that
history is marked by other forms of conflict and, unfortunately, of
confrontation between persons.

There are those who seem without further discussion to identify the
idea of class struggle with Marxism. As we know, this is incorrect and
indeed was rejected by Marx himself. In his well-known letter to
J. Weydemeyer (cited in *A Theology of Liberation,* p. 284, note 51
of the first edition), he says: "As for me, mine is not the merit to have
discovered either the existence of classes in modern society or the
struggle between them. Much before me bourgeois historians had de-

scribed the historical development of this class struggle and the bourgeois economists had studied its economic anatomy."

Marx thought that his own contribution was to have established the connection between class struggle and economic factors (as well as the dictatorship of the proletariat). He often presents these economic factors as operating historically in a deterministic manner. I am not concerned here with the important debate on this point or with the varying interpretations that the debate has produced within Marxism itself. The point I want to make is simply that an economically based determinist view of class struggle is completely alien to liberation theology.[4]

In this connection, experts on Marx have always pointed out the very limited space (a few paragraphs amid thousands of pages) given to class struggle in Marx's principal work, *Capital*. These various considerations have led to such statements as the following:

> In Marx's view, the class struggle is not an essential part of his teaching, as others sometimes think. In the *Communist Manifesto* he regards it indeed as necessary, given the fact of alienation, but it is a passing stage and by no means permanent. The truly essential focus of his humanism is the search for harmony among all through work, for an equality in that which is the distinctive element in human existence. But interpretations of Marxist thought as egalitarian are likewise shallow and without foundation. Marx recognizes the variations in gifts, qualifications, and so on. What he seeks is equality among classes in that which is specifically human: work deliberately and responsibly undertaken. [Alfonso López Trujillo, *La Concepción del Hombre en Marx* (Bogota, 1972), p. 178]

Despite all this, Marxist thought does contain expressions that turn class struggle from a simple fact into "the driving force of history" and, in philosophical versions, a "law of history." An analysis would have to be made to determine the meaning and importance of this transformation of fact into historical principle. My only concern here is to insist that this approach does not reflect my own thinking and that therefore I have never used such expressions. . . .

The Requirements of Christian Love

There is obviously no question of identifying a preferential option for the poor with an ideology or a specific political program that would serve as framework for reinterpreting the gospel or the task of the church. Nor is there any question of limiting oneself to one sector of the human race. I regard these reductive positions as utterly alien. But I have dealt with this matter on various occasions and need not insist on the point once again.

I do, however, wish to discuss a question I regard as important. I said earlier that the universality of Christian love is incompatible with any exclusion of persons but not with a preference for some. I think it worth citing here a passage from Karl Lehmann, a theologian and presently archibishop of Mainz: "There can undoubtedly be situations in which the Christian message allows of only one course of action. In these cases the church is under the obligation of decisively taking sides (see, for example, the experience of Nazi dictatorship in Germany). In these circumstances, an attitude of unconditional neutrality in political questions contradicts the command of the gospel and can have deadly consequences." (International Theological Commission, *Téologica de la Liberación* [Madrid: BAC, 1978], p. 38, note 2).

There is no passage in my own writings that so incisively stresses specificity and points to one course of action as the only possible course. But, faced with so strong a statement, I cannot but ask: Does not what held for the experience of Nazism in Europe hold also for the Latin American experience of wretchedness and oppression? In both cases, we are faced with boundary situations, but that is precisely what I said at the beginning of this section, and it is to this kind of situation that Archbishop Lehmann is referring.

The important point is that according to the German theologian there are cases in which "the Christian message allows only one course of action." Would anyone dare brand this claim unchristian and reductivist? In this case, proximity to the horror of Nazism showed that the claim is theologically acceptable in an extreme situation. In such situations, the judgment one makes depends not simply on social analysis but on the ethical reaction (see John Paul II's notion), which we experience in face of a situation that we analyze and, above all, live through. Perhaps it is this very last point—living in the situation—that makes the difference in outlooks. For there is no doubt that behind Archbishop Lehmann's words lies the complex and painful experience of the German people and German Christians.[5]

The Universality of Christian Love

All that has preceded brings me to a final, but fundamental, point. When we speak of taking social conflict (including the fact of class struggle) into account and of the necessity of overcoming the situation by getting at the causes that give rise to it, we are asserting a permanent demand of Christian love. We are thus recalling a basic injunction of the gospel: love of our enemies. In other words, a painful situation that may cause us to regard others as our adversaries does not dispense us from loving them; quite the contrary. When, therefore, I speak of social conflict, I am referring to social groups, classes, races, or cultures, and not to individuals . . .

 . . . To be a Christian is to be a witness to the resurrection and to proclaim the reign of life. We celebrate this life in the eucharist, which is the primary task of the ecclesial community. In the breaking of the bread we remember the love and fidelity that brought Jesus to his death; we remember, too, his resurrection, which was the confirmation of his mission, a mission to all and especially to the poor. At the same time, the breaking of bread is both point of departure and point of arrival for the Christian conmmunity. In it the assembled faithful express their deep communion in human suffering (often caused by the lack of food) and joyfully acknowledge the risen Lord who gives life and raises the hope of the people he has brought together by his actions and his word.

The theology of liberation seeks to provide a language for talking about God. It is an attempt to make the word of life present in a world of oppression, injustice, and death.

Notes

Introduction

1. See, for example, the article by a Canadian Sister of Charity who works in Peru that ends with a prayer-poem by a member of her catechetical group:

> We used to think God was in heaven . . . and it was only a matter of praying at night and going to Mass every now and then. Suddenly someone called us to form a Christian community. Then we discovered that we were wrong. The light came. Our happiness came through those who today represent the prophets of an ancient treasure. . . . But what pain to find out and experience the sad reality of our country: violence, exploitation and so forth. . . . Thank you, Lord. Give us strength to assume the mission you have entrusted to us, and thus to pass from oppression to the liberation of our people. [*National Catholic Reporter,* August 17, 1984, p. 13]

2. Juan Luis Segundo S.J., *Theology and the Church: A Response to Cardinal Ratzinger and a Warning to the Whole Church,* trans. John W. Diercksmeier. (Minneapolis: Winston Press, 1985), p. 65.

Chapter 1

1. On the political implications of the New Testament, see Oscar Cullmann, *The State in the New Testament* (New York: Scribner, 1956); S. G. Brandon, *Jesus and the Zealots* (Manchester: University of Manchester Press, 1967); and, John Yoder, *The Politics of Jesus* (Grand Rapids, MI: Eerdmans, 1972).

2. On the hierarchical world view see Arthur O. Lovejoy, *The Great Chain of Being* (Cambridge, MA: Harvard University Press, 1936), and Paul E. Sigmund, *Nicholas of Cusa and Medieval Political Thought* (Cambridge, MA: Harvard University Press, 1963), ch. 3. On the fusion of Stoicism and Christianity see Charles C. Cochrane, *Christianity and Classical Culture* (London: Oxford, 1944), as well as Paul E. Sigmund, *Natural Law in Political Thought* (Lanham, MD: University Press of America, 1980) (reprint of 1971 edition), ch. 2.

3. On the political implications of the Thomistic synthesis see Walter Ullmann, *A History of Political Thought: The Middle Ages* (New York: Penguin Books, 1970), ch. 6, and Paul E. Sigmund, ed., *St. Thomas Aquinas, On Ethics and Politics* (New York: W. W. Norton, 1988).

4. See my article "The Catholic Tradition and Modern Democracy," *The Review of Politics* (Fall 1987): 530–48. Paragraph 75 of *Gaudium et Spes states*, "It is in full accord with human nature that juridical-political structures should afford all their citizens the chance to participate freely and actively in establishing the constitutional bases of a political community governing the state, determining the scope and purpose of various institutions, and choosing leaders." Walter Abbott S.J., ed., *The Documents of Vatican II* (New York: The Guild Press, 1966), p. 285.

5. On the Christian-Marxist dialogue in Europe, see Alasdair MacIntyre, *Marxism and Christianity* (New York: Schocken, 1968); Ernst Bloch, *Atheism in Christianity* (New York: Herder and Herder, 1972); René Coste, *Analyse Marxiste et Foi Chretienne* (Paris: Editions Ouvrieres, 1977); Peter Hebblethwaite and James Bentley, *Between Marx and Christ* (London: Verso Publishers, 1982).

6. On the Second Vatican Council, see Xavier Rynne, *Letters from Vatican City*, 3 vols. (New York: Farrar, Straus, 1963–1968).

7. See Edward L. Cleary O.P., *Crisis and Change: The Church in Latin America Today* (Maryknoll, NY: Orbis Books, 1985), ch. 1. On the earlier history of the Catholic church in Latin America see J. Lloyd Mecham, *Church and State in Latin America* (Chapel Hill: University of North Carolina Press, 1966); and, from a liberationist point of view, Enrique Dussel, *A History of the Church in Latin America: Colonialism to Liberation (1492–1979)* (Grand Rapids, MI: Eerdmans, 1981).

8. The classic analysis of the causes of the 1964 coup is Thomas Skidmore, *Politics in Brazil, 1930–1964* (New York: Oxford University Press, 1967). On the church see Emanuel de Kadt, *Catholic Radicals in Brazil* (London: Oxford University Press, 1970), and Thomas Bruneau, *The Political Transformation of the Brazilian Catholic Church* (Cambridge: Cambridge University Press, 1974), esp. ch. 4.

9. See John Gerassi, ed., *Revolutionary Priest: The Complete Writings and Messages of Camilo Torres* (New York: Vintage, 1971).

10. The most accessible collection of Catholic social teaching since 1960 is Joseph Gremillion, ed., *The Gospel of Peace and Justice* (Maryknoll, NY: Orbis Books, 1976). *Populorum Progressio* appears at pp. 387–416.

Chapter 2

1. For excerpts from the Medellín Documents see Gremillion, *The Gospel of Peace and Justice* (Maryknoll, NY: Orbis Press, 1976), pp. 445–76. The full text has been published by the U.S. Catholic Conference as *The Church in the Present-Day Transformation of Latin America in the Light of the Council*, Vol. II: *Conclusions* (Washington, D.C., 1970).

2. Deane William Ferm, *Third World Liberation Theologies, An Introductory Survey* (Maryknoll, NY: Orbis Books, 1985), p. 17. For a list of the members and advisors of the Committee, see Enrique Dussel, *De Medellín a Puebla* (Mexico City: Centro de Estudios Ecumenicos, 1979), p. 76.

3. Quoted in Robert McAfee Brown, *Gustavo Gutierrez* (Atlanta: John Knox Press, 1980), p. 23.

4. Gustavo Gutierrez, *A Theology of Liberation* (Maryknoll, NY: Orbis Books, 1973), pp. 33–34. The official English translation of paragraph 10 of the decree has "emancipation" instead of "liberation," which is used in the Spanish version quoted by Gutierrez (*Teología de la Liberation*, Salamanca: Sigueme, 1972, p. 63).

Chapter 3

1. See "Evangelio, Politica, y Socialismos" in Carlos Oviedo Camus, ed., *Documentos del Episcopado de Chile, 1970–73* (Santiago: Ediciones Mundo, 1974), pp. 58–100. This important document is not translated or excerpted in the useful collection edited by John Eagleson, *Christians and Socialism: Documentation of the Christians for Socialism Movement in Latin America* (Maryknoll, NY: Orbis Books, 1975), which contains the original Declaration of the Eighty and subsequent exchanges with the bishops, as well as the reports on the 1972 meeting and the bishops' 1973 condemnation of the movement. One of the most active members of the group was Father Pablo Richard, who left Chile after the 1973 coup. He has published *Origen y Desarrollo del Movimiento Cristianos por el Socialismo, Chile, 1970–73* (Paris: Centre Lebret, 1975). A more balanced analysis appears in Arthur McGovern S.J., *Marxism, An American*

Christian Perspective (Maryknoll, NY: Orbis Books, 1980), ch. 6. The bishops' statement is totally misrepresented by Juan Luis Segundo S.J., *The Liberation of Theology* (Maryknoll, NY: Orbis Books, 1976) ("the bishops who claim that they cannot choose sides, come out and say that socialism cannot be an alternative to the existing capitalist system"— p. 131). For hostile views see Roger Vekemans S.J., *Teología de la Liberación y Cristianos por el Socialismo* (Bogota: Cedial, 1976), Part II, and Teresa Donoso Loero, *Los Cristianos por el Socialismo en Chile* (Santiago: El Mercurio, 1975). On the Chilean church in the Allende period, see Brian Smith, *The Church and Politics in Chile* (Princeton, NJ: Princeton University Press, 1982), Part III.

2. For the full text, see Gremillion, *The Gospel of Peace and Justice* (Maryknoll, NY: Orbis Books, 1976), pp. 485–512.

3. The Peruvian statement is summarized and contrasted with that of the Chileans in Juan Carlos Scannone, *Teología de la Liberación y Praxis Popular* (Salamanca, Ediciones Sigueme, 1976), pp. 108–16, where it is described as a "prophetic reading of the signs of the times" (p. 113). Scannone is an Argentine liberation theologian.

4. "Justice in the World" in Gremillion, pp. 513–29.

5. On Castro's visit, see Pablo Richard, ed., *Los Cristianos y la Revolución* (Santiago: Quimantu, 1973).

6. On the causes of the coup see Paul E. Sigmund, *The Overthrow of Allende and the Politics of Chile* (Pittsburgh, PA: University of Pittsburgh Press, 1977). The earlier quotations are from Eagleson, ed., *Christians and Socialism.*

7. Vekemans, pp. 312–13. For an "exposé" of Vekemans's role in Chile in the 1960s, see David Mutchler, *The Church as a Political Factor in Latin America* (New York: Praeger, 1970). Mutchler is an ex-Jesuit who seems to have had access to the confidential files of the order in Chile. His book was translated into Spanish in Prague. For Vekemans's extensively documented reply, see Roger Vekemans S.J., *D.C.—C.I.A.—CELAM; Autopsia del Mito* (Caracas: Universidad Catolica de Tachira, 1982).

8. Quoted in Enrique Dussel, *A History of the Church in Latin America* (Grand Rapids, MI: Eerdmans, 1981), p. 312.

9. CELAM, *Liberación: Dialogos en el CELAM* (Bogota: CELAM, 1974). The "hidden agenda" of the book is criticized by Philip Berryman in Sergio Torres and John Eagleson, eds., *Theology in the Americas* (Maryknoll, NY: Orbis Books, 1976), pp. 58–59.

10. Alfonso Lopez Trujillo, *De Medellín a Puebla* (Madrid: Biblioteca de Autores Cristianos, 1980). An earlier, less subtle attack by Lopez Trujillo has been translated as *Liberation or Revolution* (Huntington, IN: Our Sunday Visitor Press, 1977).

11. Gremillion, p. 597.

12. See discussion in Donald Dorr, *Option for the Poor* (Maryknoll, NY: Orbis Books, 1983), pp. 193–206.

13. For a more direct attack on the popular church quoting extensively from documents of the Christians for Socialism, see Bonaventura Kloppenburg O.F.M., *The People's Church* (Chicago: Franciscan Herald Press, 1978).

Chapter 4

1. For further discussion of the relation of Christianity and Marxism by the same author see his 1974 London Lectures on Contemporary Christianity, published as *Christians and Marxists: The Mutual Challenge to Revolution* (Grand Rapids, MI: Wm. B. Eerdmans, 1976), in which he describes what he calls the "Christian pilgrimage to Marxism" in Latin America as the result of the failure of reformist, idealist, and voluntaristic approaches to structural change. "The decision for Marxism is therefore an option for structural over against purely individual change, for revolution over against reformist, for socialism over against capitalist development or 'third' solutions, for 'scientific' over against idealistic or utopian socialism" (p. 21). This decision, he says, leaves the Christians open to develop new solutions in an undogmatic way. However, to this observer, at least, it also involves a leap of faith concerning the scientific validity of the Marxist analysis, since, in his words, "the search for an historically scientific way of making love efficacious is the ethos of Marxism" (p. 115), and in Latin America, Miguez Bonino admits that "Marxist social revolutions so far have shown certain disquieting features in relation to personal freedom, popular participation, [and] the control of power" (123), and that a Christian cannot make a group or class "exclusive and definitive bearer of evil in history" (p. 129).

2. Another reason that Assmann is regarded as radical is the exaggerated quality of his statements (what one commentator has called its "verbal overkill"). Thus, at a theological meeting in Detroit, Assmann argued that "it is impossible to be a Christian without a holistic revolutionary perspective." A few minutes later he insisted that "the opinion gaps among Christians must be bridged by scientific instruments, by the tools of analysis that will at least enable Christians to have minimal certainties vis-à-vis the world's problems," adding, in contradiction to what he had just said, that "praxis, struggle, is the basic reference for social analysis, and this means that all socio-analytical tools can never be free, liberated from ideological implications" ("Statement by Hugo Assmann," in Sergio Torres and John Eagleson, ed., *Theology in the Americas*, Maryknoll, NY: Orbis Books, 1976, pp. 300–301.)

3. Some of the most revealing statements of Segundo's views appear

in the footnotes. Consider, for example, the following lines in footnote 13 to chapter 11 of *Faith and Ideologies:*

> What are called "human rights" are certain freedoms particularly useful to the middle classes. And they have been defended by the very people who have generated poverty and misery in the past and the present—even if only by their own consumption. By creating this situation of misery, democratic institutions drain away from their own substance (since it benefits only small minorities in the end) and give rise to subversive movements. Moreover increasing degrees of repression are needed to make the people and nations in poverty accept institutionalized violence without muttering. [p. 303]

These lines were written at a time when the Uruguayan military had imprisoned or interrogated a larger percentage of the Uruguayan population than in any other country in the world, with little or no effort by the Uruguayan Catholic church to use its institutional structures to defend human rights.

4. Segundo's interpretation of Luke's "Blessed are the poor" version of the Beatitudes as announcing the kingdom exclusively to the poor, regardless of their moral status, is attacked by James T. Burtchaell C.S.C. ("How Authentically Christian Is Liberation Theology?" *The Review of Politics,* Vol. 50, No. 2, Spring 1988, 268ff.) because it is "an implausible task to square with the Christian revelation any doctrine that Jesus has disclosed a differential love for humankind." Segundo is also the liberation theologian who is singled out for attack ("a muddle of confusions") by Richard Neuhaus in *The Catholic Moment* (New York: 1988, pp. 178ff.) for its "monism" in linking the Church and social revolution in Latin America.

5. "Theologies of the Periphery and the Centre" in *Concilium,* p. 91. Earlier works by Dussel in English include *History and Theology of Liberation: A Latin American Perspective* (Maryknoll, NY: Orbis Books, 1976) (originally lectures delivered in 1972), and *Ethics and the Theology of Liberation* (Maryknoll, NY: Orbis Books, 1978) (Argentine edition, 1974). His most recent translated book is *Ethics and Community* (Maryknoll, NY: Orbis Books, 1988), an attempt to apply a community-oriented ethic to contemporary issues.

6. For Comblin's recent thinking, especially on the possibilities of socialism in the Third World, see *Tiempo de Acción* (Lima: Centro de Estudios y Publicaciones, 1986). His most recent work in English is *The Holy Spirit and Liberation* (Maryknoll, NY: Orbis Books, 1989), which discusses the activity of the Holy Spirit in the Christian Base Communities.

7. See John R. Pottenger, *The Political Theory of Liberation Theology* (Albany, NY: State University of New York Press, 1989), ch. 3 ("The Marxist-Christian Tension").

Chapter 5

1. Rosino Gibellini, *The Liberation Theology Debate* (Maryknoll, NY: Orbis Books, 1988), p. 2.

2. Claus Bussman, *Who Do You Say? Jesus Christ in Latin American Theology* (Maryknoll, NY: Orbis Books, 1985), in an otherwise favorable account criticizes Boff for linking the resurrection too closely to the liberation struggle (p. 126).

3. See the critique of *Ecclesiogenesis* in Marcello de C. Azevedo S.J., *Basic Ecclesial Communities in Brazil* (Washington, DC: Georgetown University Press, 1987), pp. 203ff.

4. Gibellini, ed., *Frontiers of Theology*, p. 90.

5. This argument is developed further in the liberationist journal *Pasos*, published in Costa Rica by DEI. Franz Hinkelammert argues in "Democracia, Estructura Economico-social, y Formación" (*Pasos*, 3, October 1985, p. 4) that

> in the bourgeois tradition private production is the principle of hierarchization of human rights, and in the socialist tradition the satisfaction of human needs determines the system of property. . . . The social system chooses those who can participate in elections on the basis of *a priori* principle. On the basis of the specific view of the general interest of the system in question, one can distinguish not only between legitimate and illegitimate majorities, but also between parties and political groups, and ultimately determine who can legitimately participate in elections.

This is the closest that liberation theology comes to a Leninist "vanguard" theory that under socialism an elite can determine who may participate in the political system.

Chapter 6

1. Enrique Dussel, *De Medellín a Puebla* (Mexico City: Editorial Edicol, 1979), p. 281. For short accounts of Puebla in English by Dussel, see his *History of the Church in Latin America* (Grand Rapids, MI: Eerdmans, 1981), pp. 229–39, and his article "Current Events in Latin America," in John Eagleson and Sergio Torres, eds., *The Challenge of Basic Christian Communities* (Maryknoll, NY: Orbis Books, 1981).

2. Gutierrez's article, "The Preparatory Document for Puebla: A Retreat from Commitment," appears as chapter 5 of Gustavo Gutierrez, *The Power of the Poor in History* (Maryknoll, NY: Orbis Books, 1983).

3. A good example of this line of thinking is Bonaventura Kloppenburg O.F.M., *The People's Church* (English translation, Chicago: Franciscan Herald Press, 1978), which concludes with fifty-three "unanswered

questions" about liberation theology, and accuses it of being an ideology rather than a theology. Kloppenburg, who like Boff and Cardinal Lorscheiter is a Franciscan, is a close associate of Lopez Trujillo. He is supposed to have written a substantial part of the Consultative Document. He has also published a critique of liberation theology, translated as *Temptations for a Theology of Liberation* (Chicago: Franciscan Herald Press, 1974).

4. Penny Lernoux, *Cry of the People* (New York: Penguin Books, 1982—hardback edition, published in 1980 by Doubleday and Company with the subtitle, *United States Involvement in the Rise of Fascism, Torture and Murder and the Persecution of the Catholic Church in Latin America*). The "smear campaign" is discussed in Lernoux's article "The Long Path to Puebla," in John Eagleson and Philip Scharper, eds., *Puebla and Beyond* (Maryknoll, NY: Orbis Books, 1979), pp. 20ff.

5. Lernoux's statements led to a libel suit against her in Colombia, initiated by Lopez Trujillo.

6. Gary MacEoin and Nivita Riley, *Puebla, A Church Being Born* (New York: Paulist Press, 1980), p. 56.

7. See Moises Sandoval, "Report from the Conference," in Eagleson and Scharper, eds., p. 30.

8. The membership of each committee, and the various drafts of their statements are given in Dussel, *De Medellín a Puebla*, pp. 563ff., along with a breakdown of the voting on each section of the Final Document.

9. The full text appears in Eagleson and Scharper, eds., pp. 122–85.

Chapter 7

1. Much of the foregoing is taken from chapter 5 of Phillip Berryman, *The Religious Roots of Rebellion: Christians in the Central American Revolution* (Maryknoll, NY: Orbis Books, 1984). See also Penny Lernoux, *Cry of the People* (New York: Penguin Books, 1982), ch. 3, and James R. Brockman, *The World Remains: The Life of Oscar Romero* (Maryknoll, NY: Orbis Books, 1982). Brockman has also published a collection of Romero's sermons, *The Church Is All of You: Thoughts of Archbishop Oscar Romero* (Minneapolis: Winston, 1984), and Orbis Books has published his four Pastoral Letters and other statements as Archbishop Oscar Romero, *Voice of the Voiceless* (Maryknoll, NY: Orbis Books, 1985).

2. See, for example, Jon Sobrino and Juan Hernandez Pico, *Theology of Human Solidarity* (Maryknoll, NY: Orbis Books, 1985), pp. 38ff.

3. In 1987 Zamora and Ungo briefly returned to San Salvador. In 1988 they announced that they would nominate a candidate to contest the 1989 presidential election.

4. Quoted from *Tricontinental* (Havana) (17), March–April 1970, pp. 61–68, in Humberto Belli, *Breaking Faith* (Westchester, IL: Crossway Press, 1985), pp. 16–17, who emphasizes its Marxist elements. This should be compared with a somewhat sanitized summary of the 1969 program in Berryman, p. 59. Berryman and Belli write about the church and the Nicaraguan revolution from very different points of view. For the origins of the FSLN see John Booth, *The End and the Beginning* (Boulder, CO: Westview Press, 1981). See also Penny Lernoux, ch. 4, and Michael Dodson and T. S. Montgomery, "The Churches in the Nicaraguan Revolution," in Thomas W. Walker, ed., *Nicaragua in Revolution* (New York: Praeger Publishers, 1982), pp. 181–99, and Dodson, "Nicaragua: The Struggle for the Church," in Daniel Levine, ed., *Religion and Political Conflict in Latin America* (Chapel Hill: University of North Carolina Press, 1986), pp. 79–105.

5. Berryman, p. 63. On Borge and Christianity, see Andrew Reding, ed., *Christianity and Revolution: Tomas Borge's Theology of Life* (Maryknoll, NY: Orbis Books, 1987). In his acknowledgments, Reding thanks Borge "for reinforcing faith in an earthly incarnation of the kingdom of God" (p. ix). As Minister of Interior Borge was responsible for extrajudicial killings and disappearances of around three hundred Nicaraguans up to March 1986 (Americas Watch, *Human Rights in Nicaragua, 1985–86,* March 1986).

6. Margaret Randall, *Cristianos en la Revolución* (Managua: Nueva Nicaragua, 1983), p. 59, which also provides useful background on the intellectual and ideological trajectory of other revolutionary Christians, including Fathers Fernando Cardenal and Uriel Molina.

7. Carta Pastoral del Episcopado Nicaraguense, *Compromiso Christiano para una Nicaragua Nueva,* Managua, 17 November 1979, *passim.*

8. Quoted in Belli, pp. 156–59. Belli also describes (p. 160) a baptism by Ernesto Cardenal in 1981 in which he commanded the spirit of capitalism and Somocismo to leave the baby. The source he cites (Randall, *Christianos y la Revolución*) does not contain it but the incident was widely discussed in Managua at the time.

9. Communiqué by the FSLN National Directorate on Religion (English translation by ANN, New Nicaragua News Agency), *passim.*

10. Belli, pp. 185–87; Belli's discussion should be compared to Berryman's criticism of the bishops' statement, pp. 253–54.

11. Gustavo Gutierrez, "Liberation Praxis and Christian Faith," in R. Gibellini, ed., *Frontiers of Theology in Latin America* (Maryknoll, NY: Orbis Books, 1979), p. 9.

12. Juan Hernandez Pico S.J., *El Papa en Nicaragua* (Madrid: Editorial IEPALA, 1983), p. 281.

13. Conferencia Episcopal de Nicaragua, *Carta Pastoral del Episcopado Nicaraguense sobre la Reconciliacion,* April 22, 1984.

14. Blaise Bonpane, *Guerrillas of Peace: Liberation Theology and the Central American Revolution* (Boston: South End Press, 1985), pp. 10–12. Bonpane's book proposes a new society with a minimum guaranteed income of $20,000 per year and a maximum of $75,000, and concludes, 'Revolution si, revolution yes, *hasta la victoria siempre*. Forward forever until victory."

15. Valdivieso's name has been given to the other major liberationist center in Managua, the Antonio Valdivieso Ecumenical Center. It has published Giulio Girardi, *Sandinismo, Marxismo, Cristianismo en la Nueva Nicaragua*, 1986, which argues for the "confluence" of Marxism, nationalism, and Christianity in *Sandinismo*.

16. See, for example, the statement in an article by Pablo Richard, a Chilean former priest now working at the liberationist center, DEI, in San Jose, Costa Rica: "Christian Democracy is progressively contradicting the processes of liberating transformation found as much in society and politics as in theology and the Church" ("Political Organization of Christians in Latin America: From Christian Democracy to a New Model," in Gregory Baum and John Coleman, eds., *The Church and Christian Democracy*, Edinburgh: T. T. Clark Ltd., 1987, p. 18).

Chapter 8

1. See, however, Brown's *Theology in a New Key, Responding to Liberation Themes* (Philadelphia: Westminster Press, 1978), for a sympathetic discussion of liberation theology that also—too briefly—attempts to summarize and respond to its major critics.

2. McGovern has recently completed another book that specifically focuses on an evaluation of liberation theology and its critics.

3. He cites a recently published interpretation of liberation theology by an American Jesuit, Roger Haight S.J., *An Alternative Vision* (New York: Paulist Press, 1985) as typical of the liberation theologians' ignorance of economics. Haight begins by avowing his own "lack of expertise in the social sciences" and "the necessity of a division of labor" (p. 3) and then proceeds to argue that poverty is "caused by human beings. There is a connection between wealth and poverty, a causal interrelationship between the extraordinary wealth of the developed sectors both inside and outside Latin America and the extensive poverty that prevails there" (p. 47). It is the nature of that asserted causal connection that Novak questions.

4. The dust jacket on Novak's book refers to "political leaders and churchmen who claim to be both Marxists and Christians." A similar error is made by an American Catholic socialist, John Cort, in *Christian*

Socialism (Maryknoll, NY: Orbis Books, 1988) when, after quoting early Gutierrez on the need to abolish private property, Cort accuses him of "imposing the European abstractions, or conclusions, of Karl Marx onto the Latin American peasants, whose actual praxis cries out for land of their own and by no means wants to be submerged in some vast collective owned and operated by the state" (p. 317).

5. The number of Brazilian bishops attending the national meetings of the Base Communities has increased from seven at the first meeting in 1975 to eighty at the 1989 meeting. Cardinal Evaristo Arns of São Paulo has been a regular participant since the first meeting.

6. There is a large empirically based literature on the Ecclesial Base Communities, especially in Brazil. Alvaro Barreiro S.J., *Basic Ecclesial Communities: The Evangelization of the Poor* (Maryknoll, NY: Orbis Books, 1982), reviews the Brazilian experience, as do Thomas Bruneau ("Basic Christian Communities in Latin America: Their Nature and Significance," in Daniel Levine, ed., *Churches and Politics in Latin America,* Beverly Hills, CA: Sage Publications, 1980, pp. 225–37, and "Brazil: The Catholic Church and Basic Christian Communities. A Case Study from the Brazilian Amazon," in Daniel Levine, ed., *Religion and Political Conflict in Latin America,* Chapel Hill: University of North Carolina, 1986, pp. 202–33) and Scott Mainwaring ("The Catholic Church, Popular Education and Political Change in Brazil," *Journal of Inter-American Studies and World Affairs* (26), Feb. 1984, 97–124, and "Brazil: The Catholic Church and the Popular Movement; Nova Iguaçu, 1974–1982," in Levine, ed., *Religion and Political Conflict,* pp. 234–94). The first Mainwaring article is followed by comments by Philip Berryman, Michael Dodson, and Daniel Levine on Mainwaring's claim that the CEBs are guilty of *basismo*—an unwillingness to become involved in larger movements for social change. The most comprehensive discussion of Brazilian theory and practice is Marcello deC. Azevedo S.J., *Basic Ecclesial Communities in Brazil* (Washington, DC: Georgetown University Press, 1987). See also Dominique Barbe, *Grace and Power* (Maryknoll, NY: Orbis Books, 1987) for a travel diary involving the Base Communities and a discussion of their relation to nonviolent politics and to Marxism. Pablo Galdames, *Faith of a People* (Maryknoll, NY: Orbis Books, 1983) is an account of Base Communities in El Salvadore between 1970 and 1980.

Chapter 9

1. For the English text see Joseph Ratzinger, *The Ratzinger Report* (San Francisco: Ignatius Press, 1985), pp. 174–86. Ratzinger claimed that the notes had been private in character and had been taken from

his desk. However, he permitted the text to be published as part of the lengthy 1984 interview with an Italian journalist, Vittorio Massi, *Rapporta sulla Fide,* which was published in English as *The Ratzinger Report.*

2. Gustavo Gutierrez, "Teología y Ciencias Sociales," *Paginas* (Lima), vol. XI, nos. 63–64 (September 1984). It has also been published in *Christus* (Mexico City), 1984; in the *Revista de Téologia* (San Salvador), no. 4, 1984; and in *Cristianismo y Sociedad* (Mexico City), no. 84, 1985, pp. 46–68.

3. When asked by this writer whether liberation theologians could support a welfare-oriented capitalism that incorporates a preferential option for the poor, Gutierrez replied, "I don't know any who do" (Georgetown University, Conference on Liberation Theology, June 10, 1985). Three years later when asked whether there could be a capitalist liberation theology, he answered, "I don't believe the capitalist system as we know it today is good for the poor. But theoretically if it is a way out of poverty, I have no problem. My question is not about capitalism. My question is about poverty" (*New York Times,* July 27, 1988). If quoted correctly this is a rare, if grudging, departure from the consistent anticapitalism of the liberation theologians.

4. "Respuesta de Leonardo Boff a la carta del Cardenal Joseph Ratzinger," *Revista Latinoamericana de Teología* (San Salvador), vol. I, no. 3 (September–December 1984), pp. 340–71. See also Leonardo and Clodovis Boff, *Liberation Theology: From Dialogue to Confrontation* (New York: Harper & Row, 1986), Part III. The text of Cardinal Ratzinger's letter is printed in Spanish in *Misión Abierta* (Madrid), no. 1, February 1985, pp. 9–13.

5. "Doctrinal Congregation Criticizes Brazilian Theologian's Book," *Origins* (Washington), vol. 14, no. 42 (April 4, 1985), pp. 683–87. For a Protestant theologian's view of the controversy ("the Boff episode as the revolt of the base" versus "the thrashing of western Christianity as it watches its millennium-long hegemony drain"), see Harvey Cox, *The Silencing of Leonardo Boff* (Oak Park, IL: Meyer Stone, 1988).

6. For the statement by Ronaldo Muñoz see "Reacciones de los teologos latinoamericanos a proposito de la 'Instruccion,'" *Revista Latinoamericana de Teología,* vol. I, no. 2 (May–August 1984), p. 239. Muñoz admits that in Chile during the period 1967–1973, "the Christian-Marxist confrontation . . . was not always carried out with sufficient maturity and critical awareness." For the two versions of Pablo Richard's response, one endorsing the Instruction "out of faithful obedience, love for the church, and intellectual honesty" and the second criticizing it as "alien and ignorant of the way of thinking of the Third World," see Roberto Jiménez, *La Teología Latinoamericana en Capilla* (Caracas: Tripode, 1987), pp. 75–79. The comments of Boff and Sobrino appear at pp.

227–30 and 240–47. Boff also argues in Leonardo and Clodovis Boff, pp. 48–49, that "in all our years of theological work" he had never met "any theologian who accepts Marxism in the totality to which the *Instruction* refers," and he describes such an attitude as "a theoretical and practical monstrosity." For Segundo's response, see Juan Luis Segundo, *Theology and the Church, A Response to Cardinal Ratzinger and a Warning to the Whole Church* (Minneapolis: Winston Press, 1985).

7. See Jiri Valenta and Herbert J. Ellison, eds., *Grenada and Soviet/Cuban Policy* (Boulder, CO: Westview Press, 1986), appendix A, document 2, pp. 292–93.

8. Frei Betto, *Fidel y la Religion: Conversaciones con Frei Betto* (Havana: Oficina del Consejo de Estado, 1986). The English translation was published by Simon and Schuster, New York, in 1987.

9. *Our Sunday Visitor,* March 2, 1986, p. 17. On the Roman Catholic church and the Castro regime, see John Kirk, *Between God and the Party: Religion and Politics in Revolutionary Cuba* (Tampa: University of South Florida Press, 1989).

10. "Theology of Liberation," *New LADOC Keyhole Series* (Lima, 1985), p. 21. The *Declaration* is translated on pp. 12–18.

11. For the comments see "Responden los Teologos de la Liberación," *Vida Nueva* (Madrid), September 1986, pp. 23–30.

12. Gustavo Gutierrez, *La Verdad los Hara Libres,* Lima: Centro de Estudios y Publicaciones, 1986.

13. "Aún Es Tiempo," *Paginas* (Lima), XL, no. 86, July 1986.

14. *Origins,* vol. 17, no. 38, March 3, 1988, pp. 641–60. I have used the Catholic Truth Society edition of *Laborem Exercens* (London, 1981).

15. Hugo Assmann, "Democracy and the Debt Crisis," *This World* (14) (Spring-Summer 1986), pp. 92–94. (For Assmann's recent thinking see *A Idolatria do Mercado,* with Franz Hinkelammert, [São Paulo: Vozes, 1989]). See also José Miguez Bonino, *Toward a Christian Political Ethics* (Philadelphia: Fortress, 1983), p. 77, where he describes the basic features of "the liberation project" as "socialist in the organization of its economy, democratic in terms of the political participation of the people, and open in the sense of ensuring the conditions for personal realization, cultural freedom and opportunity, and mechanisms for self-correction."

16. This view is shared by Daniel Levine, who concludes a review of the literature on liberation theology ("Religion and Politics: Drawing Lines, Understanding Change," in *Latin American Research Review,* vol. xx, no. 1, 1985, pp. 185–201): "Future understandings of religion, the churches, and politics in Latin America are best pursued not through ideological polemic, class analysis, or attention to institutional matters alone, but rather in the developing interplay of these planes of action

and meaning with the new structures being created at the grass roots" (p. 199).

Chapter 10

1. J. B. Libanio S.J., *Teologia da Libertação* (Sao Paulo: Editorial Loyola, 1987), p. 27.

2. Pablo Richard, "Political Organization of Christians in Latin America: From Christian Democracy to a New Model," in Gregory Baum and John Coleman, eds., *The Church and Christian Democracy (Concilium,* vol. 193 (Edinburgh: T. and T. Clark, 1987), p. 18. Richard predicted that redemocratization would lead to the decline of Christian Democracy, at the very time when they were becoming the most important parties in a number of redemocratizing Latin American countries, e.g., Chile and Guatemala.

3. Clodovis Boff. *Theology and Praxis* (Maryknoll, NY: Orbis Books, 1984), p. 203.

4. Quoted in Robert McAfee Brown, *Theology in a New Key* (Philadelphia: Westminster Press, 1978), p. 61.

5. Jack Nelson-Pallmeyer, *The Politics of Compassion* (Maryknoll, NY: Orbis Books, 1986), p. 55.

6. For the debate, see Bruce Grelle and David Krueger, eds., *Christianity and Capitalism* (Chicago: Center for the Scientific Study of Religion, 1986). For a more polemical edited collection see Franky Schaeffer, ed., *Is Capitalism Christian?* (Westchester, IL: Crossway Books, 1985). For Protestant and Catholic views favorable to "democratic" capitalism, see Robert Benne, *The Ethic of Democratic Capitalism: A Moral Reassessment* (Philadelphia: Fortress Press, 1981), and Michael Novak, *The Spirit of Democratic Capitalism* (New York: Simon and Schuster, 1982).

7. For persuasive arguments see Nathan Rosenberg and L. E. Birdzell, Jr., *How the West Grew Rich* (New York: Basic Books, 1986); Benjamin Cohen, *The Question of Imperialism* (New York: Basic Books, 1973); and Peter Berger, *The Capitalist Revolution* (New York: Basic Books, 1986).

8. See the case studies in Paul E. Sigmund, *Multinationals in Latin America: The Politics of Nationalization* (Madison: University of Wisconsin Press, 1980).

9. See Peter T. Knight, "New Forms of Economic Organization in Peru," in Abraham Lowenthal, ed., *The Peruvian Experiment* (Princeton, NJ: Princeton University Press, 1975), ch. 9.

10. See Paul E. Sigmund, *The Overthrow of Allende and the Politics of Chile* (Pittsburgh: University of Pittsburgh Press, 1977).

11. See Graeme Duncan, *Marx and Mill, Two Views of Social Conflict and Social Harmony* (Cambridge: Cambridge University Press, 1973). For the equalitarian implications of liberalism see Amy Gutmann, *Liberal Equality* (Cambridge: Cambridge University Press, 1980). For an argument that the principal difference between liberation theology and the social doctrine of the church is their attitude toward the inevitability of class conflict, see Ana Maria Ezcurra, *La Doctrina Social de la Iglesia* (Mexico City: UNAM-Nuevomar, 1986). On Marxism and contemporary liberalism, see Allen E. Buchanan, *Marx and Justice: The Radical Critique of Liberalism* (Totowa, NJ: Ronman and Littlefield, 1982) and Ellen Paul *et al.*, eds., *Marxism and Liberalism* (New York: Basil Blackwell, 1986).

12. I am aware that there is a large literature on Marx and democracy. It often quotes his 1872 speech to the First International on the possibility of arriving at socialism through parliamentary means. However, his central belief was that political institutions were part of the capitalist superstructure, and only a change in the mode of production could change the politics. After the revolution, Marx seems to have recommended a direct democracy such as the Paris commune, which "was to be a working, not a parliamentary body, executive and legislative at the same time . . . instead of deciding once in three or six years which members of the ruling class was to represent and repress the people in parliament" (*Eighteenth Brumaire*). On Marx's political theory as a mixture of majoritarian dictatorship and anarchism, see Robert C. Tucker, *The Marxian Revolutionary Idea* (New York: W. W. Norton, 1964), ch. 3. For a defense of Marx's democratic convictions, see John McMurtry, *The Structure of Marx's World View* (Princeton, NJ: Princeton University Press, 1978).

13. The best-known works in this genre are Roberto Mungabeira Unger, *Knowledge and Politics* (New York: Free Press, 1975), Alasdair MacIntyre, *After Virtue* (Notre Dame: University of Notre Dame Press, 1981) (2nd rev. ed., 1984), Michael Sandel, *Liberalism and the Limits of Justice* (New York: Cambridge University Press, 1982), and Michael Walzer, *Spheres of Justice* (New York: Basic Books, 1983). For a liberal criticism of the communitarian theories see Amy Gutmann, "Communitarian Critics of Liberalism," *Philosophy and Public Affairs* (14) 3 (Summer 1985), 308–22.

14. See Mark Roelofs, "Liberation Theology: The Recovery of Biblical Radicalism," *American Political Science Review* (82) 2 (June 1988), 549–66.

Appendix I

1. Y. Congar, *Situation et tâches présentes de la théologie* (Paris, 1967), p. 72.

2. This manner of speaking is found in the well-known work of W. W. Rostow, *The Stages of Economic Growth* (Cambridge Univ. Press, 1960).

3. Recall how Karl Marx refers the abolition of private property to the "to be" and not to the "to have" of man. See also the "to have" of the "total man" of H. LeFebre and R. Garaudy.

4. This is the profound meaning of Hegel's dialectic, Master-Slave.

5. See the inspiring three-volume work of Ernst Bloch, *Das Prinzip Hoffnung* (Frankfurt/Main, 1959), as well as Harvey Cox's preface to the English translation of Bloch, *Man on His Own* (New York, 1970).

6. For an exposition and critique of this attitude, cf. F. Cardoso and E. Faleto, *Dependencia y desarrollo en América latina* (Santiago de Chile, 1967).

7. Cf. Teotonio Dos Santos, *El nuevo carácter de la dependencia* (Santiago de Chile, 1968).

8. Cf. Felipe Herrera, "Viabilidad de una comunidad latinoamericana," in *Estudios internacionales* (Santiago de Chile, April 1967.

9. This point has been well studied in its historical genesis by O. Sunkel, *El marco histórico del proceso de desarrollo y de subdesarollo* (Santiago de Chile, 1967).

10. Cf. G. Arroyo, "Pensamiento latinoamericano sobre subdesarrollo y dependencia externa: Revisión bibliográfica," *Mensaje* 173 (Oct. 1968), 516–20.

11. Cf. A. Salazar Bondy, "La cultura de la dominación," in *Peru problema* (Lima, 1968).

12. Starting with this educational field, the most creative and fertile efforts along this line in Latin America are the experiences and works of P. Freire, which attempt to build a "pedagogy of the oppressed."

13. Cf. "Mensaje a los pueblos de América latina," in *Documentación de Medellín*. On the Latin American Bishops' Conference in Colombia, Aug.–Sept., 1968, see Renato Poblete, "Conferencia del CELAM en Medellín," *Mensaje* 173 (Oct. 1968), 495–500; also *Informations catholiques internationales* 321 (Oct. 1, 1968), 7–10, 21–25; also the Peruvian Episcopal Conference, Jan. 1969.

14. Cf. "Paz" in *Medellín;* also "Mensaje de los obispos del tercer mundo" (tr. in *Catholic Mind* 66 no. 1219 [Jan. 1968] 37–46: "A Message to the People of the Third World by Fifteen Bishops"); also "America latina, continente de violencia" (letter signed by a thousand priests).

15. Cf. "Paz" in *Medellín;* also *Conclusiones de Itapoan,* May 1968.

16. Cf. H. Borrat, "El gran impulso," *Vispera,* Oct. 1968.

17. See most of the documents of Medellín; also the Peruvian Episcopal Conference, Jan. 1969.

18. Cf. the address of Cardinal Landázuri at the University of Notre Dame in 1966; the 1968 Declaration of Peruvian Priests; the 1968 Letter of Bolivian Priests; the second Encuentro de Golconda, 1968.

19. Karl Rahner (*La riposta dei teologi* [Brescia, 1969]) speaks of the not too remote possibility that the Church might give a "univocal no" to certain tendencies or interpretations of Christianity.

Appendix II

1. The 1968 Latin American Bishops Conference of Medellín also appealed to that interpretation of Latin American reality. "We refer here in particular to the consequences for our countries of their dependence on a center of economic power around which they gravitate. The result of this is that our nations frequently are not in control of their own goods or economic decisions. As is obvious this has had its effects on their politics, given the interdependence that exists between both areas" (*Document on Peace,* section 8).

2. "This is the area of the encounter of the social sciences and Marxist analysis with theology, a critical encounter which occurs in the dynamics of an historical movement that goes beyond individual elements, dogmaticisms, and passing enthusiasms. For this reason intellectual terrorism in this area is a serious error" (*The Power of the Poor in History,* p. 192).

3. In the same text we said "If another type of analysis would be better than the one we are now using, it seems to me that it would enrich my comprehension of a reality of misery, injustice, and oppression" (*Dialogos,* p. 88).

4. "In this process of liberation there is also present, explicitly or implicitly, a transformation which one should not forget. To achieve the liberation of the subcontinent means going beyond the overcoming of economic, social, and political dependence" (*A Theology of Liberation,* p. 56).

5. Some have expressed surprise that they have not found in my work a lengthy treatment of the subject of violence, and some curious explanations have been offered for this. The reasons are simple. Theological reflection on the subject of violence, or more exactly in this case on counter-violence, has not made substantial advances since St. Thomas Aquinas. His teaching was recalled in our times by Pope Paul VI in his encyclical *Populorum Progressio,* no. 31. That text inspired what was said by the Medellín Bishops Conference in the *Document on Peace*

concerning the situation in Latin America. Later there was the document of the Nicaraguan bishops in June 1979. Also, unlike other theological approaches—that of the theology of revolution for example—my concern was to situate what takes place in Latin America within the broad focus of total liberation, and to see that process in the light of the Word of the Lord. This provides the context for discussion of matters like counter-violence that otherwise end up either bulking abnormally large or being treated solely at the level of principles. Such a fate is tragic in the case of violence.

Author and Subject Index

Index of Biblical Citations

Note: Biblical books are listed in alphabetical order.